Aus dem Institut für Softwaretechnik und Programmiersprachen
an der Technisch-Naturwissenschaftlichen Fakultät
der Universität zu Lübeck
Direktor:
Herr Prof. Dr. W. Dosch

Mechanizing the Transformation of Higher-Order Algebraic Specifications for the Development of Software Systems

Dissertation
zur
Erlangung der Doktorwürde
der Universität zu Lübeck
- Aus der Technisch-Naturwissenschaftlichen Fakultät -

Vorgelegt von

Sönke Johannes Magnussen

aus Schleswig

Lübeck, den 30. Oktober 2002

Bibliografische Information Der Deutschen Bibliothek

Die Deutsche Bibliothek verzeichnet diese Publikation in der Deutschen
Nationalbibliografie; detaillierte bibliografische Daten sind im Internet über
http://dnb.ddb.de abrufbar.

ISBN 3-8325-0152-5

Logos Verlag Berlin
Comeniushof, Gubener Str. 47,
10243 Berlin
Tel.: +49 030 42 85 10 90
Fax: +49 030 42 85 10 92
INTERNET: http://www.logos-verlag.de

Abstract

In this thesis we present a sound framework for mechanizing the transformation of algebraic specifications. The framework comprises a specification language, a formal development method and various mechanizable transformation rules. Moreover, we survey the Lübeck Transformation System LTS — a tool for the interactive development of software systems based on the described framework.

The *specification language* employs equational higher-order algebraic specifications offering a coherent basis for both problem-oriented specifications and high-level algorithms. Distinguished function symbols, so called constructors, define a generation constraint on sorts confining their interpretation to sets of constructor-reachable elements. In order to specify large software systems in a modular way, the language offers structuring concepts. The development of software aims at algorithmic specifications. This subset of algebraic specifications can be translated into a collection of modules in a functional programming language.

The thesis provides a *formal development method* for converting property oriented specifications into algorithmic specifications in a stepwise way. The property preserving refinement steps are defined by a refinement relation on specifications. The refinement relation is compatible with the structuring concepts of the specification language. This allows for a compositional derivation of software: the refinement of the involved sub-specifications result in an implementation of the overall specification. The task of formally deriving an implementation consists in the stepwise transformation of a requirement specification into an algorithmic specification. The development effort can be reduced by partially mechanizing the derivation. The thesis introduces various transformation rules that suit for mechanization and that are implemented in the Lübeck Transformation System.

The *transformation rules* describe syntactic manipulations of specification parts on different levels of abstraction. Axioms can be transformed using various algebraic and logic rules. As transformation steps on specifications we introduce enrichments and reductions of function symbols, sorts, and axioms. These transformations form a basis for wide-spanning refinement steps that make a large headway towards an algorithmic specification possible. The usage of wide-spanning transformation steps simplifies the development process by reducing the number of derivation steps to a few large steps which capture the essential design decisions. As a major contribution we mechanize wide-spanning transformation steps for fusing function compositions and for refining data structures.

Function composition supports the problem-oriented structuring of complex functions into simpler auxiliary functions. The thesis surveys the *fusion of a catamorphism* with an arbitrary function in an algebraic setting. The presented fusion theorem generalizes the well-known approach in functional programming to non-free data types and even applies to catamorphisms specified by a set of mutually recursive functions. The fusion theorem forms the basis for the corresponding fusion transformation. This step transforms an entire specification by manipulating several axioms, enriching the signature, and inserting proof obligations in case of non-free data types. Furthermore, we provide a sufficient syntactic criterion to detect catamorphisms by analysis algorithms.

For the *refinement of data structures* in the setting of algebraic specifications we first present a general theoretical basis. Then we mechanize the refinement of data structures by several transformation rules that follow the described theory and transform entire specifications. The approach is based on representation and abstraction functions which allows flexible transformations between data structures. The transformation rules comprise the general approach of algebraic implementations as well as particular situations like constructor enrichments or constructor implementations.

The suitability of the introduced framework is demonstrated by a *case study* showing the development of a software system for a booking optimizer. The software is specified in a compositional way and is transformed into an efficient algorithmic solution. The proposed transformation steps suffice to achieve a well-structured development process revealing the essential design decisions. The derivation is completely performed with LTS.

The *Lübeck Transformation System* allows for a tool supported, interactive derivation of software systems. Several analysis algorithms are applied to each loaded specification aiming at the detection of desirable or critical semantic properties. These properties support the user during the derivation process. Specifications can be refined in two different modes. The fine tuning mode focuses on single equations, which are modified by term rewriting and equational logic. In the specification mode transformation steps on entire specifications can be performed. This comprises specification enrichment and reduction as well as wide-spanning transformation steps for fusion and data structure refinement. The application conditions are either evaluated automatically by analyzing the specification or inserted into the specification as proof obligations. Additionally, the system provides a collection of strategies which combine standard transformations to wide-spanning transformation steps.

Zusammenfassung

In dieser Arbeit wird ein Rahmen für die mechanisierbare Transformation algebraischer Spezifikationen untersucht. Dieser Rahmen besteht aus einer Spezifikationssprache, einer formalen Entwicklungsmethode und verschiedenen mechanisierbaren Transformationsregeln. Darüber hinaus präsentieren wir das Lübecker Transformationssystem LTS — ein Werkzeug zur interaktiven Entwicklung von Softwaresystemen, das auf dem eingeführten Rahmen basiert.

Als *Spezifikationssprache* dienen gleichungsbasierte algebraische Spezifikationen höherer Ordnung. Diese bieten eine durchgängige Grundlage sowohl für eigenschaftsorientierte Spezifikationen als auch für eine abstrakte Beschreibung von Algorithmen. Ausgezeichnete Funktionssymbole, die sogenannten Konstruktoren, schränken die Interpretation von Sorten auf von Konstruktoren erzeugte Elemente ein. Für die modulare Spezifikation großer Softwaresysteme stellt die Sprache Strukturierungskonzepte zur Verfügung. Die Entwicklung von Software zielt auf algorithmische Spezifikationen ab. Diese Teilmenge der algebraischen Spezifikationen kann in eine Sammlung von Modulen einer funktionalen Programmiersprache übersetzt werden.

Mittels einer *formalen Entwicklungsmethode* können eigenschaftsorientierte Spezifikationen schrittweise in algorithmische Spezifikationen überführt werden. Die eigenschaftserhaltenden Verfeinerungsschritte werden durch eine Verfeinerungsrelation auf Spezifikationen festgelegt. Die Verfeinerungsrelation ist mit den Strukturierungskonzepten der Spezifikationssprache verträglich. Das erlaubt eine kompositionelle Entwicklung von Software: Die Verfeinerung der Spezifikationskomponenten führt zu einer Verfeinerung der Gesamtspezifikation. Dabei besteht die formale Herleitung einer Implementation aus der schrittweisen Transformation einer Anforderungsspezifikation in eine algorithmische Spezifikation. Der Entwicklungsaufwand kann reduziert werden, wenn Teile der Herleitung mechanisiert werden. Diese Arbeit führt verschiedenartige Transformationsregeln ein, die sich für eine Mechanisierung eignen und im Lübecker Transformationssystem implementiert sind.

Die *Transformationsregeln* beschreiben die syntaktische Manipulation von Spezifikationsteilen auf verschiedenen Abstraktionsstufen. Die Axiome können mit Hilfe verschiedener algebraischer und logischer Regeln umgeformt werden. Als Transformationsschritte auf Spezifikationen führen wir die Anreicherung und Reduzierung von Funktionssymbolen, Sorten und Axiomen ein. Diese Transformationen bilden die Basis für weitreichende Verfeinerungsschritte, die einen großen Fortschritt in Richtung einer algorithmischen Spezifikation ermöglichen. Der Gebrauch von weitreichenden Transformationsschritten vereinfacht den Entwicklungsprozess, indem die Anzahl der Herleitungsschritte auf wenige reduziert wird, die wichtige Entwurfsentscheidungen beinhalten. Als einen wesentlichen Beitrag dieser Arbeit mechanisieren wir weitreichende Transformationsschritte für das Verschmelzen von Funktionskompositionen und für die Verfeinerung von Datenstrukturen.

Die Funktionskomposition unterstützt die problemorientierte Strukturierung von komplexen Funktionen in einfachere Hilfsfunktionen. Diese Arbeit untersucht die *Verschmelzung eines Catamorphismus* mit einer beliebigen Funktion in einem algebraischen Umfeld. Der vorgestellte Verschmelzungssatz verallgemeinert den bekannten Ansatz aus der funktionalen Programmierung auf nicht-freie Datentypen und deckt außerdem Catamorphismen ab, die durch eine Menge von verschränkt rekursiven Funktionen definiert werden. Der Verschmelzungssatz bildet die Grundlage für eine Transformationsregel. Diese verfeinert ganze Spezifikationen durch die Manipulation von Gesetzen, Anreicherung der Signatur und Einfügen von Beweisverpflichtungen im Fall nicht-freier Datentypen in einem Schritt. Darüber hinaus wird ein syntaktisches Kriterium für die Erkennung von Catamorphismen durch Analyse-Algorithmen aufgestellt.

Zur *Verfeinerung von Datenstrukturen* im Rahmen algebraischer Spezifikationen präsentieren wir zunächst die theoretischen Grundlagen. Dann mechanisieren wir Verfeinerungen von Datenstrukturen durch mehrere Transformationsregeln, die dem theoretischen Ansatz folgen und ganze Spezifikationen in einem Zug verfeinern. Der Ansatz basiert auf Repräsentations- und Abstraktionsfunktionen, was die flexible Transformationen von Datenstrukturen unterstützt. Die Transformationsregeln umfassen den allgemeinen Ansatz der algebraischen Implementierung sowie spezielle Regeln für die Anreicherung oder Reduzierung von Konstruktoren.

Die Angemessenheit des eingeführten Rahmens wird anhand einer Fallstudie demonstriert, in der ein optimierendes Buchungssystem entwickelt wird. Die Software wird in einer kompositionellen Weise spezifiziert und in eine effiziente algorithmische Lösung umgeformt. Die eingeführten Transformationsregeln reichen für einen wohlstrukturierten Entwicklungsprozess aus, der die wesentlichen Entwurfsentscheidungen offenlegt. Die Entwicklung wurde vollständig mit dem Lübecker Transformationssystem durchgeführt.

Das *Lübecker Transformationssystem* ermöglicht die rechnergestützte, interaktive Herleitung von Softwaresystemen. Jede geladene Spezifikation wird einem Analyseprozess unterzogen mit dem Ziel, wünschenswerte oder kritische semantische Eigenschaften der Spezifikation zu erkennen. Das Ergebnis der Analyse unterstützt den Benutzer bei der weiteren Entwicklung. Spezifikationen können in zwei verschiedenen Modi verfeinert werden: Der Modus für feine Veränderungen fokussiert auf die Herleitung einzelner Gesetze, die mit Term- und Gleichungsmanipulationen transformiert werden. Im Spezifikationsmodus können Transformationsschritte auf ganzen Spezifikationen durchgeführt werden. Das umfasst sowohl Anreicherungen und Reduzierungen als auch weitreichende Transformationsschritte zur Verschmelzung von Funktionskompositionen und zur Verfeinerung von Datenstrukturen. Die Anwendbarkeitsbedingungen werden entweder automatisch durch die Analyse der Spezifikation evaluiert oder als Beweisverpflichtungen in die Spezifikation eingefügt. Zusätzlich stellt das System eine Sammlung von Strategien zur Verfügung, um Standardtransformationen zu weitreichenden Transformationsschritten zu kombinieren.

Acknowledgment

The development of this thesis has been made possible by the help of many people. Herewith, I would like to express my gratitude for all their contributions to this work.

First of all I have to thank my supervisor Prof. Dr. Walter Dosch for guiding me through my research and the development of this thesis. Without his help, especially in the early years, I would not have been able to decide which directions are worth pursuing and what is important in academic research. I am grateful for his awareness that research requires an exchange of ideas and that writing papers clarifies one's own ideas. His questions and his intuitions during discussions have always been a source of inspiration to me. For all this I wish to thank him.

I am sincerely grateful to Prof. Dr. Rudolf Berghammer for his willingness to co-referee this thesis. He has read my work in detail and has provided many useful remarks. In fact his influence reaches even further. It was during the writing of my Master's thesis under supervision of Prof. Dr. Rudolf Berghammer that I discovered how enjoyable doing research can be.

I owe special thanks to Dr. Clemens Grelck, Annette Stümpel, Andreas Vox and Bernd Wiedemann for countless informal discussions about the theory and practice of developing software, transformational programming, fusion techniques, and data structure refinements. Moreover, I thank Dietmar Wolf for taking care of my workstations and installing and implementing various tools and scripts required for the development of LTS and Kathrin Janfeld and Hedwig Hellkamp for all kinds of assistance in managing daily work.

Many thanks to Dr. Clemens Grelck, my uncle John Shevlin, Annette Stümpel and Andreas Vox for carefully reading the manuscript, for suggesting improvements, and for correcting several mistakes concerning the English language.

I am grateful to students who helped to improve LTS towards a usable transformation system. Martin Krüger, Eva Lange and Johannes Textor contributed their experiences with the Lübeck Transformation System when working through various case studies. Jan Balster has assisted in developing an early version of the code generator. Caroline Kühnel and Kai Trojahner have implemented first prototypes of the graphical user interface.

Finally, I thank my parents and my family for their mental support and for making an academic education possible. In particular, I thank my beloved friend Irid Joswig; through her love and support, she gave me the motivation to complete this thesis.

Contents

Chapter 1

Introduction

The quality of software systems depends on many criteria. The choice of an adequate software process model is essential in meeting quality requirements. When aiming at a rigorous notion of correctness, formal software development [80] provides an appropriate process model, which ensures that the final implementation fulfills the requirements given by a formal specification.

1.1 Formal software development

In general, formal software development consists of a sequence of property preserving refinement steps starting with a problem-oriented specification and ending with an efficient implementation. There are essentially two different techniques guaranteeing the correctness of this *stepwise refinement* process: In the *invent and verify* approach [14, 58] the developer invents the next version and proves afterwards that the step preserves the specified properties. In the approach of *transformational programming* [8, 69] transformation rules [33, 74] describe syntactic manipulations which preserve the properties under certain application conditions. Invent and verify steps keep a maximum of freedom in refining a specification, but require an a-posteriori verification of each transition. Transformation steps are confined to the available set of transformation rules. They are proved to be correct once and forever; so the generated implementation is correct by construction. Simple proof obligations cover the application conditions. Moreover, in the transformational approach design decisions are documented by the choice of the transformation rules. This leads to a better understanding and justification of the developed software. Furthermore, the software development can be replayed if the requirements change. In general the development effort can be reduced by preferring transformation steps over invent and verify steps.

The trustworthiness of the development process relies on carefully dealing with proofs, syntactic manipulations and application conditions. Handling these book-keeping tasks and error-sensitive manipulations with paper and pencil is tedious, time-consuming, and error-prone. As a consequence, formal system development without computer assistance is limited to small scaled software systems. Only by mechanical assistance, formal software development can be extended to medium and large scaled software systems. This simplifies the process by automatic book-keeping, mechanization of the manipulation tasks and automatic validation of application conditions. Computer assistance also minimizes various types of errors that may occur during the development process. Systems that support the development process of transformational programming are called *transformation systems* .

Aiming at a high degree of assistance a transformation system should reduce user interaction to the essential design decisions. This can be achieved by validating application conditions automatically and by reducing the number of small refinement steps.

Wide-spanning transformations possibly composed from several small transformation steps make a large headway towards an implementation. Making use of wide-spanning transformation steps achieves a development consisting of a few transformation steps which reflect the essential design decisions. The transformation rules strongly depend on the underlying specification or programming language used during the formal development process. Consequently, an approach for mechanizing transformational programming must provide an entire framework comprising a formal specification language and a set of correct transformation rules which suit for being mechanized by a transformation system.

In this thesis, we present a framework for transformational programming serving as theoretical foundation of a transformation system. Since we aim at a rigorous notion of correctness, the framework offers precise mathematical definitions and a clear distinction between syntax and semantics. As specification language we use equational algebraic specifications [55, 85] extended by higher-order sorts and functions. The framework allows for expressing problem-oriented specifications as well as high-level algorithms. A separation of function symbols that construct the elements, so called constructors, leads to generation constraints for defining data structures. In order to structure the specification of large software systems the specification language provides structuring concepts. A refinement relation on algebraic specifications determines possible refinement steps that preserve the properties of the original specification. Transformation rules which realize wide-spanning transformation steps, but still are eligible to mechanization within a transformation system form a major contribution of this thesis. Basic transformation rules comprise specification enrichments, specification reductions and various logic and algebraic rules manipulating terms and equations. The introduced wide-spanning transformation rules can be classified into two categories.

Fusion   Function composition forms a short and concise way of specifying complex functions composed from several auxiliary functions. For efficiency reasons in most cases one aims at fusing the auxiliary functions achieving a compact axiomatization. This eliminates the intermediate data structures emerging in between the auxiliary functions. If the innermost auxiliary function embodies a catamorphism, i.e. a recursive function following the data structure, the fusion theorem for catamorphisms can be applied. In this thesis, we introduce a theoretical foundation for fusion in algebraic theories based on algebra homomorphisms. In contrast to fusion techniques for functional programming [60] the approach also covers catamorphisms over non-free data structures and generalizes the fusion theorem to catamorphisms consisting of several mutually recursive functions. Based on this theoretical foundation a fusion transformation rule is introduced manipulating several equations and the interface of the corresponding specification in one go. For mechanizing the fusion step a sufficient syntactic criterion for the detection of catamorphisms is given.

Data structure refinements Often data structures are defined in an abstract way in the requirement specification. In order to achieve an efficient implementation a refinement of the data structures is desirable. The thesis contains a theoretical foundation of algebraic data structure refinements which also handles higher-order types. Several transformation rules are given manipulating entire specifications for the refinement of the specified data structures. The soundness of the rules relies on the theoretical framework. Simple data structure transformations introduce, enrich or reduce the set of constructors responsible for the generation of data types. More sophisticated refinements either implement the constructors by terms which represent the embedding of the corresponding elements into another data type or by new function symbols describing the representation or abstraction functions of the data structure refinement.

The feasibility of the approach is demonstrated by means of the Lübeck Transformation System, a tool for supporting the interactive derivation of software systems. The integration of the framework into the transformation system is surveyed, and its assistance in developing software systems is illustrated. Besides the manipulation tasks performing the transformation steps the system analyses desirable or critical semantic properties of specifications which guide the developer in making further design decisions.

1.2 Overview of the thesis

The thesis is organized as follows. In Chapter 2, we define the syntax and semantics of basic algebraic specifications with higher-order sorts, function symbols, and universally quantified equations.

Viewing basic specifications as atoms we introduce in Chapter 3 structuring concepts for algebraic specifications. System specifications are constructed from specification fragments using specification combinators.

We proceed in Chapter 4 with a catalogue of standard specifications which will be used in examples of following chapters.

Chapter 5 surveys the general approach of a compositional development of software systems. It is described how large systems can be specified and stepwise refined in a compositional way. Moreover, we present a collection of machine checkable criteria revealing desirable or critical properties of specifications. Stepwise development is characterized by the successive application of transformation rules.

In Chapter 6, we present the basic transformation rules for manipulating entire specifications, equations, and terms.

The fusion transformation step for catamorphisms follows in Chapter 7. After giving a semantic justification on the basis of algebra homomorphisms a syntactic treatment of the fusion transformation is presented. This includes a sufficient and machine checkable criterion for catamorphisms as well as a syntactic rule transforming entire basic specifications for performing a fusion step.

Another class of wide-spanning transformation steps is given by data structure refinements treated in Chapter 8. Starting with a general semantic foundation of data structure refinements, a description of several distinct data structure refinements in terms of transformation rules on entire basic specifications is provided. The correctness of the rules is proved by reducing the transformations to the general semantic framework of refining data structures given at the beginning of the chapter.

The suitability of the approach introduced in the previous chapters is illustrated in Chapter 9 by a case study. We specify and design a booking optimizer maximizing the benefit of product combinations. Here, a compositional system specification is given and an efficient algorithmic solution is derived by applying the given transformation rules.

In Chapter 10, an overview of the Lübeck Transformation System (LTS) is given. The characteristic features of the system are summarized followed by an outline of the transformation process. This includes an explanation of the life-cycle of a specification residing in the system. A short summary of the implementation of LTS completes this chapter.

The assistance of the system for transformational derivations is illustrated in Chapter 11. We explicate how the supported transformation steps can be performed with the system and how transformation steps can be combined to transformation strategies. Moreover, the system guidance by property checking is explained in more detail.

Finally, we conclude in Chapter 12 with a summary of the proposed approach and discuss experiences and short comings. We finish with an outlook on potential future work.

1.3 Related work

Formal software development by refinement has a long tradition and various approaches have emerged. The early work of Hoare [45] and the stepwise refinement method of Dijkstra [23] form the beginning of a long history. Back and Wright [5] introduced the refinement calculus, which is based on Dijkstra's weakest precondition calculus. These model oriented methods suit for the development of algorithms but data structures cannot be refined. Algebraic specifications provide a framework for both algorithms and data structures. An early algebraic approach is given by Broy [14] using algebraic specifications.

In the area of computer support for formal software development many approaches arose in the last decades. Several systems were proposed differing, among others, in the language, the area of support, and the degree of mechanization. In the following, we will discuss existing systems and classify them into three transformational approaches according to Feather[33] and system support for the invent and verify paradigm.

Extended Compilation   A completely mechanized support of programming is a compiler where the source code is parsed, context checked, optimized and translated into target code. This process is fully automatic; since the input is already source code, there are no proper refinement steps. From the user's point of view extended compilation is similar to usual compilation. The difference consists of automatic source code transformations with minor user interaction before code generation. The user has to annotate the source code with some strategy for its automatic transformation before code generation. In contrast to normal compilation the input specification is more abstract although still very similar to source code. The transformation steps may concern efficiency aspects. User interaction is avoided and there is no clear distinction with code optimization. This approach was early adopted by Paige and Koenig [68] where transformation techniques like finite differencing are used to optimism SETL programs [68]. The approach was implemented in the RAPTS system, a prototype for the transformation of SETL programs. A common optimization technique that can be seen as extended compilation is deforestation for functional programs [84]. Here, intermediate data structures are automatically eliminated in order to improve efficiency. A weaker technique, the so called short cut deforestation, is implemented in the Glasgow Haskell Compiler [39].

Due to the limited expressibility of the specification language extended compilation is not suitable for formal system development since requirements can hardly be described in a property oriented way. The framework introduced in this thesis provides a more powerful specification language covering both requirement specifications and executable programs.

Metaprogramming   The metaprogramming model uses a possibly non-algorithmic specification as starting point. The specification can be refined by transformation steps aiming at an efficient implementation. Compared with extended compilation, metaprogramming requires a higher degree of interaction. The user transforms the input specification by giving structured transformation commands. So the user actually "programs" the construction of an implementation, which is the reason for the notion of 'metaprogramming'. As a consequence, metaprogramming can deal with more abstract specifications at the expense of a higher degree of interaction. The granularity of transformation steps is rather fine. Therefore, strategies are used to combine fine grained transformation steps in a certain control flow automatically. At some point the user decides to generate code from the refined algorithmic specification.

One early realization of this approach is the transformation system of Burstall and Darlington [17]. Their system supports fold and unfold steps of recursively defined first order functions. The steps are interactively invoked by the user. The system has a low degree of interaction; transformations aim at improving efficiency of functional programs.

The CIP system [7] deals with more powerful, language dependent specifications and programs. The system supports a large variety of transformation steps; it was primarily used for program derivations in the wide-spectrum language CIP-L [6]. Derivations with the CIP system consist of many small transformation steps which cause confusingly long developments. By simple user defined strategies wide-spanning transformation steps can be constructed, but there are no built-in transformation steps that manipulate entire specifications at once.

The ULTRA system [70, 43] developed at the University of Ulm has a more sophisticated graphical user interface and can be used to transform simple specifications based on Haskell [39] programs. As in the CIP system derivations consists of many small transformation steps. The graphical user interface leads to more a comfortable usage of transformational programming.

A generic approach to metaprogramming is provided by the TAS system [56, 57]. It is based on the Isabelle theorem prover [72] and offers a sophisticated user interface following the principle of direct manipulation. The user can define new transformation rules whose correctness can be proved by Isabelle itself. The system is flexible as the user may extend the range of possible transformation steps. This enables the generation of wide-spanning transformation steps in principle. In contrast to our approach, transformation steps cannot handle entire specifications, which precludes wide-spanning transformations concerning entire specifications.

All approaches for metaprogramming described sofar have in common that they are unable to handle data structure refinements. Such refinement steps require an explicit definition of data structures within the specification and transformation steps manipulating entire specifications.

Synthesis   The synthesis approach provides far reaching transformation steps with a high degree of user interaction. Besides the specification the synthesis model additionally uses a knowledge base of algorithm design principles, e.g. divide-and-conquer, which may also be provided by the user. The design principles are described either by a set of higher-order patterns [49] or by a collection of complex algorithm design principles [79]. The user instantiates tactics found in the knowledge base, which are applied to the specifications. The degree of user interaction is high because the user must apply the right tactics in a right instantiation. The granularity of refinement steps is rather coarse. Depending on the abstractness of the rules, it is possible to derive a program in one step.

Manna and Waldinger presented an early synthesis system called DEDALUS [59]. Theorem proving rules and techniques are used for synthesis, and proof obligations can be handled within the same framework. The transformation steps embody rather small refinements, whereas wide-spanning transformation steps are not supported.

Dold [24] performs an application of algorithm design pattern by the proof system PVS [66]. Here the user has to instantiate the pattern manually for an application; there is no automatic utility.

The KIDS system [78] synthesizes software using a knowledge base of algorithmic design principles. The user applies such principles to problem specifications by instantiating them. The system also supports transformational derivation techniques like partial evaluation and finite differencing. A formal specification can be transformed into a program by interactively applying a sequence of high-level transformations followed by several optimization steps. The successor system Specware [51] is similar to KIDS. The system synthesizes software by providing composition and transformation operators for building specifications and refinements. Specification diagrams and diagram refinements are used for software development in the large. Both systems use a basis of prefabricated design principles which describe algorithmic schemes and solutions like divide-and-conquer in a highly parameterized way. As a consequence, a lot of user interaction is necessary to instantiate the pattern. Moreover, the instantiation may cause proof obligations that cannot be solved automatically.

Invent and verify In the invent and verify approach mechanical support consists mainly of proving the correctness of a refinement step. Hence, a system requires two inputs, viz. the original specification and the refined specification, which may be a program. In general the specification consists of several logical formulae which describe the requirements. A proof system verifies that the refined specification actually meets the requirements. The abstraction level of the input specification may be rather high. Therefore, a high degree of user interaction is required since the user has to invent each refinement step and, depending on the degree of user interaction of the proof system, has to handle the proof obligations. The granularity of refinement steps depends on the invent steps. The user may provide the system with a correct program in one step, but may also invent small refinements such that the proofs become simple.

Extended ML [52], for short EML, supports the specification of signatures and modules. It extends Standard ML by specification constructs like axioms, but provides no mechanization of transformation steps. Formulas in EML are based on expressions of data type `bool`. This integrates them into SML, but makes the underlying semantics more complex.

An approach of supporting algebraic program derivation by the proof system PVS [66, 67] is described in [9]. Here the PVS system is used for proving the correctness of refinements in a stepwise development of functional programs starting with an algebraic specification. Whereas PVS only provides a simple user interface based on the editor emacs, both the INKA system [1] and the KIV system [76] provide a more elaborated graphical user interface. Both systems offer assistance in proving and managing structured algebraic specifications. The Isabelle system [72] is a generic proof system which can also be used to mechanize correctness proofs of refinement steps. In fact Isabelle is also used in the TAS system [57] to prove application conditions for transformation rules. Such kind of assistance by proof systems is also sensible for other approaches of transformational programming. However, this assistance only covers part of the development process and, in general, does not support genuine transformation steps.

Part I

Foundations

Chapter 2

Basic Algebraic Specifications

In this chapter we will introduce the syntax and semantics of algebraic specifications. Algebraic specifications [85, 55] have a long tradition and are based on the theory of predicate logic [83] and universal algebra [62]. The signatures of algebraic specifications are many-sorted and generation constraints of sorts may confine the models to Herbrand models.

Our approach extends classical algebraic specifications in the extension to higher-order concepts. Besides the basic sorts we consider derived sorts which are constructed using Cartesian products and function building. The sorts are used to define functionality for function symbols possibly achieving higher-order function symbols. The approach is similar to [61] and [47]. A subset of function symbols are designated as constructors which generate the elements of the carriers. An algebraic specification consists of a signature and a set of universally quantified higher-order equations between terms. The terms are built from variables and function symbols, by currying, tupling, function application and function composition.

The semantics of an algebraic specification uses the notion of an algebra. Each basic sort is interpreted as a non-empty set and the interpretation of the derived sorts are inductively defined on the interpretation of their constituent sorts. Each function symbol is interpreted as a total function operating on the sorts of its functionality. Furthermore, the generation constraints confine the interpretations of constructor sorts to elements that are reachable by a term construction. This provides the possibility of using induction for proving properties of a model.

Finally, we introduce some advanced semantic concepts which will be used for a refinement relation in Chapter 5 and complex transformation steps in Chapters 7 and 8. We define subalgebras and homomorphisms on higher-order algebras and introduce an equivalence relation on the elements of derived sorts. Moreover, we weaken the notion of equality which leads to behavioural equivalences [11] of algebras.

In order to simplify the following definitions and lemmas we will use indexed families along with some set theoretic operations and notations, see Appendix A.

2.1   Syntax

The syntax of algebraic specifications is based on the notion of a signature providing sorts and sorted function symbols. By designating a subset of constructors, the semantic definition in Section 2.2 can take generation constraints into account. Terms are built as usual extended by currying function symbols and by function composition. Formulae embody universally quantified equations between terms, and specifications consist of a signature and a set of formulae. Furthermore, we introduce some implicit extensions for specifications covering the axiomatization of the conditional and standard function symbols for projection.

2.1.1   Signatures and terms

We define a signature as a triple of sorts, function symbols and constructor function symbols. Terms and formulae can be constructed inductively from function symbols and variables.

The functional closure of a set of sorts is generated by forming function and tuple sorts.

Definition 2.1.1 (Functional closure, result sort)
Let S be a set of basic sorts. Then the *functional closure* $S^{\times,\to}$ of S is defined as the least set with

(i) $S \subseteq S^{\times,\to}$ (basic sort)

(ii) If $n \geq 2$ and $s_1, \ldots, s_n \in S^{\times,\to}$, then $(s_1, \ldots, s_n) \in S^{\times,\to}$.   (tuple sort)

(iii) If $s_1, s_2 \in S^{\times,\to}$, then $(s_1 \to s_2) \in S^{\times,\to}$.   (function sort)

The elements of $S^{\times,\to}$ are called the *derived sorts*. For a function sort $(s_1 \to s_2)$ we call s_1 the *argument sort* and s_2 the *result sort*.   □

We drop brackets with usual conventions: For example, $s_1 \to s_2$ denotes $(s_1 \to s_2)$ and $s_1 \to s_2 \to s_3$ abbreviates $(s_1 \to (s_2 \to s_3))$.

The syntax of algebraic specifications is based on a signature which provides the basic sorts and function symbols.

Definition 2.1.2 (Signature)
A *signature* $\Sigma = (S, F, C)$ consists of

- a non-empty set $S = SC \,\dot\cup\, SL$ of *basic sorts* composed from the disjoint sets of *constructor sorts* SC and *loose sorts* SL,

- an $S^{\times,\to}$-indexed family F of *function symbols* F_s of *functionality* s, and

- an $S^{\times,\to}$-indexed subfamily $C \subseteq F$ of *constructors* C_s. We assume $C_s \neq \emptyset$ with either $s \in SC$ or $s = (s_1 \to s_2)$ and $s_2 \in SC$, and $C_s = \emptyset$ for all $s \in S^{\times,\to}$ with non constructor result sort.

The function symbols $F \setminus C$ are called *operations*. The class of all signatures is denoted by SIG. □

The signature comprises higher-order function symbols since functionalities range over derived sorts. Loose sorts are basic sorts without constructors. Whenever the family C of constructors is irrelevant, we shortly write $\Sigma = (S, F)$.

In order to structure signatures we introduce the usual set operations for signatures.

Definition 2.1.3 (Set operations on signatures)
For signatures $\Sigma_1 = (S_1, F_1, C_1)$ and $\Sigma_2 = (S_2, F_2, C_2)$ we define:

(i) $\Sigma_1 \cup \Sigma_2 = (S_1 \cup S_2, F_1 \cup F_2, C_1 \cup C_2)$ (union)

(ii) $\Sigma_1 \cap \Sigma_2 = (S_1 \cap S_2, F_1 \cap F_2, C_1 \cap C_2)$ (intersection)

(iii) $\Sigma_1 \setminus \Sigma_2 = (S_1 \setminus S_2, F_1 \setminus F_2, C_1 \setminus C_2)$ (difference)

(iv) $\Sigma_1 \subseteq \Sigma_2$ iff $S_1 \subseteq S_2$ and $F_1 \subseteq F_2$. (subsignature)

(v) $\Sigma_1 \supseteq \Sigma_2$ iff $S_1 \supseteq S_2$ and $F_1 \supseteq F_2$. (supersignature)

□

The difference of two signatures does in general not yield a signature. The set operations can be propagated in a unique way to signature fragments.

Definition 2.1.4 (Signature fragments)
The set of *signature fragments SIGfrag* is inductively defined by

(i) $SIG \subseteq SIGfrag$

(ii) If $\Sigma_1^{frag}, \Sigma_2^{frag} \in SIGfrag$, then $\Sigma_1^{frag} \setminus \Sigma_2^{frag} \in SIGfrag$. □

Signature fragments can be expanded to signatures.

Definition 2.1.5 (Spanned signature)
The *spanned signature* of a signature fragment $\Sigma^{frag} \subseteq \Sigma'$ *wrt.* a signature Σ' is the smallest signature $\Sigma'' \subseteq \Sigma'$ with $\Sigma^{frag} \subseteq \Sigma''$ and is denoted by $[\Sigma^{frag}]_{\Sigma'}$. □

The constructors will be used to generate the elements of the sorts belonging to SC. A signature can be restricted to the relevant subsignature generating the data structures.

Definition 2.1.6 (Constructor signature)
Let $\Sigma = (S, F, C)$ be a signature. The *constructor signature* is defined as $\Sigma_C = (S, C, C)$.
$\square$

A signature and a family of sets of variables form the basis for constructing terms.

Definition 2.1.7 (Basis)
A *basis* (Σ, X) consists of a signature $\Sigma = (S, F)$ and an $S^{\times, \rightarrow}$-indexed family X of pairwise disjunct sets X_s of *variables* such that $F \cap X = \emptyset$.
$\square$

Terms are built from the function symbols and variables of a basis respecting their functionalities and sorts.

Definition 2.1.8 ((Σ, X)-Term)
Let (Σ, X) be a basis. The $S^{\times, \rightarrow}$-indexed family $T(\Sigma, X)$ of (Σ, X)-*terms* over the basis (Σ, X) is defined inductively as follows:

(i) $X \subseteq T(\Sigma, X)$ (variable)

(ii) $F \subseteq T(\Sigma, X)$ (function symbol)

(iii) If $n \geq 2$ and $t_f \in T(\Sigma, X)_{(s_1, \ldots, s_n) \rightarrow s}$, then $(@t_f) \in T(\Sigma, X)_{(s_1 \rightarrow \ldots \rightarrow s_n \rightarrow s)}$.
                                                                             (currying)

(iv) If $n \geq 2$ and $t_i \in T(\Sigma, X)_{s_i}$, $1 \leq i \leq n$, then $(t_1, \ldots, t_n) \in T(\Sigma, X)_{(s_1, \ldots, s_n)}$.
                                                                               (tuple)

(v) If $t_f \in T(\Sigma, X)_{(s_1 \rightarrow s_2)}$ and $t_a \in T(\Sigma, X)_{s_1}$, then $(t_f(t_a)) \in T(\Sigma, X)_{s_2}$.
                                                                           (application)

(vi) If $t_f \in T(\Sigma, X)_{(s_1 \rightarrow s_2)}$ and $t_g \in T(\Sigma, X)_{(s_2 \rightarrow s_3)}$, then $(t_g \circ t_f) \in T(\Sigma, X)_{(s_1 \rightarrow s_3)}$.
                                                                     (function composition)
$\square$

In the following we will drop brackets in writing terms with usual conventions i.e. $t_f\, t_a$ denotes $t_f(t_a)$ and $t_f {\circ} t_g {\circ} t_h$ abbreviates $((t_f {\circ} t_g) {\circ} t_h)$. Moreover, we simplify the treatment of constants $f \in F_s$ by setting $f() = f$. The syntactic equality of two terms of the same sort is denoted by $\mathrel{\widehat{=}}$.

Constructor terms are generated from variables, constructors, tuples and applications only.

Definition 2.1.9 ((Σ, X)-Constructor term)
The $S^{\times, \rightarrow}$-indexed family $T^{cons}(\Sigma, X)$ of (Σ, X)-*constructor terms* over the basis $(\Sigma = (S, F, C), X)$ is defined inductively as follows:

(i) $X \subseteq T^{cons}(\Sigma, X)$ (variable)

(ii) $C \subseteq T^{cons}(\Sigma, X)$ (constructor)

(iii) If $n \geq 2$ and $t_i \in T^{cons}(\Sigma, X)_{s_i}$, $1 \leq i \leq n$, then $(t_1, \ldots, t_n) \in T^{cons}(\Sigma, X)_{(s_1, \ldots, s_n)}$. (tuple)

(iv) If $t_f \in C_{(s_1 \rightarrow s_2)}$ and $t_a \in T^{cons}(\Sigma, X)_{s_1}$, then $(t_f(t_a)) \in T^{cons}(\Sigma, X)_{s_2}$. (application)

□

The family of constructor terms forms a subfamily of the family of all terms over the same basis.

Terms that can be built without variables of constructor sorts are called constructor ground.

Definition 2.1.10 (Σ-Ground term, (Σ, X)-Constructor ground term)
Let (Σ, X) be a basis.

a) $T_G(\Sigma) = T(\Sigma, \emptyset)$ is the $S^{\times, \rightarrow}$-indexed family of Σ-*ground terms*.

b) $T_G^{cons}(\Sigma, X) = T^{cons}(\Sigma, X^-)$ with $X_{sc}^- = \emptyset$ for all constructor sorts sc and $X_s^- = X_s$ for all non constructor sorts is the $S^{\times, \rightarrow}$-indexed family of (Σ, X)-*constructor ground terms*. □

In order to reason about terms, we define the set of variables occurring in a term.

Definition 2.1.11 (Variables of a (Σ, X)-term)
For a basis (Σ, X), the $S^{\times, \rightarrow}$-indexed family $Var : T(\Sigma, X) \rightarrow \mathcal{P}(X)$ yields the family of sets of variables occurring in a term:

(i) $Var_s(x) = \begin{cases} \{x\} & \text{if } x \in X_s \\ \emptyset & \text{if } x \notin X_s \end{cases}$ (variable)

(ii) $Var_s(f) = \emptyset$ (function symbol)

(iii) $Var_s(@t_f) = Var_s(t_f)$ (currying)

(iv) $Var_s(t_1, \ldots, t_n) = \bigcup_{i=1}^{n} Var_s(t_i)$ (tuple)

(v) $Var_s(t_f(t_a)) = Var_s(t_f) \cup Var_s(t_a)$ (application)

(vi) $Var_s(t_g \circ t_f) = Var_s(t_f) \cup Var_s(t_g)$ (function composition)

□

2.1.2   Formulae and specifications

For the specification of properties we introduce a notation of formulae based on equational logic.

Definition 2.1.12 ((Σ, X)-Formulae with free variables)
The set of (Σ, X)-*formulae* $\mathcal{F}(\Sigma, X)$ over the basis (Σ, X) is inductively defined:

(i) If $s \in S^{\times, \rightarrow}$ and $t_1, t_2 \in T(\Sigma, X)_s$, then $(t_1 = t_2) \in \mathcal{F}(\Sigma, X)$.   (equation)

(ii) If $\varphi \in \mathcal{F}(\Sigma, X)$ and $x \in X_s$, then $(\forall x : s\ \varphi) \in \mathcal{F}(\Sigma, X)$.   (quantification)

$\square$

In the following we will simplify the notation of formulae with the usual conventions. For example $\forall x_1 : s_1, x_2 : s_2\ \varphi$ abbreviates $(\forall x_1 : s_1\ (\forall x_2 : s_2\ \varphi))$ and $\forall x_1, x_2 : s_1$ denotes $(\forall x_1 : s_1\ (\forall x_2 : s_1\ \varphi))$.

The variables occurring in a formula can be separated in free and bounded variables.

Definition 2.1.13 (Free variables, Closed formulae)
Let (Σ, X) be a basis.

a) The $S^{\times, \rightarrow}$-indexed families $Free, Bound : \mathcal{F}(\Sigma, X) \rightarrow \mathcal{P}(X)$ of *free* and of *bound* variables are inductively defined:

(i)
$$\begin{aligned} Free_s(t_1 = t_2) &= Var_s(t_1) \cup Var_s(t_2) \\ Bound_s(t_1 = t_2) &= \emptyset \end{aligned}$$ (equation)

(ii)
$$\begin{aligned} Free_s(\forall x : s'\ \varphi) &= Free_s(\varphi) \backslash \{x\} \\ Bound_s(\forall x : s'\ \varphi) &= Bound_s(\varphi) \cup (\{x\} \cap X_s) \end{aligned}$$ (quantification)

b) A formula $\varphi \in \mathcal{F}(\Sigma, X)$ with $Free(\varphi) = \emptyset$ is called *closed*. $\square$

Finally, we can define algebraic specifications consisting of a signature and a set of closed formulae.

Definition 2.1.14 (Algebraic specifications)
For a basis (Σ, X) an (*algebraic*) *specification* (Σ, E) consists of a signature Σ and a set E of closed (Σ, X)-formulae called *axioms*. The class of all algebraic specifications over the basis (Σ, X) is denoted by $SPEC(\Sigma, X)$ and the class of all specifications is abbreviated by $SPEC$. $\square$

In the following when writing formulae of an algebraic specification, the quantification ranging over all variables occurring in the terms will be omitted. Moreover, we call closed (Σ, X)-formulae also equations.

2.1.3   Translations and manipulations

We provide some definitions for translating and manipulating signatures, terms, formulae and specifications.

Translations

For the transformation of signatures a sort morphism translates the derived sorts.

Definition 2.1.15 (Sort morphism)
Let S_1, S_2 be two sets of sorts. A sort mapping $\iota : S_1 \rightarrow S_2^{\times, \rightarrow}$ is extended to a *sort morphism* $\iota : S_1^{\times, \rightarrow} \rightarrow S_2^{\times, \rightarrow}$ by setting

(ii) $\iota((s_1, \ldots, s_n)) = (\iota(s_1), \ldots, \iota(s_n))$ and   (tuple sort)

(iii) $\iota((s_1 \rightarrow s_2)) = (\iota(s_1) \rightarrow \iota(s_2))$.   (function sort)

$\square$

A sort morphism can be propagated to signatures by joining it with a compatible mapping for the function symbols.

Definition 2.1.16 (Signature morphism)
Let $\Sigma_1 = (S_1, F_1)$ and $\Sigma_2 = (S_2, F_2)$ be signatures. A *signature morphism* $\delta : (S_1, F_1) \rightarrow (S_2, F_2)$ consists of a sort morphism $\delta : S_1^{\times, \rightarrow} \rightarrow S_2^{\times, \rightarrow}$ and an (equally denoted) $S_1^{\times, \rightarrow}$-indexed family $\delta : F_1 \rightarrow F_2$ of functions $\delta_s : F_{1,s} \rightarrow F_{2,\delta(s)}$. The set of all signature morphisms is denoted by *SigMorph* . $\square$

The image of a signature under a signature morphism does not necessarily form a signature. Imagine that a sort $sb \in S$ is mapped by a signature morphism to (s_1, s_2) . If s_1, s_2 are not in the image of δ the image is not a signature. Therefore, we define the image of a signature morphism as the smallest signature comprising the images of the sub morphisms.

Definition 2.1.17 (Image signature)
For signatures Σ_1, Σ_2 and a signature morphism $\delta : \Sigma_1 \rightarrow \Sigma_2$ the *image signature* $\delta(\Sigma_1)$ of Σ_1 under δ is defined by $[(\delta(S), \delta(F), \delta(C))]_{\Sigma_2}$. $\square$

Signature translations are signature morphisms mapping basic sorts to basic sorts.

Definition 2.1.18 (Signature translation)
For two signatures $\Sigma_1 = (S_1, F_1)$ and $\Sigma_2 = (S_2, F_2)$ a signature morphism $\delta : \Sigma_1 \rightarrow \Sigma_2$ is called a *signature translation* , if $\delta(S_1) \subseteq S_2$ holds. $\square$

A signature morphism can be extended to a supersignature.

Definition 2.1.19 (Canonical extension of signature morphism)
The *canonical extension* of a signature morphism $\delta : \Sigma \rightarrow \Sigma_1$ by a supersignature $\Sigma' \supseteq \Sigma$ written $[\delta]_{\Sigma'} : \Sigma' \rightarrow \Sigma_1 \cup \Sigma'$ is defined by

(i) $[\delta]_{\Sigma'}(sb) = \begin{cases} \delta(sb) & \text{if } sb \in S \\ sb & \text{otherwise} \end{cases}$

(ii) $[\delta]_{\Sigma'}((s_1, \ldots, s_n)) = ([\delta]_{\Sigma'}(s_1), \ldots, [\delta]_{\Sigma'}(s_n))$

(iii) $[\delta]_{\Sigma'}((s_1 \rightarrow s_2)) = ([\delta]_{\Sigma'}(s_1) \rightarrow [\delta]_{\Sigma'}(s_2))$

(iv) $[\delta]_{\Sigma'}(f) = \begin{cases} \delta(f) & \text{if } f \in F \\ f & \text{otherwise} \end{cases}$

$\square$

Two signature morphisms with equal domains can be combined, if they are domain compatible.

Definition 2.1.20 (Domain compatible, combine signature morphism)
Let $\Sigma = (S, F)$, $\Sigma_1 = (S_1, F_1)$ and $\Sigma_2 = (S_2, F_2)$ be signatures. Two signature morphisms $\delta_1 : \Sigma \rightarrow \Sigma_1$ and $\delta_2 : \Sigma \rightarrow \Sigma_2$ are called *domain compatible wrt.* $\Sigma = (S, F)$, if for all $s \in S$ it is $\delta_1(s) \in S_1$ or $\delta_2(s) \in S_2$.

The *combine signature morphism* $[\delta_1, \delta_2] : \Sigma_1 \rightarrow \Sigma_1$ of two domain compatible signature morphisms δ_1, δ_2 is defined by

$$[\delta_1, \delta_2](s) = \begin{cases} [\delta_1]_{\Sigma \cup \Sigma_2}(\delta_2(s')) & \text{if there is } s' \in S \text{ such that } s = \delta_1(s') \\ s & \text{otherwise} \end{cases}$$

for all $s \in S_1$ and

$$[\delta_1, \delta_2](f) = \begin{cases} [\delta_1]_{\Sigma \cup \Sigma_2}(\delta_2(f')) & \text{if there is } f' \in F \text{ such that } f = \delta_1(f') \\ f & \text{otherwise} \end{cases}$$

for all $f \in F_1$. $\square$

A signature morphism can be extended to a basis morphism providing a mapping on variables.

Definition 2.1.21 (Basis morphism)
Let (Σ_1, X_1) and (Σ_2, X_2) be bases. A *basis morphism* $\hat{\delta} : (\Sigma_1, X_1) \rightarrow (\Sigma_2, X_2)$ consists of a signature morphism $\delta : \Sigma_1 \rightarrow \Sigma_2$ and an (equally denoted) $S_1^{\times, \rightarrow}$-indexed family $\delta : X_1 \rightarrow X_2$ of functions $\delta_s : X_{1,s} \rightarrow X_{2,\delta(s)}$. $\square$

If the sets of variables of the family X_1 form subsets of the sets of variables of the family X_2 respecting the signature morphism, a canonical basis morphism can be defined.

Definition 2.1.22 (Canonical basis morphism)
Let (Σ_1, X_1) and (Σ_2, X_2) be bases. For a signature morphism $\delta : \Sigma_1 \rightarrow \Sigma_2$ with $X_{1,s} \subseteq X_{2,\delta(s)}$ for all $s \in S_1^{\times, \rightarrow}$ the *canonical basis morphism* is defined by $\delta(\Sigma_1, X_1) = (\delta(\Sigma_1), X_1)$. $\qquad\square$

In the sequel we will implicitly extend signature morphisms to basis morphisms using the canonical basis morphism if no basis morphism is given.

A basis morphism extends in a unique way to a translation of terms, formulae and specifications.

Definition 2.1.23 (Translation of terms, formulae and specifications)
Let $(\Sigma_1, X_1), (\Sigma_2, X_2)$ be bases and $\delta : (\Sigma_1, X_1) \rightarrow (\Sigma_2, X_2)$ be a basis morphism.

a) The *translation* $\hat{\delta} : T(\Sigma_1, X_1) \rightarrow T(\Sigma_2, X_2)$ *of terms* is given by an $S_1^{\times, \rightarrow}$-indexed family of functions $\hat{\delta}_s : T(\Sigma_1, X_1)_s \rightarrow T(\Sigma_2, X_2)_{\delta(s)}$ which is inductively defined as follows:

  (i) $\hat{\delta}(x) = \delta(x)$ $\hfill$ (variable)

  (ii) $\hat{\delta}(f) = \delta(f)$ $\hfill$ (function symbol)

  (iii) $\hat{\delta}(@t_f) = @(\hat{\delta}(t_f))$ $\hfill$ (currying)

  (iv) $\hat{\delta}(t_1, \ldots, t_n) = (\hat{\delta}(t_1), \ldots, \hat{\delta}(t_n))$ $\hfill$ (tuple)

  (v) $\hat{\delta}(t_f(t_a)) = (\hat{\delta}(t_f))(\hat{\delta}(t_a))$ $\hfill$ (application)

  (vi) $\hat{\delta}(t_g \circ t_f) = \hat{\delta}(t_g) \circ \hat{\delta}(t_f)$ $\hfill$ (function composition)

b) The *translation* $\hat{\delta} : \mathcal{F}(\Sigma_1, X_1) \rightarrow \mathcal{F}(\Sigma_2, X_2)$ *of* (Σ_1, X_1)-*formulae* is inductively defined as follows:

  (i) $\hat{\delta}(t_1 = t_2) = (\delta(t_1) = \delta(t_2))$ $\hfill$ (equation)

  (ii) $\hat{\delta}(\forall x : s\ \varphi) = \forall \delta(x) : \delta(s)\ \hat{\delta}(\varphi)$ $\hfill$ (quantification)

  Sets of formulae are translated by setting $\hat{\delta}(E) = \{\hat{\delta}(\varphi) \mid \varphi \in E\}$.

c) The *translation* $\hat{\delta} : SPEC(\Sigma_1, X_1) \rightarrow SPEC(\Sigma_2, X_2)$ *of specifications* is defined by $\hat{\delta}(\Sigma_1, E) = (\delta(\Sigma_1), \hat{\delta}(E))$.

In the following we simplify notations and write δ instead of $\hat{\delta}$. $\qquad\square$

Manipulations

Variables in a term can be substituted by terms of appropriate sort. This forms the foundation of term rewriting. A substitution maps variables to terms of appropriate sort.

Definition 2.1.24 (Substitution, constructor-ground substitution)
For a basis $(\Sigma = (S, F, C), X)$, a *substitution* $\sigma : X \rightarrow T(\Sigma, X)$ associates variables with (Σ, X)-terms of appropriate sort. The set of all substitutions wrt. a basis (Σ, X) is denoted by $SUBST(\Sigma, X)$.

Let $x_i \in X_{s_i}$ and $t_i \in T(\Sigma, X)_{s_i}$ for $1 \leq i \leq n$. By $\sigma = \{x_1 \mapsto t_1, \ldots, x_n \mapsto t_n\}$ we denote a substitution with $\sigma(x_i) = t_i$ for $1 \leq i \leq n$ and $\sigma(y) = y$ for all $y \in X \setminus \{x_1, \ldots, x_n\}$.

A substitution σ is called *constructor ground*, if $\sigma(X) \subseteq T_G^{cons}(\Sigma, X)$.   □

A substitution can be propagated to terms.

Definition 2.1.25 (Application of substitution)
Let (Σ, X) be a basis and $\sigma : X \rightarrow T(\Sigma, X)$ a substitution.

a) The *application of a substitution to a term* $\hat{\sigma} : T(\Sigma, X) \rightarrow T(\Sigma, X)$ is defined inductively:

   (i) $\hat{\sigma}(x) = \sigma(x)$ (variable)

   (ii) $\hat{\sigma}(f) = f$ (function symbol)

   (iii) $\hat{\sigma}(@t_f) = (@\hat{\sigma}(t_f))$ (currying)

   (iv) $\hat{\sigma}(t_1, \ldots, t_n) = (\hat{\sigma}(t_1), \ldots, \hat{\sigma}(t_n))$ (tuple)

   (v) $\hat{\sigma}(t_f(t_a)) = (\hat{\sigma}(t_f))(\hat{\sigma}(t_a))$ (application)

   (vi) $\hat{\sigma}(t_g \circ t_f) = (\hat{\sigma}(t_g) \circ \hat{\sigma}(t_f))$ (function composition)

   We simplify the notation and abbreviate $\hat{\sigma}(t)$ by $t\sigma$.

b) The *application of a substitution to a formula* $\hat{\sigma} : \mathcal{F}(\Sigma, X) \rightarrow \mathcal{F}(\Sigma, X)$ is defined inductively:

   (i) $\hat{\sigma}(t_1 = t_2) = (\sigma(t_1) = \sigma(t_2))$ (equation)

   (ii) $\hat{\sigma}(\forall x : s\, \varphi) = \forall x : s\, \hat{\sigma'}(\varphi)$ (quantification)

   with $\sigma'(y) = \begin{cases} y & \text{if } x = y \\ \sigma(y) & \text{otherwise} \end{cases}$

   We simplify the notation and abbreviate $\hat{\sigma}(\varphi)$ by $\varphi\sigma$.   □

In order to navigate in terms and replace designated subterms, we introduce a notion of positions of a term.

Definition 2.1.26 (Positions of a term)
The set of positions $Pos : T(\Sigma, X) \rightarrow \mathcal{P}(\mathbb{N}^*)$ of a term is defined inductively:

(i) $Pos(x) = \langle\rangle$ $\hspace{6cm}$ (variable)

(ii) $Pos(f) = \langle\rangle$ $\hspace{5.5cm}$ (function symbol)

(iii) $Pos((@t_f)) = \langle\rangle \cup \{\langle 1\rangle \& p \mid p \in Pos(t_f)\}$ $\hspace{3cm}$ (currying)

(iv) $Pos((t_1, \ldots, t_n)) = \langle\rangle \cup \bigcup_{i=1}^{n} \{\langle i\rangle \& p \mid p \in Pos(t_i)\}$ $\hspace{2cm}$ (tuple)

(v) $Pos((t_f(t_a))) = \langle\rangle \cup \{\langle 1\rangle \& p \mid p \in Pos(t_f)\} \cup \{\langle 2\rangle \& p \mid p \in Pos(t_a)\}$ $\hspace{0.5cm}$ (application)

(vi) $Pos((t_g \circ t_f)) = \langle\rangle \cup \{\langle 1\rangle \& p \mid p \in Pos(t_g)\} \cup \{\langle 2\rangle \& p \mid p \in Pos(t_f)\}$
$\hspace{7cm}$ (function composition)

$\square$

For each position of a term, we can retrieve the subterm at that position.

Definition 2.1.27 (Subterm at position)
For a basis (Σ, X), a term $t \in T(\Sigma, X)$ and a position $p \in Pos(t)$ the *subterm at position* p (written $t|_p$) is defined inductively:

(i') $t|_{\langle\rangle} = t$ $\hspace{6.5cm}$ (epsilon)

(iii) $(@t_f)|_{\langle 1\rangle \& p} = t_f|_p$ $\hspace{5cm}$ (currying)

(iv) $(t_1, \ldots, t_n)|_{\langle i\rangle \& p} = t_i|_p$ $\hspace{4.5cm}$ (tuple)

(v) $(t_f(t_a))|_{\langle i\rangle \& p} = \begin{cases} t_f|_p & \text{if } i = 1 \\ t_a|_p & \text{if } i = 2 \end{cases}$ $\hspace{3cm}$ (application)

(vi) $(t_g \circ t_f)|_{\langle i\rangle \& p} = \begin{cases} t_g|_p & \text{if } i = 1 \\ t_f|_p & \text{if } i = 2 \end{cases}$ $\hspace{2.5cm}$ (function composition)

$\square$

Given a term and a position of the term, the specified subterm can be replaced by a term of appropriate sort.

Definition 2.1.28 (Replacement of subterm at position)
Let (Σ, X) be a basis, $t \in T(\Sigma, X)$ a term and $p \in Pos(t)$ a position such that $t|_p \in T(\Sigma, X)_s$ and $t' \in T(\Sigma, X)_s$. The *replacement $t[t']_p$ of the subterm of t at a position p with t'* is defined inductively:

(i') $t[t']_{\langle\rangle} = t'$ $\hspace{6.5cm}$ (epsilon)

(iii) $(@t_f)[t']_{\langle 1 \rangle \& p} = @(t_f[t']_p)$ (currying)

(iv) $(t_1, \ldots, t_n)[t']_{\langle i \rangle \& p} = (t_1, \ldots, t_{i-1}, t_i[t']_p, t_{i+1}, \ldots, t_n)$ (tuple)

(v) $(t_f(t_a))[t']_{\langle i \rangle \& p} = \begin{cases} (t_f[t']_p)(t_a) & \text{if } i = 1 \\ t_f(t_a[t']_p) & \text{if } i = 2 \end{cases}$ (application)

(vi) $(t_g \circ t_f)[t']_{\langle i \rangle \& p} = \begin{cases} (t_g[t']_p) \circ t_f & \text{if } i = 1 \\ t_g \circ (t_f[t']_p) & \text{if } i = 2 \end{cases}$ (function composition)

$\square$

2.1.4   Implicit extensions

The formulae of algebraic specifications are based on equations. This renders the theory and the mechanization easier, but leads to a lack of expressibility. For example, conditionals can not conveniently be expressed in the equational logic. In order to improve the practical usage of algebraic specifications, we introduce standard function symbols for conditionals and projections.

Conditionals

In the sequel we assume that the following signature constituents are available in each specification:

$$bool \in S$$
$$true, false \in C_{bool} \subseteq F_{bool}$$

Moreover, we assume that for all sorts $s \in S^{\times, \rightarrow}$ there is a *conditional*

$$\textbf{if } \_ \textbf{ then } \_ \textbf{ else } \_ \in F_{(bool,s,s) \rightarrow s}$$

available. The notation **if** _ **then** _ **else** _ introduces a ternary operation with infix notation. The following axioms are implicitly added to all specifications guaranteeing the intended behaviour of the conditional:

$$\forall x, y : s \ \ \textbf{if } true \textbf{ then } x \textbf{ else } y \ = \ x,$$
$$\forall x, y : s \ \ \textbf{if } false \textbf{ then } x \textbf{ else } y \ = \ y$$

Projections

In order to simplify the usage of tuples we assume for all sorts $s_1, \ldots, s_n \in S^{\times, \rightarrow}$ and indices $1 \leq i \leq n$ the operation

$$\#_i \in F_{(s_1, \ldots, s_n) s_i}$$

for *projections* to be part of the signature. As properties for the provided function symbols we assume that the axioms

$$\forall x_1 : s_1, \ldots, x_n : s_n \ \ \#_i(x_1, \ldots, x_n) \ = \ x_i \quad (1 \leq i \leq n)$$

are added to the specification. The application of the projection function symbol $\#_i$ to an n-tuple yields the i-th element of the tuple.

2.2 Semantics

We will now approach the semantic aspects of algebraic specifications. We will define algebras of a signature and will introduce models that satisfy the axioms of a specification and the generation constraints. We follow a loose semantics approach rather than an initial algebra approach [41]. For the relation between algebras we study homomorphisms and subalgebras. Finally, a notion of behavioural equivalence of algebras modulo a set of equations is defined.

2.2.1 Algebras and models

We introduce the basic semantic concepts of algebraic specifications extended by higher-order sorts and function symbols. The semantics of an algebraic specification comprises the class of all constructor generated models.

An algebra provides interpretations for the constituents of a signature.

Definition 2.2.1 (Σ-Algebra)

a) For a signature $\Sigma = (S, F)$ a Σ-*algebra* $\mathcal{A} = (S^{\mathcal{A}}, F^{\mathcal{A}})$ consists of the families $S^{\mathcal{A}} = (s^{\mathcal{A}})_{s \in S^{\times, \rightarrow}}$ and $F^{\mathcal{A}} = (f^{\mathcal{A}})_{f \in F}$ providing

   (i) for each basic sort $sb \in S$ a non-empty *carrier set* $sb^{\mathcal{A}}$,

   (ii) for each tuple sort $s = (s_1, \ldots, s_n) \in S^{\times, \rightarrow}$ the Cartesian product $s^{\mathcal{A}} = s_1^{\mathcal{A}} \times \cdots \times s_n^{\mathcal{A}}$

   (iii) for each function sort $s = s_1 \rightarrow s_2 \in S^{\times, \rightarrow}$ the set $s^{\mathcal{A}} = [s_1^{\mathcal{A}} \rightarrow s_2^{\mathcal{A}}]$ of all total functions with domain $s_1^{\mathcal{A}}$ and range $s_2^{\mathcal{A}}$, and

   (iv) for each function symbol $f \in F_s$ an element $f^{\mathcal{A}} \in s^{\mathcal{A}}$ of the corresponding carrier set.

b) The carrier $s^{\mathcal{A}}$ resp. the function $f^{\mathcal{A}}$ are called the *interpretations* of sort s resp. of function symbol f in the Σ-algebra $\mathcal{A}$.   □

Algebras can be confined by a subsignature.

Definition 2.2.2 (Σ-Reduct)
Let $\Sigma_1 = (S_1, F_1)$ be a subsignature of $\Sigma = (S, F)$. The Σ_1-*reduct* $\mathcal{A}|_{\Sigma_1} = (S^{\mathcal{A}|_{\Sigma_1}}, F^{\mathcal{A}|_{\Sigma_1}})$ of a Σ-algebra $\mathcal{A} = (S^{\mathcal{A}}, F^{\mathcal{A}})$ is a Σ_1-algebra keeping all carriers and functions of the subsignature:
$$s^{\mathcal{A}|_{\Sigma_1}} = s^{\mathcal{A}} \quad \text{and} \quad f^{\mathcal{A}|_{\Sigma_1}} = f^{\mathcal{A}}.$$
□

In order to define the interpretation of terms in an algebra, we need a notion for providing values for variables.

Definition 2.2.3 (Valuation)
Let (Σ, X) be a basis. A *valuation* $v : X \rightarrow S^{\mathcal{A}}$ of X in a Σ-algebra $\mathcal{A}$ associates variables with elements of appropriate sorts.   □

A valuation can be modified updating the value associated with a variable.

Definition 2.2.4 (Valuation modification)
Let $v : X \rightarrow S^{\mathcal{A}}$ be a valuation of X in a Σ-algebra $\mathcal{A}$, $x \in X_s$ a variable and $a \in s^{\mathcal{A}}$ an element of the appropriate carrier set. The *valuation modification of v at x with a* is defined as follows:

$$v[x \leftarrow a](y) = \begin{cases} a & \text{if } x = y \\ v(y) & \text{otherwise} \end{cases}$$

□

For the interpretation of the curried function symbols we need to define currying of functions.

Definition 2.2.5 (Currying of functions)
Let $f : M_1 \times \cdots \times M_n \rightarrow M$ be an n-ary function, $n \geq 2$. The *curried function* $@f : M_1 \rightarrow \cdots \rightarrow M_n \rightarrow M$ validates for all $a_i \in M_i$, $(1 \leq i \leq n)$:

$$(@f)\,(a_1)\ldots(a_n) = f(a_1, \ldots, a_n)$$

□

Given a valuation a value of the corresponding carrier set is assigned to each term.

Definition 2.2.6 (Value of term)
The *value $t^{\mathcal{A}}[v]$ of a term* $t \in T(\Sigma, X)$ wrt. a valuation $v : X \rightarrow S^{\mathcal{A}}$ is inductively defined as follows:

(i) $x^{\mathcal{A}}[v] = v(x)$ (variable)

(ii) $f^{\mathcal{A}}[v] = f^{\mathcal{A}}$ (function symbol)

(iii) $(@t_f)^{\mathcal{A}}[v] = @(t_f^{\mathcal{A}}[v])$ (currying)

(iv) $(t_1, \ldots, t_n)^{\mathcal{A}}[v] = (t_1^{\mathcal{A}}[v], \ldots, t_n^{\mathcal{A}}[v])$ (tuple)

(v) $(t_f(t_a))^{\mathcal{A}}[v] = t_f^{\mathcal{A}}[v](t_a^{\mathcal{A}}[v])$ (application)

(vi) $(t_g \circ t_f)^{\mathcal{A}}[v] = (t_g^{\mathcal{A}}[v]) \circ (t_f^{\mathcal{A}}[v])$ (function composition)

□

Based on values of terms, we can define a satisfaction relation of formulae.

Definition 2.2.7 (Satisfaction relation)
A formula $\varphi \in \mathcal{F}(\Sigma, X)$ is said to be *satisfied* in a Σ-algebra $\mathcal{A}$ wrt. a valuation v from X in $\mathcal{A}$ (short: $\mathcal{A} \models_v \varphi$) if we have:

(i) $\mathcal{A} \models_v (t_1 = t_2) :\Leftrightarrow t_1^{\mathcal{A}}[v] = t_2^{\mathcal{A}}[v]$ and (equation)

(ii) $\mathcal{A} \models_v (\forall x : s \; \varphi) :\Leftrightarrow$ For all $a \in s^{\mathcal{A}}$ it is $\mathcal{A} \models_{v[x \leftarrow a]} \varphi$. (quantification)

A formula $\varphi \in \mathcal{F}(\Sigma, X)$ is *satisfied on principle* in a Σ-algebra $\mathcal{A}$ (denoted by $\mathcal{A} \models \varphi$), if for all valuations v from X in $\mathcal{A}$ it is $\mathcal{A} \models_v \varphi$. □

The satisfaction of closed formulae is independent of the valuation. In the following we will denote the satisfaction of closed formulae also by $\mathcal{A} \models \varphi$.

Lemma 2.2.8 (Properties of Σ-algebras)
Let $\mathcal{A}$ be a Σ-algebra, v a valuation of X in $\mathcal{A}$, $x \in X_{s_1}$ and $t_f, t_g \in T(\Sigma, X \setminus \{x\})_{s_1 \rightarrow s_2}$. The following properties hold for terms of appropriate sorts:

a) $\mathcal{A} \models_v \forall x : s_1 \; t_f(x) = t_g(x)$ if and only if $\mathcal{A} \models_v t_f = t_g$.

b) $\mathcal{A} \models_v t_i = t_i'$ for all $1 \leq i \leq n$ if and only if $\mathcal{A} \models_v (t_1, \ldots, t_n) = (t_1', \ldots, t_n')$.

c) $\mathcal{A} \models_v (t_g \circ t_f)(t_a) = t_g(t_f(t_a))$

d) $\mathcal{A} \models_v (@f)t_1 \ldots t_n = f(t_1, \ldots, t_n)$ □

The satisfaction of formulae lays the basis for defining the models of an algebraic specification.

Definition 2.2.9 (Model)
A Σ-algebra $\mathcal{A}$ is called a *model* of an algebraic specification (Σ, E), if for all formulae $\varphi \in E$ $\mathcal{A} \models \varphi$ holds. The class of all models of (Σ, E) is denoted by $MOD(\Sigma, E)$. □

Models that interpret the constants *true* and *false* equally are useless for an implementation. Since we cannot axiomatize that each model must distinguish the interpretations of *true* and *false*, we define specifications to be inconsistent if they have only models that interpret *true* and *false* equally.

Definition 2.2.10 (Consistent, inconsistent)
An algebraic specification (Σ, E) is called *consistent*, if there is a model $\mathcal{A} \in MOD(\Sigma, E)$ with $true^{\mathcal{A}} \neq false^{\mathcal{A}}$. Otherwise the specification is called *inconsistent*. □

Since we head for implementations of algebraic specifications in programming languages, we are interested in carriers that can be generated by constructors.

Definition 2.2.11 (Generated model, semantics)
Let $(\Sigma = (S, F, C), E)$ be an algebraic specification.

a) A model $\mathcal{M}$ of (Σ, E) is called a *generated model* of (Σ, E), if for all constructor sorts $sc \in SC$ the carrier set $sc^{\mathcal{M}}$ is the least set wrt. set inclusion satisfying

$$C_{sc}^{\mathcal{M}} \subseteq sc^{\mathcal{M}} \quad \text{and} \quad c^{\mathcal{M}}(s^{\mathcal{M}}) \subseteq sc^{\mathcal{M}} \text{ for all } c \in C_{(s \to sc)}.$$

b) The *semantics* of the specification (Σ, E) is defined by the class $CGEN(\Sigma, E)$ of all generated models of (Σ, E). □

The class of algebras contributing to the semantics is confined by the axioms. Formulae that can be added to a specification achieving the same semantics are called theorems.

Definition 2.2.12 (Theorem)
A (Σ, X)-formula φ is called a *theorem* of an algebraic specification (Σ, E) (denoted by $E \models \varphi$), if $CGEN(\Sigma, E) = CGEN(\Sigma, E \cup \{\varphi\})$. □

A minimal specification contains no theorems.

Definition 2.2.13 (Minimal specification)
A specification (Σ, E) is called *minimal*, if there is no formula $\varphi \in E$ such that φ is a theorem of $(\Sigma, E \setminus \{\varphi\})$. □

The theorems are not necessary for the axiomatization, but they contribute to a better understanding and ease the development of an implementation.

2.2.2 Homomorphisms and subalgebras

A homomorphism is a family of mappings between the carrier sets of two Σ-algebras which is compatible with all operations.

Definition 2.2.14 (Σ-Homomorphism)
Let $\mathcal{A}$ and $\mathcal{B}$ be Σ-algebras with $\Sigma = (S, F)$. A Σ-*homomorphism* $\varphi : \mathcal{A} \to \mathcal{B}$ is an $S^{\times, \to}$-indexed family of mappings $\varphi_s : s^{\mathcal{A}} \to s^{\mathcal{B}}$ with

- $\varphi_s(f^{\mathcal{A}}) = f^{\mathcal{B}}$ for all $f \in F_s$,

- $\varphi_{(s_1,\ldots,s_n)}((a_1,\ldots,a_n)) = (\varphi_{s_1}(a_1),\ldots,\varphi_{s_n}(a_n))$ for all $a_i \in s_i^{\mathcal{A}}, 1 \leq i \leq n$,

- $\varphi_{s_2}(f(a)) = \varphi_{(s_1 \to s_2)}(f)(\varphi_{s_1}(a))$ for all $f \in (s_1 \to s_2)^{\mathcal{A}}$ and $a \in s_1^{\mathcal{A}}$. □

Surjective homomorphisms are compatible with the formation of terms.

Lemma 2.2.15 (Homomorphisms distribute with interpretation of terms)
Let (Σ, X) be a basis, $\varphi : \mathcal{A} \to \mathcal{B}$ a surjective Σ-homomorphism from $\mathcal{A}$ to $\mathcal{B}$, and
$v : X \to S^{\mathcal{A}}$ a valuation of X in $\mathcal{A}$. Let the valuation $v' : X \to S^{\mathcal{B}}$ of X in $\mathcal{B}$ be given by
$v'(x) = \varphi(v(x))$. Then φ is compatible with the interpretation of terms:

(i) $\varphi_s(x^{\mathcal{A}}[v]) = x^{\mathcal{B}}[v']$ (variable)

(ii) $\varphi_s(f^{\mathcal{A}}[v]) = f^{\mathcal{B}}[v']$ (function symbol)

(iii) $\varphi_{s_1 \to \cdots \to s_n \to s}((@t_f)^{\mathcal{A}}[v]) = @(\varphi_{(s_1,\ldots,s_n) \to s}(t_f^{\mathcal{B}}[v']))$ (currying)

(iv) $\varphi_{(s_1,\ldots,s_n)}((t_1,\ldots,t_n)^{\mathcal{A}}[v]) = (\varphi_{s_1}(t_1^{\mathcal{A}}[v]),\ldots,\varphi_{s_n}(t_n^{\mathcal{A}}[v]))$ (tuple)

(v) $\varphi_{s_2}((t_f(t_a))^{\mathcal{A}}[v]) = \varphi_{s_1 \to s_2}(t_f^{\mathcal{A}}[v])(\varphi_{s_1}(t_a^{\mathcal{A}}[v]))$ (application)

(vi) $\varphi_{(s_1 \to s_3)}((t_g \circ t_f)^{\mathcal{A}}[v]) = \varphi_{(s_2 \to s_3)}(t_g^{\mathcal{A}}[v]) \circ \varphi_{(s_1 \to s_2)}(t_f^{\mathcal{A}}[v])$ (function composition)

$\square$

Moreover, surjective homomorphisms preserve the satisfaction of formulae.

Lemma 2.2.16 (Property preservation)
Let $\varphi : \mathcal{A} \to \mathcal{B}$ be a surjective Σ-homomorphism and ξ a closed (Σ, X)-formulae. Then
$\mathcal{A} \models \xi$ implies $\mathcal{B} \models \xi$. $\square$

An algebra can be embedded into a "larger" algebra of the same signature that comprises
supersets for all its carriers.

Definition 2.2.17 (Embedded algebra)
A Σ_1-algebra $\mathcal{A}$ with $\Sigma_1 = (S_1, F_1)$ is said to be *embedded* into a Σ_2-algebra $\mathcal{B}$ *via* a sort
morphism $\iota : S_1^{\times, \to} \to S_2^{\times, \to}$ (written $\mathcal{A} \overset{\iota}{\subseteq} \mathcal{B}$), if $sb^{\mathcal{A}} \subseteq \iota(sb)^{\mathcal{B}}$ holds for all basic sorts
$sb \in S_1$. $\square$

The inclusion relation for basic sorts induces further properties for the derived sorts.
However, the inclusion relation can not be transfered to higher function types, since the
equality of functions demands equal domains and ranges. Therefore we introduce an
equivalence notion for comparing functions of higher types.

Definition 2.2.18 (Equivalence on embedded sorts)
Let the Σ_1-algebra $\mathcal{A}$ be embedded in the Σ_2-algebra $\mathcal{B}$ via the sort morphism $\iota : S_1^{\times, \to} \to S_2^{\times, \to}$. The *equivalence on embedded sorts* $^{\mathcal{A}}\asymp^{\mathcal{B}}$ is a family of $S_1^{\times, \to}$-indexed relations
$^{\mathcal{A}}\asymp_s^{\mathcal{B}} \subseteq s^{\mathcal{A}} \times \iota(s)^{\mathcal{B}}$ with

(i) $a \; ^{\mathcal{A}}\asymp_{sb}^{\mathcal{B}} b \Leftrightarrow a = b$,

(ii) $(a_1,\ldots,a_n) \; ^{\mathcal{A}}\asymp_{(s_1,\ldots,s_n)}^{\mathcal{B}} (b_1,\ldots,b_n) \Leftrightarrow a_i \; ^{\mathcal{A}}\asymp_{s_i}^{\mathcal{B}} b_i$ for all $1 \leq i \leq n$,

(iii) $f \,^{A}\!\asymp^{B}_{(s_1 \to s_2)} g \Leftrightarrow \forall a \colon s_1^{A} \; \forall b \colon \iota(s_1)^{B} \; a \,^{A}\!\asymp^{B}_{s_1} b \to f(a) \,^{A}\!\asymp^{B}_{s_2} g(b)$.   □

Now we can prove that for each function of the embedded algebra there is an equivalent function in the original algebra which describes a kind of subset property for higher types.

Lemma 2.2.19 (Subset condition for embedded algebras)
Let $\mathcal{A} \overset{\iota}{\subseteq} \mathcal{B}$. For each $g \in (s_1 \to s_2)^{\mathcal{A}}$ there is a function $h \in (s_1 \to s_2)^{\mathcal{B}}$ such that $g \,^{A}\!\asymp^{B}_{s_1 \to s_2} h$.   □

Based on the definition of embedded algebras we introduce subalgebras. A subalgebra additionally satisfies the compatibility of the operations.

Definition 2.2.20 (Subalgebra)
Given two signatures $\Sigma_1 = (S_1, F_1, C_1)$ and $\Sigma_2 = (S_2, F_2, C_2)$, a Σ_1-algebra $\mathcal{A}$ is said to be a *subalgebra* of a Σ_2-algebra $\mathcal{B}$ *via* a signature morphism $\delta : \Sigma_1 \to \Sigma_2$, if we have $\mathcal{A} \overset{\delta}{\subseteq} \mathcal{B}$ and $f^{\mathcal{A}} \,^{A}\!\asymp^{B}_{s} \delta(f)^{\mathcal{B}}$ for all $f \in F_{1,s}$.   □

The image of a homomorphism is defined by the images of the carrier sets.

Definition 2.2.21 (Image)
Let $\Sigma = (S, F)$ be a signature and $\varphi : S^{\mathcal{A}} \to S^{\mathcal{B}}$ a family of mappings $\varphi_s : s^{\mathcal{A}} \to s^{\mathcal{B}}$. The *image* $\varphi(\mathcal{A})$ of $\mathcal{A}$ under φ is a structure $\mathcal{C} = (S^{\mathcal{C}}, F^{\mathcal{C}})$ with $s^{\mathcal{C}} = \varphi_s(s^{\mathcal{A}})$ and $f^{\mathcal{C}} \,^{C}\!\asymp^{B}_{s} f^{\mathcal{B}}$ for all $s \in S^{\times, \to}$ and $f \in F$.   □

The image of a homomorphism forms a Σ-algebra which is a subalgebra of the target algebra of the homomorphism.

Lemma 2.2.22 (Image is subalgebra)
Let $\varphi : \mathcal{A} \to \mathcal{B}$ be a Σ-homomorphism. The image $\varphi(\mathcal{A})$ forms a subalgebra of $\mathcal{B}$.   □

Homomorphisms and subalgebras lay the foundation for fusion techniques and data structure refinements.

2.2.3   Congruences and behavioural semantics

In order to partition carriers into classes of behavioural equivalence we introduce congruences. The congruences can be established by equations between constructor terms. The following definitions are based on the notion of behavioural specifications [11] extended to higher-order specifications.

A congruence is an equivalence relation on the carrier sets of an algebra which is compatible with forming tuples and functions of the carriers.

Definition 2.2.23 (Σ-Congruence)
A Σ-*congruence* $\approx^{\mathcal{A}}$ on a Σ-algebra $\mathcal{A}$ with $\Sigma = (S, F)$ is an $S^{\times,\rightarrow}$-indexed family of equivalence relations $\approx_s^{\mathcal{A}}$ on $s^{\mathcal{A}}$ validating:

(ii) If $a_i \approx_{s_i}^{\mathcal{A}} b_i$ for $1 \leq i \leq n$, then $(a_1, \ldots, a_n) \approx_{(s_1, \ldots, s_n)}^{\mathcal{A}} (b_1, \ldots, b_n)$.

(iii) If $g \approx_{(s_1 \rightarrow s_2)}^{\mathcal{A}} h$ and $a \approx_{s_1}^{\mathcal{A}} b$, then $g(a) \approx_{s_2}^{\mathcal{A}} h(b)$. □

A congruence can be used to build the quotient algebra using the equivalence classes as carrier sets.

Definition 2.2.24 (Quotient algebra)
Let $\mathcal{A}$ be a Σ-algebra with $\Sigma = (S, F)$ and $\approx^{\mathcal{A}}$ a Σ-congruence on $\mathcal{A}$. The *quotient algebra* $\mathcal{A}/_{\approx} = (S^{\mathcal{A}/\approx}, F^{\mathcal{A}/\approx})$ is given by

a) $s^{\mathcal{A}/\approx} = s^{\mathcal{A}}/_{\approx_s^{\mathcal{A}}}$,

b) $f^{\mathcal{A}/\approx}([a]_{\approx_{s_1}^{\mathcal{A}}}) = [f^{\mathcal{A}}(a)]_{\approx_{s_2}^{\mathcal{A}}}$. □

Since $\approx$ is a congruence, the functions of the quotient algebra are well defined, and the structure $\mathcal{A}/_{\approx}$ forms a Σ-algebra.

A congruence can be used to reduce an algebra to the behaviour viewed modulo a congruence.

Definition 2.2.25 (Behaviour wrt. a congruence)
The *behaviour* of a Σ-algebra $\mathcal{A}$ wrt. a Σ-congruence $\approx$ is given by the quotient algebra $\mathcal{A}/_{\approx}$. □

In the following we head for a syntactic representation of the congruence by a set of equations.

Definition 2.2.26 (Equivalence relation on terms)
Let E be a set of (Σ, X)-formulae. The $S^{\times,\rightarrow}$-indexed family $\sim^E$ of *induced equivalence relations* $\sim_s^E$ on $T(\Sigma, X)_s$ is defined inductively:

(i') If $l = r \in E$ with $l, r \in T(\Sigma, X)_s$, then for all $\sigma \in SUBST(\Sigma, X)$ it is $l\sigma \sim_s^E r\sigma$.
(substitution)

(iii) If $t_f \sim_{(s_1, \ldots, s_n) \rightarrow s}^E t_f'$, then $@t_f \sim_{(s_1 \rightarrow \cdots \rightarrow s_n \rightarrow s)}^E @t_f'$.
(currying)

(iv) If $t_i \sim_{s_i}^E t_i'$ for all $1 \leq i \leq n$, then $(t_1, \ldots, t_n) \sim_{(s_1, \ldots, s_n)}^E (t_1', \ldots, t_n')$.
(tuple)

(v) If $t_f \sim_{(s_1 \rightarrow s_2)}^E t_f'$ and $t_a \sim_{s_1}^E t_a'$, then $t_f(t_a) \sim_{s_2}^E t_f'(t_a')$.
(application)

(vi) If $t_f \sim^E_{(s_1 \to s_2)} t'_f$ and $t_g \sim^E_{(s_2 \to s_3)} t'_g$, then $(t_g \circ t_f) \sim^E_{(s_1 \to s_3)} (t'_g \circ t'_f)$.

(function composition)

□

Terms identified by equivalence relation induced by a set of equations have the same interpretation in an algebra satisfying these equations.

Lemma 2.2.27 (Equality on carriers follows induced equivalence relation)
Let E be a set of (Σ, X)-formulae. The induced equivalence relation $\sim^E$ relates terms with equal interpretation in algebras satisfying E:

$$t_1 \sim^E_s t_2 \Leftrightarrow \text{for all } \mathcal{A} \in MOD(\Sigma, E) \text{ and all valuations } v \text{ of } X \text{ in } \mathcal{A} \text{ it is } t_1^{\mathcal{A}}[v] = t_2^{\mathcal{A}}[v] .$$

□

Using an equivalence relation on terms, we can construct an equivalence relation on the carrier set of a Σ-algebra.

Definition 2.2.28 (Induced equivalence relation)
Let $\mathcal{A}$ be a Σ-algebra and E a set of (Σ, X)-formulae. The *induced $S^{\times, \to}$-indexed family of equivalence relations* $\approx^E_s$ on $s^{\mathcal{A}}$ is defined inductively on the structure of derived sorts:

(i′) If $t_1 \sim^E_s t_2$, then $t_1^{\mathcal{A}}[v] \approx^E_s t_1^{\mathcal{A}}[v]$ for all $v : X \to S^{\mathcal{A}}$.   (term equivalence)

(ii) $(a_1, \ldots, a_n) \approx^E_{(s_1, \ldots, s_n)} (b_1, \ldots, b_n)$ iff $a_i \approx^E_{s_i} b_i$ for all $1 \le i \le n$.   (tuple sort)

(iii) $g \approx^E_{(s_1 \to s_2)} h$ iff for all $a, b \in s_1^{\mathcal{A}}$ $a \approx^E_{s_1} b$ implies $g(a) \approx^E_{s_2} h(b)$.   (function sort)

□

The induced equivalence relation is by definition compatible with the functions of the carriers of higher sorts and therefore $\approx^E$ builds a Σ-congruence for all Σ-algebras. As a consequence the equivalence relation $\sim^E$ induces a Σ-congruence.

A Σ-congruence induces a weaker satisfaction relation on formulae by claiming the equivalence wrt. $\approx^E$ instead of equality.

Definition 2.2.29 (Behavioural satisfaction)
Let $\mathcal{A}$ be a Σ-algebra and $\approx^{\mathcal{A}}$ a Σ-congruence on $\mathcal{A}$. The *behavioural satisfaction* of a formula $\varphi \in \mathcal{F}(\Sigma, X)$ wrt. $\approx^{\mathcal{A}}$ written $\mathcal{A} \models^{\approx}_v \varphi$ is defined as follows:

a) $\mathcal{A} \models^{\approx}_v (t_1 = t_2) \Leftrightarrow t_1^{\mathcal{A}}[v] \approx_{\mathcal{A}} t_2^{\mathcal{A}}[v]$.

b) $\mathcal{A} \models^{\approx}_v (\forall x : s \; \varphi) \Leftrightarrow$ for all $a \in s^{\mathcal{A}}$ we have $\mathcal{A} \models^{\approx}_{v[x \leftarrow a]} \varphi$.   □

The behavioural satisfaction is equivalent to the standard satisfaction of the quotient algebra.

Lemma 2.2.30 (Behavioural satisfaction relates to standard satisfaction)
Let $\mathcal{A}$ be a Σ-algebra and $\approx^{\mathcal{A}}$ a Σ-congruence on $\mathcal{A}$. For all closed formulae $\varphi \in \mathcal{F}(\Sigma, X)$ we have

$$\mathcal{A} \models^{\approx^{\mathcal{A}}} \varphi \iff \mathcal{A}/_{\approx^{\mathcal{A}}} \models \varphi. \qquad \square$$

A Σ-congruence which is induced by a set of formulae provides an equivalence relation on Σ-algebras of behavioural equivalence.

Definition 2.2.31 (Behavioural equivalence)
Let $\mathcal{A}, \mathcal{B}$ be two Σ-algebras, E a set of (Σ, X)-formulae, and $\approx^{\mathcal{A}}, \approx^{\mathcal{B}}$ the induced congruences on $\mathcal{A}, \mathcal{B}$, respectively. The algebras $\mathcal{A}, \mathcal{B}$ are called *behavioural equivalent*, if $\mathcal{A}/_{\approx_{\mathcal{A}}} = \mathcal{B}/_{\approx_{\mathcal{B}}}$ holds. $\qquad \square$

The behaviour of algebras wrt. a set of equations can be used to enlarge the interpretations of an algebraic specification by admitting all algebras that are behaviourally equivalent to a regular model of the semantics of an algebraic specification.

Definition 2.2.32 (Behavioural models)
Let (Σ, E) be an algebraic specification and $E_C \subseteq E$ the subset of all Σ_C-equations (constructor equations) of E. The class of all *behavioural models* is defined as

$$BEH(\Sigma, E) = \{\mathcal{A} \mid \mathcal{A} \text{ is a } \Sigma\text{-algebra and } \mathcal{A}/_{\approx^{E_C}} \in CGEN(\Sigma, E)\} \qquad \square$$

This definition points out all constructor equations of an algebraic specification for defining a congruence on the carriers. Such equations restrict the carriers to equivalence classes of the term algebra. Since the term algebras behave equivalently modulo the induced congruence of E_C, the behavioural semantics also includes such algebras. This enables an implementation of such specifications by term algebras.

If there are non-constructor equations that cause non-free interpretations only, term algebras are not in the set of behavioural models. Hence, the use of behavioural interpretations by constructor equations does not guarantee the existence of term models.

Chapter 3

Structuring Concepts for Algebraic Specifications

We extend basic specifications by a distinguished subsignature declaring the visible sorts and function symbols. Algebraic specifications with hiding serve as basic building blocks for structuring composite specifications. The specification language consists of specification expressions formed by hiding, renaming, parameterization, parameter instantiation, union and extension. The introduced concepts are similar to the parameterized module language of Loeckx et al. [55] where large systems can be constructed by a specification expression with fragments of specifications as atoms. Specification expressions can be reduced to basic algebraic specifications as introduced in Chapter 2 extended by hiding. Finally, we will discuss semantic aspects of the structuring concept.

3.1 Specifications with hiding

Algebraic specifications with hiding may distinguish a subsignature of visible sorts and function symbols.

Definition 3.1.1 (Algebraic specifications with hiding)
Let (Σ, E) be an algebraic specification, and Σ_v the *visible subsignature* of Σ. The triple (Σ, E, Σ_v) is called an *algebraic specification with hiding*. □

The semantics of an algebraic specification with hiding comprises the class of all constructor generated models restricted to the visible subsignature.

Definition 3.1.2 (Semantics of specification with hiding)
The *semantics of an algebraic specification with hiding* (Σ, E, Σ_v) is defined by the class

$$HGEN(\Sigma, E, \Sigma_v) = \{ \mathcal{A}|_{\Sigma_v} \mid \mathcal{A} \in CGEN(\Sigma, E) \} .$$ □

The reduction by the visible signature may hide constructor symbols of the specification. As a consequence, the carriers of the reduct are in general not generated by the constructors of the visible signature.

3.2 Structuring algebraic specifications

Large specifications can be structured into subspecifications; vice versa, existing subspecifications can be combined into larger specifications using combining operators. By this principle composite specifications are structured in a syntactic way. For the time being, the structure of a composite specification does not impose an additional structure on the class of models. The semantics of a structured specification is determined by the corresponding flat specification with hiding.

3.2.1 Specification fragments

Specification fragments form the atoms for the specification language structuring specifications in a syntactic way. Based on the definition of signature fragments we introduce specification fragments with hiding.

Definition 3.2.1 (Specification fragments with hiding)
A *specification fragment with hiding* (Σ, E, Σ_v) *wrt.* a signature Σ' consists of a signature fragment $\Sigma \subseteq \Sigma'$, a set E of (Σ', X)-formulae and a subsignature Σ_v of Σ'. We denote the set of specification fragments by $SPEC_{frag}$. $\qquad \square$

Partial specifications can be combined by set oriented operations.

Definition 3.2.2 (Operations on specification fragments)
For specification fragments $P_1 = (\Sigma_1, E_1, \Sigma_{v,1})$, $P_2 = (\Sigma_2, E_2, \Sigma_{v,2})$ wrt. a common signature Σ', for all signature fragments $\Sigma_h = (S_h, F_h, C_h)$ a signature fragment of Σ' and signature morphisms $\delta : \Sigma' \rightarrow \Sigma''$ we define the following operations:

a) $P_1 \cup P_2 = (\Sigma_1 \cup \Sigma_2, E_1 \cup E_2, \Sigma_{v,1} \cup \Sigma_{v,2})$ $\qquad\qquad\qquad$ (union)

b) $P_1 \setminus P_2 = (\Sigma_1 \setminus \Sigma_2, E_1 \setminus E_2, [\Sigma_{v,1} \setminus \Sigma_{v,2}]_{\Sigma'})$ $\qquad\qquad$ (difference)

c) $P_1 \setminus_{sig} \Sigma_h = (\Sigma_1, E_1, [\Sigma_{v,1} \setminus \Sigma_h]_{\Sigma'})$ $\qquad\qquad\qquad$ (hiding)

d) $\delta(P_1) = (\delta(\Sigma_1), \delta(E_1), \delta(\Sigma_{v,1}))$ $\qquad\qquad\qquad\qquad$ (translation)

$\hfill \square$

3.2.2 Specification expressions

A specification morphism is a signature morphism that respects the validity of the axioms.

Definition 3.2.3 (Specification morphism)
Let (Σ_1, E_1) and (Σ_2, E_2) be specifications. A signature morphism $\delta : \Sigma_1 \to \Sigma_2$ is called a *specification morphism* $\delta : (\Sigma_1, E_1) \to (\Sigma_2, E_2)$, if for all $\mathcal{A} \in CGEN(\Sigma_2, E_2)$ there is $\mathcal{B} \in CGEN(\Sigma_1, E_1)$ such that $\mathcal{B}$ is a subalgebra of $\mathcal{A}$ via δ. $\square$

We will now define the expressions of the specification language. A specification expression can be reduced to a basic specification with hiding.

Definition 3.2.4 (Specification expression, local environment)
The set of *specification expressions SpecExpr* and the *local environment* of a specification expression $env : SpecExpr \to SPEC_{frag}$ are defined by mutual induction as follows:

a) If $SE = (\Sigma, E, \Sigma_v) \in SPEC_{frag}$, then (specification fragment)

- $SE \in SpecExpr$
- $env(SE) = (\Sigma, E, \Sigma_v)$.

b) If $SE \in SpecExpr$ with $env(SE) = (\Sigma, E, \Sigma_v)$ and $\Sigma_h \in SIGfrag$, then (hiding)

- $(SE \textbf{ hide } \Sigma_h) \in SpecExpr$
- $env(SE \textbf{ hide } \Sigma_h) = env(SE) \setminus \Sigma_h$.

c) If $SE \in SpecExpr$ with $env(SE) = (\Sigma, E, \Sigma_v)$ and $\delta : \Sigma \to \Sigma'$ is a signature morphism, then (translation)

- $SE(\delta) \in SpecExpr$
- $env(SE(\delta)) = (\delta(\Sigma), \delta(E), \delta(\Sigma_v))$.

d) If $SE, SP \in SpecExpr$ with $env(SE) = (\Sigma, E, \Sigma_v)$, and $env(SP) = (\Sigma_P, E_P, \Sigma_{v,P})$, then (parameterization)

- $SE[: SP] \in SpecExpr$
- $env(SE[: SP]) = (\Sigma \cup \Sigma_P, E \cup E_P, \Sigma_v \cup \Sigma_{v,P})$.

e) If $SE = SE'[: SP] \in SpecExpr$, $SP_{act} \in SpecExpr$, and $\delta : SP \to SP_{act}$ a specification morphism, then (parameter instantiation)

- $SE[SP_{act} \textbf{ fit } \delta] \in SpecExpr$
- $env(SE[SP_{act} \textbf{ fit } \delta]) = \delta(env(SE')) \cup env(SP_{act})$.

f) If $SE_1, SE_2 \in SpecExpr$ such that $env(SE_1)$ and $env(SE_2)$ are specifications, then (union)

- $(SE_1 + SE_2) \in SpecExpr$
- $env(SE_1 + SE_2) = env(SE_1) \cup env(SE_2)$.

g) If $SE_1, SE_2 \in SpecExpr$ such that $env(SE_1)$ is a specification, then   (extension)

- $(SE_1; SE_2) \in SpecExpr$
- $env(SE_1; SE_2) = env(SE_1) \cup env(SE_2)$.

The operators for constructing specification expressions, i.e. hiding, translation, parameterization, parameter instantiation, union and extensions, are called *specification combinators*.   □

The parameter instantiation follows the pushout construction [32, 77]. Given a specification expression SP_{act} and a specification morphism $\delta : SP \to SP_{act}$, the instantiated specification $SE(SP_{act})$ is the pushout of the commuting diagram Fig. 3.1.

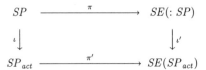

Figure 3.1: Push out construction

For specifying software systems we are interested in specification expression that yield an algebraic specification.

Definition 3.2.5 (Syntactically complete specification expression)
A specification expression SE is called *syntactically complete*, if $env(SE)$ is an algebraic specification with hiding.   □

The meaning of specification expressions is then defined by the semantics of the local environment.

Definition 3.2.6 (Semantics of specification expression)
The *semantics of a* of a syntactically complete specification expression $SE \in SpecExpr$ is defined by
$$HGEN(SE) = HGEN(env(SE)).$$ □

In order to simplify specification expressions we introduce global environments mapping specification names to specification expressions.

Definition 3.2.7 (Global environment)
Let NA be a set of specification names. A *global environment* is a function $GE : NA \to SpecExpr$.   □

If we assume a global environment and no cyclic dependencies between specification names, we can extend Definition 3.2.4 to names of specifications. Since *env* then depends on GE, we write env^{GE} instead of *env* and since *SpecExpr* then depends on *NA* we write $SpecExpr(NA)$ instead of *SpecExpr*.

h) If $SN \in NA$, then (specification name)

- $SN \in SpecExpr$
- $env^{GE}(SN) = env^{GE}(GE(SN))$.

A global environment models the state of a transformation system and makes reuse of specifications more comfortable. For the successive construction of a specification expressions we define named specifications.

Definition 3.2.8 (Named specifications)
Let $SE \in SpecExpr$ be a syntactically complete specification expression. Then

$$\textbf{spec} \quad name = SE$$

is a called a *named specification* with name *name*. □

Named specifications can be used to construct a global environment. The successive construction of an acyclic global environment by named specifications results again in a global environment without cyclic dependencies.

3.2.3 Semantic aspects of structuring specifications

The most common way of combining specifications is vertical composition which leads to an architecture of layers:

For $0 \leq i \leq n-1$ each layer i serves as interface for the next layer $i+1$. Vice versa, for the layer $i+1$ only the signature of the layer i is visible.

Vertical composition can be modeled by specification expressions. The $layer_0$ is a syntactically complete specification expression, and for $i > 0$ each layer can be modeled by the specification expression

$$\textbf{spec } layer_i = layer_{i-1} \; ; (\Sigma, E) \; \textbf{hide } SYM(env^{GE}(layer_{i-1}))$$

where $layer_{i-1}$ is the expression of imported specifications and (Σ, E) the new part of the specification which is visible to the layer $i+1$ and $SYM(env^{GE}(layer_{i-1}))$ consists of all symbols occurring in the imported signatures.

When using hierarchies of specifications the notation of hierarchy preservation and persistence [86] is of importance. The hierarchy preservation is not relevant in our approach, because we control the construction of elements of the carrier sets by constructors, which can be constrained such that constructors for a sort can only be defined in specification parts that contain also that sort. As a consequence each hierarchical composition in our approach is hierarchy preserving.

For the development of software it is important that the new part of a hierarchy of specifications has no impact on the semantics of the imported specification. This means that for each model of the imported specification there is a model of the overall specification that comprises the former model.

Definition 3.2.9 (Persistence, primitive specification)
Let (Σ_p, E_p) ; (Σ_1, E_1) be an extension. Then (Σ_p, E_p) is called the *primitive specification*. The extension is called *persistent* if

$$\forall \mathcal{A} \in CGEN(\Sigma_p, E_p) \; \exists \mathcal{B} \in HGEN((\Sigma_p, E_p) ; (\Sigma_1, E_1)) : \mathcal{A} = \mathcal{B}|_{\Sigma_p} . \qquad \Box$$

The extension concept used in the definition of the semantics in Subsection 3.2.2 does not cover the persistence. This semantic aspect is not decidable, but there are sufficient criteria for specifications that show an algorithmic form guaranteeing persistence.

Chapter 4

A Catalogue of Standard Specifications

In this chapter we will introduce several basic specifications defining standard data structures along with the characteristic operations. These specifications are implemented by most of the common programming languages; hence they can serve as foundation for the development of a software system.

We begin with elementary specifications for Boolean values and natural numbers. We then introduce some parameterized container specifications. In order to prepare a medium-sized case study we finally present specifications for handling XML documents and trees.

4.1 Elementary specifications

We start with the standard specification *Bool* (see Fig. 4.1) for truth values which is needed for the implicit extensions described in Subsection 2.1.4. This specification must be imported into each specification where conditional terms with the **if-then-else** construct are used.

With this specification we introduce a concrete syntax of noting down specifications. Keywords like **spec** are printed boldface. Constructor sorts are introduced along with their constructors separated by the symbol |. For the sort *bool* the constructors *true* and *false* are declared. The new operations along with their argument and result sorts are enumerated after the keyword **ops**. The axioms following the keyword **axioms** are equations; the universal quantifier ranges over all variables declared after the keyword **vars**. Each axiom is named which eases references in the text.

The specification *Elem* (see Fig. 4.2) consists of a loose sort along with an equality predicate showing the properties of an equivalence relation. This specification is mainly used as parameter for parameterized specifications.

Based on the specification of Boolean values we present the specification *Nat* (see Fig. 4.3) for natural numbers along with some auxiliary operations.

```
spec   Bool =
sorts  bool = true | false
ops      not :  (bool)bool,
         and :  (bool, bool)bool,
          or :  (bool, bool)bool,
        impl :  (bool, bool)bool
vars   x : bool
axioms
          not1 :  not(true) = false,
          not2 :  not(false) = true,
          and1 :  and(true, x) = x,
          and2 :  and(false, x) = false,
           or1 :  or(true, x) = true,
           or2 :  or(false, x) = x,
         impl1 :  impl(true, x) = x,
         impl2 :  impl(false, x) = true
end
```

Figure 4.1: Specification of Boolean values

The introduced operations are axiomatized by constructor patterns covering all cases. This axiomatization enables a direct implementation in the programming language SML [73]. The axiomatization of *Nat* is minimal. For the purpose of program derivation additional theorems like the commutativity and associativity of the operations *add* and *mult* and order axioms of the comparison operation *le* are sensible.

4.2   Container specifications

Container specifications describe data structures that store elements. Several kinds of specifications are considered differing in the construction principle and the interface.

```
spec     Elem = Bool +
sorts    elem
ops       eqEl : (elem, elem)bool
vars     c, d, e : elem
axioms
            eqEl1 : eqEl(c, c) = true,
            eqEl2 : eqEl(c, d) = eqEl(d, c),
            eqEl3 : impl(and(eqEl(c, d), eqEl(d, e)), eqEl(c, e)) = true
end
```

Figure 4.2: Specification of elements with an equality predicate

```
spec   Nat = Bool ;
sorts    nat = zero | succ(nat)
ops      add :  (nat, nat)nat,
         mult :  (nat, nat)nat,
         eqnat :  (nat, nat)bool,
         le :  (nat, nat)bool,
         lt :  (nat, nat)bool
vars   m : nat, n : nat
axioms
         add1 :   add(zero, n) = n,
         add2 :   add(succ(m), n) = succ(add(m, n)),
         mult1 :   mult(zero, n) = zero,
         mult2 :   mult(succ(m), n) = add(mult(m, n), n),
         eqnat1 :   eqnat(zero, zero) = true,
         eqnat2 :   eqnat(zero, succ(n)) = false,
         eqnat3 :   eqnat(succ(m), zero) = false,
         eqnat4 :   eqnat(succ(m), succ(n)) = eqnat(m, n),
         le1 :   le(zero, n) = true,
         le2 :   le(succ(m), zero) = false,
         le3 :   le(succ(m), succ(n)) = le(m, n),
         lt1 :   lt(m, n) = and(le(m, n), not(eqnat(m, n)))
end
```

Figure 4.3: Specification of natural numbers

4.2.1 Sets

The specification for finite sets (see Fig. 4.4) is parameterized with the specification *Elem* introduced in Subsection 4.1. Hence using this specification requires an instantiation with a sort and an equality predicate. Parameter specifications are noted in square brackets behind the specification name. Finite sets of sort *set* are constructed with the constant *empty* for an empty set, *single* for forming a singleton set, and *union* for the union of two sets. The data type *set* is non-free, since the axioms *ass*, *comm* and *neutr* constrain the constructor *union* to be associative and commutative with *empty* as neutral element.

The semantics of this specification comprises models based on finite sets as well as finite multisets. Multisets can be excluded by imposing additional axioms.

4.2.2 Lists

A standard data structure for storing values in a linear order is given by the specification *List* for lists (see Fig. 4.5). We choose an axiomatization with constructors *nil* for the empty list and *cons* attaching an element to the front. The parameter specification consists of an arbitrary sort *T* only. Unnamed specification parts can be introduced in

```
spec FinSet[Elem] = Nat;
sorts      set = empty | single(elem) | union(set, set)
ops    iselem :  (elem, set)bool,
          insert :  (elem, set)set
vars x, y : elem, p, q, r, s : set
axioms
            ass :   union(union(p, q), r) = union(p, union(q, r)),
          comm :   union(p, q) = union(q, p),
          neutr :  union(p, empty) = p,
       iselem1 :  iselem(x, empty) = false,
       iselem2 :  iselem(x, single(y)) = eqEl(x, y),
       iselem3 :  iselem(x, union(s, p)) = or(iselem(x, s), iselem(x, p)),
       insert1 :  insert(x, p) = union(single(x), p)
end
```

Figure 4.4: Specification of finite sets

curly brackets.

The result of the operation *first* is not specified for empty lists. This would require additional information about the sort T e.g. an error constant. This under-specification could be solved by using error algebras [40] which introduce explicit error elements on sorts. A similar problem occurs with the operation *rest*. In contrast to the sort *elem* we have a designated constant *nil* of sort *list*. The axiomatization settles the rest of the empty list to be the empty list again.

```
spec List[{sorts T}] = Nat;
sorts      list = nil | cons(T, list)
ops    conc :  (list, list)list
          first :  (list)T
           rest :  (list)list,
        length :  (list)nat
vars l, k : list, x, y : T
axioms
         conc1 :  conc(nil, l) = l,
         conc2 :  conc(cons(x, k), l) = cons(x, conc(k, l)),
         first1 :  first(cons(x, l)) = x,
         rest1 :  rest(nil) = nil,
         rest2 :  rest(cons(x, l)) = l,
       length1 :  length(nil) = zero,
       length2 :  length(cons(x, l)) = succ(length(l))
end
```

Figure 4.5: Specification of finite lists

Given a list with elements of sort $T1$ and a function $f : T1 \rightarrow T2$, we specify a map function for lists (see Fig. 4.6) applying the function f to each element of the list. As parameters two sorts $T1$ and $T2$ have to be provided. The specification *Map* imports the necessary list specifications by instantiating the specification *List* with $T1$ and with $T2$. The keyword **fit** introduces the signature morphism required for intantiating parameters. In order to distinguish the function symbols of $T1$-lists and $T2$-lists we rename the function symbols by the qualifiers $L1$ and $L2$. When using function symbols of lists we prefix them with $L1.$ or $L2.$, respectively. For example $L1.nil$ denotes the empty $T1$-list and $L2.nil$ the empty $T2$-list.

---

spec $Map[\{\textbf{sorts } T1\}][\{\textbf{sorts } T2\}] =$
      $L1$ **as** $List[\{\textbf{sorts } T1\}$ **fit** $T/T1]+$
      $L2$ **as** $List[\{\textbf{sorts } T2\}$ **fit** $T/T2];$
sorts $F = (T1) \rightarrow T2$
ops $map : (F, L1.list)L2.list$
vars $l : L1.list, x : T1, f : F$
axioms
     $map1 : map(f, L1.nil) = L2.nil,$
     $map2 : map(f, L1.cons(x, l)) = L2.cons(f(x), map(f, l))$
end

Figure 4.6: Specification of a map function for lists

The defined sort F is an abbreviation for the function sort $(T1) \rightarrow T2$. The argument sort $T1$ is put in brackets for syntax reasons only unifying the notation with function sorts with multiple argument sorts. Due to the function sort F and the function symbol *map*, *Map* is a higher-order specification. The function symbol *map* is given with two arguments. The curried version $@map : F \rightarrow L1.list \rightarrow L2.list$ can be achieved by currying the function symbol.

4.2.3 Collections

Collections (see Fig. 4.7) form a hybrid of sets and lists; they are constructed by *clear* for the empty collection, *newColl* forming singletons and an associative constructor *addAll* joining two collections. Similar to sets collections are parameterized by the specification *Elem*. The equality function symbol for the element sort is needed to specify a membership operation *contains*.

The semantics of *Collection* comprises models based on finite sets as well as lists. As the main difference compared to the specification *FinSet* the operation *addAll* is not commutative. The specification *Collection* thus leaves more freedom in implementing the data structure.

Again we provide the higher-order function *map* for the data structure of collections (see Fig. 4.8). The specification is similar to the specification *Map*. Here the function symbol

```
spec Collection[Elem] = Nat;
sorts        coll = clear | newColl(elem) | addAll(coll, coll)
ops    contains :  (elem, coll)bool,
          addElem :  (elem, coll)coll
vars x, y : elem, s, p, q : coll
axioms
              ass :  addAll(addAll(s, p), q) = addAll(s, addAll(p, q)),
           neutr1 :  addAll(clear, p) = p,
           neutr2 :  addAll(p, clear) = p,
        contains1 :  contains(x, clear) = false,
        contains2 :  contains(x, newColl(y)) = eqEl(x, y),
        contains3 :  contains(x, addAll(s, p)) = or(contains(x, s), contains(x, p)),
         addElem1 :  addElem(x, s) = addAll(newColl(x), s)
end
```

Figure 4.7: Specification of collections

map is specified for the constructors of collections instead of lists.

4.2.4   Stacks

The specification for a stack module (see Fig. 4.9) uses a sort *elem* as parameter sort. The sort *stack* is a constructor sort with the constructors *empty* and *push* .

We cannot specify the behaviour of the access operation *top* for the empty stack since there is no error constant available. This problem is similar to that of the function symbol *first* of specification *List* .

```
spec MapColl[Elem1][Elem2] =
        S1 as Collection[Elem1]+
        S2 as Collection[Elem2];
sorts    F = (elem1) → elem2
ops    map :  (F, S1.coll)S2.coll
vars p, q : S1.coll, x : elem1, f : F
axioms
        map1 :  map(f, S1.clear) = S2.clear,
        map2 :  map(f, S1.newColl(x)) = S2.newColl(f(x)),
        map3 :  map(f, S1.addAll(p, q)) = S2.addAll(map(f, p), map(f, q))
end
```

Figure 4.8: Specification of a map functional for collections

> **spec** *Stack*[{**sorts** *elem*}] = *Bool*;
> **sorts**   *stack* = *empty* | *push*(*elem*, *stack*)
> **ops**   *isempty* :   (*stack*)*bool*,
>   *top* :   (*stack*)*elem*,
>   *pop* :   (*stack*)*stack*
> **vars**   *s*, *t* : *stack*, *c*, *d*, *e* : *elem*
> **axioms**
>   *isempty*1 :   *isempty*(*empty*) = *true*,
>   *isempty*2 :   *isempty*(*push*(*e*, *s*)) = *false*,
>   *top*2 :   *top*(*push*(*e*, *s*)) = *e*,
>   *pop*1 :   *pop*(*empty*) = *empty*,
>   *pop*2 :   *pop*(*push*(*e*, *s*)) = *s*
> **end**

Figure 4.9: Specification of stacks

4.2.5   Arrays

Arrays embody a standard data structure implemented ready-made in most programming languages. We provide a specification *Array* of arrays (see Fig. 4.10) using the constructors *init* for initial array and *put* for the modification of the array at one index. Indices are modeled by natural numbers.

The operation *isdef* tests whether an array position has been initialized by a value. As the parameter sort is general and no error constants are specified, the operation *lookup* remains under-specified for the initial array.

The data type *array* is non-free. The axiom *put*1 indicates that updates overwrite former updates at the same index. Moreover, the array is independent of the sequence of updates to different array positions.

> **spec** *Array*[{**sorts** *elem*}] = *Nat*;
> **sorts**   *array* = *init* | *put*(*array*, *nat*, *elem*)
> **ops**   *lookup* : (*nat*, *array*)*elem*,
>   *isdef* : (*nat*, *array*)*bool*
> **vars**   *a*, *b* : *array*, *c*, *d*, *e* : *elem*, *m*, *n* : *nat*
> **axioms**
>   *put*1 : *put*(*put*(*a*, *m*, *c*), *n*, *e*) = **if** *eqNat*(*m*, *n*) **then** *put*(*a*, *n*, *e*)
>   **else** *put*(*put*(*a*, *n*, *e*), *m*, *c*),
>   *lookup*1 : *lookup*(*n*, *put*(*a*, *m*, *e*)) = **if** *eqNat*(*n*, *m*) **then** *e* **else** *lookup*(*n*, *a*),
>   *isdef*1 : *isdef*(*n*, *init*) = *false*,
>   *isdef*2 : *isdef*(*n*, *put*(*a*, *m*, *e*)) = **if** *eqNat*(*n*, *m*) **then** *true* **else** *isdef*(*n*, *a*)
> **end**

Figure 4.10: Specification of arrays

This specification of arrays does not reflect the finite index intervals of arrays used in programming languages. Bounded arrays can be specified by introducing a constant m_{upb} : nat denoting the highest index of an array. The behaviour of the operations must then be specified distinguishing the cases of allowed and out-of-bound indices.

Specifications based on arrays are close to an efficient implementation. In most cases algorithms using arrays are rather complicated. Therefore, we tend to use abstract data types in requirement specifications and to implement them later as arrays (see Chapter 8).

4.3   Specifications for XML handling

In order to prepare the case study described in Chapter 9 we will introduce some specifications for handling with XML documents and XML trees. The XML documents are used to capture information embodying user requests for a server. Processing a request requires parsing of the corresponding XML document.

The range of the full XML standard [75] is quite extensive. In order to focus on the essential concepts and complexity of specifications we will reduce XML documents to XML constituents with element content containing only tags between begin-tag and end-tag. Then the information is given by the attributes of the tags. Furthermore, we distinguish between empty tags and non-empty tags.

The following example shows a simple XML document with a non-empty tag `flight` and an empty tag `hotel`:

```
<flight attr="LH3305"> <hotel attr="plaza"/> </flight>
```

A document type is determined by the two sorts *tag* for non-empty tags and *attr* for information content. Additionally, we assume an equality predicate on the sort *tag* for testing whether two tags are equal. The specification *DocType* reuses the specification *Elem* from Subsection 4.1 specifying a loose sort with an equality predicate:

spec *DocType* = (*Elem*)[*elem*/*tag*, *eqEl*/*eqTag*];
sorts *attr*
end

For the internal use of XML structures we represent XML documents by XML trees distinguishing non-empty and empty tags. The specification *XMLTree* is parameterized by the document type:

spec *XMLTree*[*DocType*] =
sorts   *XMLTree* = *Leaf*(*tag*, *attr*) | *CTree*(*tag*, *attr*, *XMLTreeList*),
    XMLTreeList = *noTree* | *appTree*(*XMLTree*, *XMLTreeList*)
end

XML documents (see Fig. 4.11) are in most cases represented in "sequential form" by a sequence of characters. After a scanning process we view an XML document as a sequence of tags. The following specification for XML documents is parameterized by the document type and defines two constructor sorts *token* and *xmldoc*. A token is either a begin-tag of a non-empty tag, an end-tag or a singleton tag. An XML document is a sequence of tokens where the empty sequence is *EoF* (end of file) and a non-empty document can be constructed by inserting one token in the beginning of a XML document.

$$
\begin{aligned}
&\textbf{spec} \;\; XMLDoc[DocType] = \\
&\textbf{sorts} \quad token = btag(tag, attr) \mid etag(tag) \mid stag(tag, attr), \\
&\qquad\qquad xmldoc = EoF \mid insert(token, xmldoc) \\
&\textbf{ops} \quad appTag : (xmldoc, token) \\
&\textbf{axioms} \\
&\qquad appTag1 : \;\; appTag(EoF, t) = insert(t, EoF), \\
&\qquad appTag2 : \;\; appTag(insert(u, d), t) = insert(u, appTag(d, t)) \\
&\textbf{end}
\end{aligned}
$$

Figure 4.11: Specification of XML documents

The operation *appTag* appends one token at the end of an XML document.

In order to operate on XML documents, a parser is needed checking the syntactical correctness of the XML document and constructing the corresponding XML tree. The parser (see Fig. 4.12) again is parameterized by the document type. The sort *token* embodies the possible tags of an XML document (recall that we only consider documents with element content). With the constructor *stag* we describe an empty single tag and *btag(t)* and *etag(t)* are the begin and the end tag of tag *t*. A sequence of tokens is axiomatized by using the specification *List* providing the sort *token* as element sort. Moreover, the specification *XMLTree* is imported. The parser is axiomatized as a simple recursive descent parser where the operations *dropTree* and *dropTrL* are used to check whether the incoming document is well-formed. For this task we use a stack where the unclosed begin-tags occurring during parsing are stored. For stacks we import the specification *Stack* of Subsection 4.2.

The introduced specifications serve as a basis library of standard specifications for describing software systems. Due to the limited space of this thesis it is not possible to provide a full library covering a large area of applications. Instead, we will emphasize on the method of developing software systems and hence only illustrate a selection of reusable and parameterized standard specifications. Most of them will be used in examples given in the following chapters.

spec *XMLParser[DocType]* =
    XMLDoc[DocType] +
    XMLTree[{**sorts** *attr, tag* **ops** *eqTag* : (*tag, tag*)*bool*}
        fit *attr/attr, tag/tag, eqTag/eqTag*] +
    Stack[{**sorts** *tag*} **fit** *elem/tag*];
ops   *mkSTree* : (*tag, attr, XMLTreeList*)*XMLTree*,
      parse : (*TL.list*)*XMLTree*,
    parseTrL : (*TL.list*)*XMLTreeList*,
    dropTree : (*stack, TL.list*)*TL.list*,
     dropTrL : (*TL.list*)*TL.list*
vars *s* : *stack, v* : *attr, t, a* : *tag, xl* : *TL.list, xtl* : *XMLTreeList*
axioms
    mkSTree1 : *mkSTree*(*t, v, noTree*) = *Leaf*(*t, v*)
    mkSTree2 : *mkSTree*(*t, v, appTree*(*xt, xtl*)) = *CTree*(*t, v, appTree*(*xt, xtl*))
       parse1 : *parse*(*TL.insert*(*btag*(*t, v*), *xl*)) = *CTree*(*t, v, parseTrL*(*xl*)),
       parse2 : *parse*(*TL.insert*(*stag*(*t, v*), *xl*)) = *Leaf*(*v*),
    parseTrL0 : *parseTrL*(*TL.EoF*) = *noTree*,
    parseTrL1 : *parseTrL*(*TL.insert*(*btag*(*t, v*), *xl*)) =
        appTree(*parse*(*TL.insert*(*btag*(*t, v*), *xl*)),
          parseTrL(*dropTree*(*push*(*t, empty*), *xl*))),
    parseTrL2 : *parseTrL*(*TL.insert*(*etag*(*t*), *xl*)) = *noTree*,
    parseTrL3 : *parseTrL*(*TL.insert*(*stag*(*t, v*), *xl*)) =
        appTree(*parse*(*TL.insert*(*btag*(*t*), *xl*)),
          parseTrL(*dropTree*(*empty, TL.insert*(*btag*(*t*), *xl*)))),
    dropTree1 : *dropTree*(*empty, xl*) = *xl*,
    dropTree2 : *dropTree*(*push*(*a, s*), *TL.insert*(*btag*(*t, v*), *xl*)) =
        dropTree(*push*(*t, push*(*a, s*)), *dropTrL*(*xl*)),
    dropTree3 : *dropTree*(*push*(*a, s*), *TL.insert*(*etag*(*t*), *xl*)) =
        if *eqTag*(*a, t*) **then** *dropTree*(*s, xl*) **else** *TL.EoF*,
    dropTree4 : *dropTree*(*push*(*a, s*), *TL.insert*(*stag*(*t, v*), *xl*)) =
        dropTree(*push*(*a, s*), *xl*),
    dropTrL1 : *dropTrL*(*TL.insert*(*btag*(*t, v*), *xl*)) =
        dropTrL(*dropTree*(*push*(*t, empty*), *xl*)),
    dropTrL2 : *dropTrL*(*TL.insert*(*etag*(*t*), *xl*)) = *TL.insert*(*etag*(*t*), *xl*),
    dropTrL3 : *dropTrL*(*TL.insert*(*stag*(*t, v*), *xl*)) = *dropTrL*(*xl*)
end

Figure 4.12: Specification of an XML parser

Part II

Mechanized Derivation of Software Systems

Chapter 5

A Formal Development Method

Software systems can be specified in a compositional manner. The structuring concepts introduced in Chapter 3 play a decisive role in coping with large systems and suffice to construct well-known architectural or design patterns. Specifications that show an algorithmic shape can be implemented in a functional programming language. An algorithmic specification can be derived from a requirement specification by stepwise refinement applying a sequence of property preserving transformations rules. The preservation of properties is described by a refinement relation on basic specifications which is compatible with building specification expressions. The mechanization of the development process can be assisted by sufficient syntactic criteria for desirable or critical properties of specifications. The mechanized transformation of specifications is performed on a development graph encapsulating the structure of the specification along with refinements of sub-specifications. Transformation rules consist of syntactic manipulation schemes that differ in the semantic effect on the manipulated specification.

Convention: For obvious reasons, we assume in the sequel of this thesis that all specifications are finite, that is, they have a finite signature and a finite set of axioms.

5.1 An algebraic approach of compositional development

Most approaches to compositional system development favour object-oriented concepts widely used for the graphical development of user interfaces [13] . We consider components of a compositional development in a more general sense. Algebraic specifications serve as specification components which can be combined to composite system specifications. We will discuss several design principles and show how they can be described by specification expressions. The development of an implementation of a composite system specification aims at an equally structured system of algorithmic specifications which form a subset of algebraic specifications. The development process respects the compositional structure enabling the separate implementation of the involved components. The approach is similar to the idea of Goguen and Tracz [42] of providing a module connection language that allow the construction of systems by building expressions of predefined modules. Bidoit, Sannella and Tarlecki [12] introduce a semantics based approach to component-oriented software development in an algebraic setting using the common algebraic specification language CASL .

5.1.1 Requirements specification

Named specifications serve as definitions for components. Parameterization establishes explicit context dependencies which must be provided when deploying the specification component. Well known design and architectural patterns can be modeled by specification components.

Algebraic specifications as components

A component covers a common abstract idea of a strongly coherent part of a software system. A specification component describes the requirements of a component by an exported signature and by a set of axioms possibly deploying other component specifications and distinguishing context dependencies by parameter specifications.

Definition 5.1.1 (Specification component)

A *specification component wrt.* a global environment $GE : NA \rightarrow SpecExpr(NA)$ is a named specification of the form

$$\textbf{spec}\ \ compName = (SE\ ;\ (\Sigma, E))[:SP_1]\dots[:SP_n]$$

with *context dependencies* $SP_1, \dots, SP_n$, an *import* SE and a *new specification part* (Σ, E). The specification names occurring in SE are called *imported specification components*. In the following we will write specification components in the form

$$\textbf{spec}\ \ compName[SP_1]\dots[SP_n] = (SE\ ;\ (\Sigma, E)). \qquad \square$$

Clearly, specification components are based on a global environment. The specification expression SE comprises specification components of the global environment which is constructed using the specification combinators. The new specification part is used to glue the specification components together. The axioms of the new specification part combine the function symbols of the imported specification components to new function symbols. Here a readable axiomatization is desirable. For example, function composition suits well for combining function symbols in a clear and concise way. The new signature defines the exported interface of the specification component.

Inserted into the global environment, the specification component is a unit of composition, since it can be used in the context of a specification expression. Specification components can be deployed in a flexible way using renaming, hiding and enrichments for specializing the behaviour but keeping the intended behaviour fixed by the axioms.

Our view of specification components is similar to the definition of a software component given by Szyperski [82], page 34:

> "A software component is a unit of composition with contractually specified interfaces and explicit context dependencies only. A software component can be deployed independently and is subject to composition."

However, Szyperski assumes that software components are available in an executable form. Such components are independent of other components and can be combined at runtime using reflection. Our approach is based on specifications of components and on a procedure of achieving implementations of specification components.

Design and architecture of system specifications

The power of specification expressions is demonstrated by examples for common architectural and design patterns [18, 37].

For the development of compositional systems we expect that there is a global environment containing standard specifications which are parameterized in order to be useful for multiple applications.

In the following we will demonstrate how common architectures can be described using specification expressions.

Layering A layered architecture consists of $n > 1$ layers (see Subsection 3.2.3) where each layer offers services for the layer above using services of the layer below. Each layer consists of several specifications at the same level of abstraction. The services inside a layer may depend on each other. A layer maps a high level service to more primitive services. Hence a layer combines the services of a lower layer in order to provide a high level service. It is important that each layer only uses services from the same layer or from the layer directly below. If a layer needs a service from a layer beneath the preceding layer, the service can be passed through if the layer below provides a service that directly calls the service from the layer beneath.

A layered architecture of the form

$layer_4$ {	$spec_{4,1}$	$spec_{4,2}$	$spec_{4,3}$
$layer_3$ {	$spec_{3,1}$		$spec_{3,2}$
$layer_2$ {	$spec_{2,1}$	$spec_{2,2}$	
$layer_1$ {	$spec_{1,1}$	$spec_{1,2}$	$spec_{1,3}$

can be modeled with algebraic specifications using simple specification expression. For example the specification components $spec_{4,1}$ and $spec_{3,1}$ can be modeled by the following named specifications:

> **spec** $spec_{4,1} = spec_{3,1} + spec_{3,2}$; $(\Sigma_{4,1}, E_{4,1})$ **hide** $(SYM(spec_{3,1} + spec_{3,2}))$
> **spec** $spec_{3,1} = spec_{2,1} + spec_{2,2}$; $(\Sigma_{3,1}, E_{3,1})$ **hide** $(SYM(spec_{2,1} + spec_{2,2}))$

Pipes and filters Imagine a stream of data has to be processed by a function. For the specification of such a function it is sensible to decompose the processing into several subtasks. Each processing step can be modeled by a function of lower complexity possibly being imported by named specifications of the global environment. The single processing functions are called filters and are connected by pipes.

With algebraic specifications we can model sequential composition and tupling by formulae using function composition. The auxiliary functions are imported from named specifications of the global environment and new functions can be specified by using function composition. These axioms serve as glue for plugging the imported specifications together.

The following abstract specification imports the specifications $spec_1, \ldots, spec_n$ which provide interfaces for function symbols $f_1, \ldots, f_{n_f}$ and $h_1, \ldots, h_{n_h}$. These functions are used as auxiliary functions for axiomatizing the function symbols f, h and g.

> **spec** $PandF = spec_1 + \cdots + spec_n$;
> **ops** f : $(s_1)s_2,$
> $\quad\quad\;\; h$: $(s_1)s_3,$
> $\quad\quad\;\; g$: $(s_1)(s_2, s_3)$
> **vars** $x : s_1$
> **axioms**
> $$f = f_1 \circ \cdots \circ f_{n_f},$$
> $$h = h_1 \circ \cdots \circ h_{n_h},$$
> $$g(x) = (f(x), h(x))$$
> **end**

This specification is in algorithmic form if the auxiliary function symbols are. Yet, it does not suit for implementation, because the overhead for constructing and holding the intermediate data structures may lead to an inefficient implementation. Therefore, transformation steps for fusing these function symbols are desirable. We will introduce transformation steps on specifications for fusion in Chapter 7.

Strategy When specifying components, in many situations one wants to leave open which variant of a certain set of functions are applied in the specification. In this situation parameterization is sensible in order to leave open which strategy is used when deploying the specification component:

> **spec** $Appl[Strategy] = expr$; (Σ, E)

For the deployment of such a component a specification has to be provided that can be adapted via a specification morphism to the specification *Strategy*. Hence, for an instantiation of *Appl* it must be assured that the axioms of the specification *Strategy* hold.

5.1.2 System implementation

System specifications describe the structure and the behaviour of a software system in an axiomatic way. A system implementation provides an algorithmic specification which respects the structure and the behaviour of the system specification. Such a system implementation must consist of basic specifications that show an algorithmic form. Aiming at a compositional development process we gain a system implementation by refining the involved basic specifications to an algorithmic form. This algorithmic form depends on the structure of the axioms

For algorithmic specifications, we aim at an axiomatization where the function symbols are defined by patterns similar to function definitions in STANDARD ML [63, 73]. Therefore, the equations must have a constructive shape.

Definition 5.1.2 (Constructive)
A (Σ, X)-equation $f(tc) = r$ is called *constructive for* a function symbol $f \in F$, if the two conditions $tc \in T^{cons}(\Sigma, X)$ and $Var(r) \subseteq Var(tc)$ hold. □

Different constructive equations for the same function symbol contribute to the definition of this function symbol in an algorithmic way.

Definition 5.1.3 (Contributing axioms)
For a function symbol $f \in F$ *the set of constructive equations* for f is denoted by E_f. □

Function declarations in SML require left-linear equations.

Definition 5.1.4 (Left-linear)
A (Σ, X)-equation $l = r$ is called *left-linear*, if each variable occurs at most once on the left-hand side l. □

In SML, functions can be declared by a sequence of left-linear, constructive equations. When executing a function call the first equation that matches the argument is taken for evaluation. This procedure leads to a deterministic evaluation even if there are several equations that match the argument. Opposite to this sequential strategy, in model theory we consider sets of equations that must be satisfied simultaneously. Hence, overlapping constructive equations may cause inconsistencies. Therefore, we provide a syntactic property for non-overlapping equations.

Definition 5.1.5 (overlapping, non-overlapping)
Two constructive equations $f(tc_1) = tr_1$ and $g(tc_2) = tr_2$ are called *overlapping*, if there are substitutions σ_1, σ_2 with $f(tc_1)\sigma_1 \hat{=} g(tc_2)\sigma_2$. A set of equations is called *non-overlapping*, if each two distinct equations are not overlapping. □

Finally, we can define algorithmic function symbols.

Definition 5.1.6 (Algorithmic function symbol)
A function symbol $f \in F$ is said to be specified *algorithmically*, if the set E_f of constructive equations for f is not empty, non-overlapping, and each equation in E_f is left-linear.   □

An algorithmic specification contains algorithmic operations only and no superfluous equations.

Definition 5.1.7 (Algorithmic specification)
A specification (Σ, E) with $\Sigma = (S, F, C)$ is called an *algorithmic specification*, if

a) all operations $f \in F \setminus C$ are specified algorithmically,

b) there are no loose types in S, and

c) each equation of E is either a data structure constraint or it contributes to the definition of a function symbol in F.   □

Based on these definitions for basic specifications we can explain algorithmic system specifications.

Definition 5.1.8 (Algorithmic system specification)
A system specification $SY = \textbf{spec}\ name[SP] = SE\ ;\ (\Sigma, E)$ with $\Sigma = (S, F, C)$ is called *algorithmic wrt.* a global environment GE, if

a) $env^{GE}(SY)$ is algorithmic,

b) each imported specification is algorithmic,

c) for each $f \in F \setminus C$ it is $E_f \neq \emptyset$, and

d) each equation of E either consist of two constructor terms or it contributes to the definition of a function symbol in F.   □

The last condition prevents that imported function symbols are implemented in the new specification part. For each new function symbol there must be an implementation given by a set of contributing equations in the new specification part.

An implementation of a structured specification is an algorithmic specification that keeps the structure and respects the axioms. More specifically, a *system implementation* of a system specification **spec** $name[SP] = SE\ ;\ (\Sigma, E)$ is an algorithmic system specification **spec** $name_{im}[SP] = SE_{im}\ ;\ (\Sigma_{im}, E_{im})$ such that all axioms of E are respected and for all imported specifications occurring in SE there is a system implementation in SE_{im}. We have not yet defined what the term *are respected* means. We will go into the preservation of properties in the next section.

The next subsection describes a possibility to achieve an implementation by stepwise refinement steps.

5.1.3 Development by stepwise refinement

The development of a software system starts with a top-down analysis fixing the requirements of the system. The overall system specification is constructed by composing predefined standard specification components and demand driven new specification components. Algebraic specification fragments serve as building blocks which are composed to system specifications.

The stepwise derivation of a system implementation starts with an initial requirement system specification P_1. This specification is transformed by several refinement steps towards a final algorithmic system specification P_n. This resulting algorithmic system specification can be translated into a functional program and executed.

$$P_1 \twoheadrightarrow P_2 \twoheadrightarrow \cdots \twoheadrightarrow P_{n-1} \twoheadrightarrow P_n \stackrel{codegen}{\longrightarrow} FP$$

The derivation steps $P_i \twoheadrightarrow P_{i+1}$ preserve the properties of the initial requirement specification when applying correctness preserving transformation rules. These transformation rules consist of syntactic manipulation schemes which can easily be mechanized. Application conditions can automatically be evaluated by sufficient syntactic criteria or can be inserted as new axioms into the specification.

For the generation of code we use Standard ML as target language. For algorithmic specifications we generate data types for each constructor sort and pattern defined functions for each operation. Data type constraints are omitted achieving an implementation that is behavioural equivalent to the algorithmic specification if the induced equivalence relation forms a congruence. The structure of the system specification is reflected by generating a module for each involved specification name.

In the remainder of this chapter we will provide a refinement relation for basic algebraic specifications as well as for specification expressions which preserves the properties. Heading for a mechanization of the development process we consider syntactic properties of specifications which can be used for user guidance. We introduce the notion of a development graph serving as an environment for a mechanized derivation. Moreover, we give an overview and a classification of transformation rules discussed in more details in the following chapters.

5.2 Preservation of properties

In this section we will manifest the property preserving framework for the transformational derivation of specifications. We introduce a transitive refinement relation on basic specifications and lift it to structured specifications such that the relation is compatible with forming specification expressions.

5.2.1 A refinement relation for basic specifications

For the refinement of algebraic specifications we provide a refinement relation.

Definition 5.2.1 (Refinement relation)
A specification (Σ_1, E_1) *is refined to* a specification (Σ_2, E_2) using a signature morphism $\delta : \Sigma_1 \to \Sigma_2$ denoted by $(\Sigma_1, E_1) \overset{\delta}{\twoheadrightarrow} (\Sigma_2, E_2)$, if for all algebras $\mathcal{B} \in CGEN(\Sigma_2, E_2)$ there is an algebra $\mathcal{A} \in CGEN(\Sigma_1, E_1)$ and a Σ_2-congruence $\approx^{\mathcal{B}}$ such that $\mathcal{A}$ is a subalgebra of $\mathcal{B}/_{\approx^{\mathcal{B}}}$ via δ. If $\delta = id$ we denote the refinement relation by $\twoheadrightarrow$. We call (Σ_1, E_1) the *source specification* and (Σ_2, E_2) the *target specification*.   □

The refinement relation follows the concept of model inclusion since a refinement step narrows the class of models. The refinement relation generalizes the model inclusion to behavioural equivalent subalgebras possibly translated by signature morphisms. This comprises also embedding steps claiming that the models of the source specification must occur as subalgebra in some model of the refined specification.

A correct transition step follows the refinement relation.

Definition 5.2.2 (Correct transition step)
A transition step from a specification (Σ_1, E_1) to a specification (Σ_2, E_2) is called *correct* , if there is a signature morphism $\delta : \Sigma_1 \to \Sigma_2$ such that $(\Sigma_1, E_1) \overset{\delta}{\twoheadrightarrow} (\Sigma_2, E_2)$.   □

A stepwise development process is based on the transitivity of the refinement relation.

Lemma 5.2.3 (Reflexivity and transitivity of $\twoheadrightarrow$)
For algebraic specifications (Σ_1, E_1), (Σ_2, E_2), (Σ_3, E_3) and signature morphisms $\delta_1 : \Sigma_1 \to \Sigma_2$ and $\delta_2 : \Sigma_2 \to \Sigma_3$ we have

   a) $(\Sigma_1, E_1) \overset{id}{\twoheadrightarrow} (\Sigma_1, E_1)$ (reflexive)

   b) If $(\Sigma_1, E_1) \overset{\delta_1}{\twoheadrightarrow} (\Sigma_2, E_2)$ and $(\Sigma_2, E_2) \overset{\delta_2}{\twoheadrightarrow} (\Sigma_3, E_3)$, then $(\Sigma_1, E_1) \overset{\delta_2 \circ \delta_1}{\twoheadrightarrow} (\Sigma_3, E_2)$.
                                                                      (transitive)

                                                                                   □

If two specifications refine each other, we call these specifications equivalently axiomatized.

Definition 5.2.4 (Equivalently axiomatized)
Two specifications (Σ_1, E_1) and (Σ_2, E_2) are called *equivalently axiomatized* , if $(\Sigma_1, E_1) \overset{\delta_1}{\twoheadrightarrow} (\Sigma_2, E_2)$ and $(\Sigma_2, E_2) \overset{\delta_2}{\twoheadrightarrow} (\Sigma_1, E_1)$ for some signature morphisms $\delta_1 : \Sigma_1 \to \Sigma_2$ and $\delta_2 : \Sigma_2 \to \Sigma_1$.   □

If the axioms of a specification are consequences of the axioms of another specification, the latter refines the former specification.

Lemma 5.2.5 ($\twoheadrightarrow$ follows logical consequence)
Let (Σ_1, E_1) and (Σ_2, E_2) be algebraic specifications and $\delta : \Sigma_1 \rightarrow \Sigma_2$ a signature morphism. If $E_2 \models \delta(E_1)$, then $(\Sigma_1, E_1) \overset{\delta}{\twoheadrightarrow} (\Sigma_2, E_2)$. $\quad\square$

This lemma suggests an invent and verify approach to system development. If a refinement is invented and it is proved that the original properties hold in the refined specification, the refinement step is correct.

5.2.2 Refinement of structured specifications

The refinement relation on structured specifications follows the refinement relation on basic specifications by using the environment of structured specifications.

Definition 5.2.6 (Refinement relation on structured specifications)
A syntactically complete specification expression SE_1 *is refined by* a syntactically complete specification expression SE_2 *via* a signature morphism $\delta : Sig(SE_1) \rightarrow Sig(SE_2)$ *in* a global environment GE, if $env^{GE}(SE_1) \overset{\delta}{\twoheadrightarrow} env^{GE}(SE_2)$. The refinement of specification expressions is denoted by $SE_1 \overset{\delta}{\twoheadrightarrow}_{GE} SE_2$. $\quad\square$

In the following we will omit GE if the context is clear. The refinement relation is only defined on syntactically complete specification expressions.

We show that the refinement relation is compatible with the construction of specification expressions. For expressions built by translations we assume that the signature morphism and the refinement morphism are domain compatible.

Lemma 5.2.7 (Refinement relation compatible with specification expression)

Let SE_1, SE_1', SE_2, SE_2' be syntactically complete specification expressions, SE a specification expression, Σ_2 a signature, and $\delta : SIG(SE_1) \rightarrow \Sigma_2$ a signature morphism. Assume $SE_1 \overset{\delta_1}{\twoheadrightarrow} SE_1'$ and $SE_2 \overset{\delta_2}{\twoheadrightarrow} SE_2'$ such that δ and δ_1 are domain compatible wrt. the signature of SE_1. Then we have the following refinements:

a) $(SE_1 \text{ hide } \Sigma_h) \overset{\delta_1}{\twoheadrightarrow} (SE_1' \text{ hide } \delta_1(\Sigma_h))$ $\hfill$ (hiding)

b) $SE_1(\delta) \overset{[\delta,\delta_1]}{\twoheadrightarrow} SE_1'(\delta)$ $\hfill$ (translation)

c) $SE_1[: SE] \overset{\delta_1}{\twoheadrightarrow} SE_1'[: SE]$ $\hfill$ (parameterization)
$\quad SE[: SE_2] \overset{\delta_2}{\twoheadrightarrow} SE[: SE_2']$

d) $SE_1[SE \text{ fit } \delta] \stackrel{[\delta, \delta_1]}{\rightarrowtail} SE'_1[SE \text{ fit } \delta]$ \hfill (parameter instantiation)

   $SE[SE_2 \text{ fit } \delta] \stackrel{\delta_2}{\rightarrowtail} SE[SE'_2 \text{ fit } (\delta_2 \circ \delta)]$

e) $(SE_1 + SE) \stackrel{\delta_1}{\rightarrowtail} (SE'_1 + \delta_1(SE))$ \hfill (union)

   $(SE + SE_2) \stackrel{\delta_2}{\rightarrowtail} (\delta_2(SE) + SE'_2)$

f) $(SE_1 \; ; \; SE) \stackrel{\delta_1}{\rightarrowtail} (SE'_1 \; ; \; \delta_1(SE))$ \hfill (extension)

   $(SE \; ; \; SE_2) \stackrel{\delta_2}{\rightarrowtail} (\delta_2(SE) \; ; \; SE'_2)$ \hfill □

Lemma 5.2.7 enables a modular development process where sub-specifications can be refined independently of the environment. Such a procedure preserves the structure of the requirement system specification and renders the independent development of the involved named specifications possible.

5.3 Mechanizing the refinement process

As described in Subsection 5.1.3 we head for a mechanization of the development process. Sufficient syntactic criteria for semantic properties of specifications can be applied for user guidance and assistance. A development graph is used for book-keeping of the development state. Refinements can be performed by applying correctness preserving transformation rules to the involved specification components or by manipulating the development graph.

5.3.1 User guidance by analysis

Several properties of specifications may guide and assist the refinement process. The algorithmic properties introduced in Subsection 5.1.2 reflect the syntactic shape of specifications that can easily be translated to an SML program. In the following we introduce further properties providing pre-requisites for the application of certain transformation steps or revealing potentially problematic axiomatizations that may cause inconsistencies.

A complete case analysis on constructor sorts can be achieved by a set of constructor terms.

Definition 5.3.1 (Complete set of constructor terms)
A family of constructor terms $CT \subseteq T^{cons}(\Sigma, X)$ is called *complete*, if for every $t \in T^{Cons}(\Sigma, X)$ there is a substitution $\sigma \in SUBST(\Sigma, X)$ and a term $t' \in CT$ such that $t \cong t'\sigma$. \hfill □

If an operation is axiomatized constructively, we can decide whether the set of constructive equations forms a complete case analysis.

Definition 5.3.2 (Specified completely)
A function symbol $f \in F$ is said to be *specified completely* in a basic specification (Σ, E), if for all constructor terms $tc \in T^{Cons}(\Sigma, X)$ there is a substitution $\sigma \in SUBST(\Sigma, X)$ and an equation $f(tc_1) = r \in E_f$ such that $(tc_1)\sigma \stackrel{\wedge}{=} tc$.   □

If a function symbol is specified completely, we can condense a complete case analysis out of the corresponding constructive equations.

The set of equations of a specification can be directed from left to right which yields a term rewriting system [22].

Definition 5.3.3 (Associated term rewriting system)
The *term rewriting system* $(\Sigma, \mathcal{R})$ associated with an algebraic specification (Σ, E) has the set of rewrite rules $\mathcal{R} = \{(l \rightarrow r) | (l = r) \in E\}$.   □

There are several syntactic properties of term rewriting systems which can be used to assist the refinement process. For example, non-termination of the associated term rewriting system may cause inconsistencies. Therefore, the termination properties of a specification are of interest. The termination of a term rewriting system can be proved using a reduction order.

Definition 5.3.4 (Reduction order)
A family of strict orders $\prec^{wf} \subseteq T(\Sigma, X) \times T(\Sigma, X)$ is called a *reduction order*, if it

- is *well-founded*: every $\prec^{wf}_s$ is well founded on $T(\Sigma, X)_s$.

- is *compatible* with the construction of terms:

  (iii) If $t_f \prec^{wf}_{(s_1,\ldots,s_n) \rightarrow s} t'_f$, then $(@t_f) \prec^{wf}_{(s_1, \rightarrow, \ldots, \rightarrow s_n \rightarrow s)} @(t'_f)$.   (currying)

  (iv) If $t_1 \prec^{wf}_{s_1} t'_1, \ldots, t_n \prec^{wf}_{s_n} t'_n$, then $(t_1, \ldots, t_n) \prec^{wf}_{(s_1,\ldots,s_n)} (t'_1, \ldots, t'_n)$.   (tuple)

  (v) If $t_f \prec^{wf}_{(s_1 \rightarrow s_2)} t'_f$ and $t_a \prec^{wf}_{s_1} t'_a$, then $(t_f(t_a)) \prec^{wf}_{s_2} (t'_f(t'_a))$.   (application)

  (vi) If $t_f \prec^{wf}_{(s_1 \rightarrow s_2)} t'_f$ and $t_g \prec^{wf}_{(s_2 \rightarrow s_3)} t'_g$, then $(t_g \circ t_f) \prec^{wf}_{(s_1 \rightarrow s_3)} (t'_g \circ t'_f)$.
                                    (function composition)

- is *closed under substitutions*: If $t_1 \prec^{wf}_s t_2$, then $t_1 \sigma \prec^{wf}_s t_2 \sigma$ for all $\sigma SUBST(\Sigma, X)$. □

The associated term rewriting system of a specification is terminating if for all rules the term at the right hand side is smaller than the left term. Hence rewriting in left-right direction makes progress towards termination.

Definition 5.3.5 (Terminating equation)
An equation $l = r \in E$ is called *terminating* wrt. a reduction order $\prec^{wf}$ on $T(\Sigma, X)$, if $r \prec^{wf}_s l$ holds for appropriate sort s. A set E of (Σ, X)-equations is called *terminating* if all equations in E are terminating.   □

Non termination of the associated term rewriting system may cause inconsistent specifications. As we head for sufficient syntactic criteria for the termination of the term rewriting system associated with a specification, we use syntactic orders [4] for checking the termination of the equations.

Another source of inconsistent specifications are data structure constraints. Data structure constraints offer the possibility to specify non-free data structure. Equations describing data structure constraints consist of two constructor terms.

Definition 5.3.6 (Data structure constraint)
A (Σ, X)-equation $l = r$ is called a *data structure constraint* , if l and r are both constructor terms.   □

For the detection of contradictions and empty model classes in specifications it is sensible to consider critical pairs and the confluence of the resulting term rewriting system [48] . The text book [4] introduces the detection of critical pairs of a rewrite system.

5.3.2   Environment of compositional developments

The development of software systems from specifications is a complex task. In order to cope with the complexity it is sensible to confine sub-developments to the relevant parts of the structured specification. In our development method sub-developments concern imported named specifications which are available via the global environment. However, named specifications of the environment may be shared in different sub-specifications. If a refined specification is updated in the global environment, the refinement would be overtaken in all specifications. In order to enable the choice, where to overtake a refined specification we introduce refinement graphs storing refinements between named specifications. The refinement is adopted by exchanging imported specifications along the refinement relation. The state of a development is given by a development graph encapsulating the structure of the overall system and performed refinements.

Development graphs have first been proposed in [2, 50] in order to manage structured specifications in combination with structured verification when changing involved specifications. Our notion of development graphs differs in the granularity of edges, since we consider global links only. Moreover, we use specification names as nodes rather than pairs of sets of sentences and a derivation relation. In addition we assume a global environment binding specification names to structured specifications.

The global environment imposes an import graph reflecting the structure of the imports.

Definition 5.3.7 (Import graph)
The *import graph* (NA, I) of a global environment $GE : NA \rightarrow SpecExpr(NA)$ consists of the set NA of nodes and $I \subseteq NA \times NA$ of directed edges with

$$(name_1, name_2) \in I \quad \text{iff} \quad name_2 \text{ occurs in the import of } GE(name_1) . \qquad \square$$

A refinement graph encapsulates refinement relations between specification components of the global environment.

Definition 5.3.8 (Refinement graph)
For a global environment $GE : NA \to SpecExpr(NA)$ a *refinement graph* (NA, R) consists of the set of names NA of the global environment as nodes and a set of labeled edges $R \subseteq NA \times SigMorph \times NA$ such that $(m_1, \delta, m_2) \in R$ iff $GE(m_1) \overset{\delta}{\twoheadrightarrow} GE(m_2)$. □

The development graph embodies the development state and consists of a global environment, a root specification and a refinement graph.

Definition 5.3.9 (Development graph)
A *development graph* $G = (NA, GE, SN, GR)$ consists of

- a set NA of specification names,

- a global environment $GE : NA \to SpecExpr(NA)$,

- a *root specification name* $SN \in NA$, and

- a refinement graph $GR = (NA, R)$. □

The import graph is implicitly contained in the development graph by the global environment.

The root specification defines the interfaces of the system specifications. Requirement specifications have no proper predecessor in the refinement relation.

A development graph serves as central data structure for the development of an implementation. The development graph is manipulated by extension, by new refinements and by replacements exchanging an imported specification by a refined specification. Refinements of specifications are performed by stepwise refinement applying a sequence of transformation steps following the refinement relation.

Definition 5.3.10 (Manipulations of development graph)
Let $G = (NA, GE, SN, GR)$ be a development graph and $spec\ name[SP] = SE$; (Σ, E) a specification component abbreviated by P. The development graph G can be manipulated by the following steps:

a) An *extension of the global environment by* P results in the development graph $G' = (NA \cup \{name\}, GE', SN, GR)$ with

$$GE' : NA \cup \{name\} \to SpecExpr(NA \cup \{name\}) \text{ such that}$$

$$GE'(N) = \begin{cases} \mathbf{spec}\ name[SP] = SE \ ; \ (\Sigma, E) & \text{if } N = name \\ GE(N) & \text{otherwise} \end{cases} .$$

b) An *extension of the importing of name* $\in NA$ *by* $N \in NA$ such that *name* is not reachable from N via GE leads to the development graph

$$G' = (NA, GE[name \leftarrow P'], SN, GR)$$

such that

$$P' = \textbf{spec } name = (SE + N) \; ; (\Sigma, E) \, .$$

c) If $GE(N_1) \overset{\delta}{\twoheadrightarrow} GE(N_2)$, then an *extension of a specification refinement* (N_1, δ, N_2) is given by

$$G' = (NA, GE, SN, GR \cup \{(N_1, \delta, N_2)\}).$$

d) If $(N_1, N_2, \delta) \in GR$ and N_1 is imported by *name* , then a *replacement of an imported specification* N_1 *by a refined specification* N_2 at a position p of SE is given by the development graph $G' = (NA, GE[name \leftarrow P'], SN, GR)$ such that

$$P' = \textbf{spec } name = SE[N_2]_p \; ; (\Sigma, E) \, . \qquad \Box$$

In the case study of Chapter 9 an example of a development graph is given in Fig. 9.13. The illustrated development graph is manipulated replacing an imported specification by its refinement.

At the beginning of a development the refinement graph consists of the system specification with all subcomponents and an empty refinement graph. The procedure of finding a system implementation consists of a sequence of refinement steps. New refinements of specification components are generated by applying a sequence of correctness preserving transformation steps to the specification, rename it and enrich the development graph by the resulting specification and a refinement edge.

5.3.3   Mechanizable transformation steps

We explicate the mechanized transformation of specifications and distinguish four kinds of transformation steps.

For mechanizing transformation steps syntactic manipulation rules are required. These rules are applied to a specification. A transformation rule is correct, if it yields refinement for all possible instantiations. Transformation steps on specification components manipulate the new specification part only. Imported and parameter specifications serve as environment providing generation constraints and equations for the transformation steps. Local transformation steps affect only one axiom or exchange an axiom by a set of axioms. Such local steps suit for the derivation of an algorithmic axiomatization of an operation or for achieving a more efficient axiomatization. A global step transforms the entire new part of the specification; it affects not only one axiom, but may manipulate several axioms and the signature.

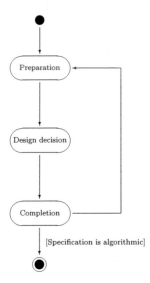

Figure 5.1: Procedure of stepwise refinement

In general the development process is manifested by a sequence of design decisions which have to be prepared and completed by enriching and exchanging the syntactic representation. The general procedure is illustrated in Fig. 5.1.

The outer loop of the process comprises the essential refinement steps that contribute to the understanding of the overall development. Possible refinements of this kinds are fold/unfold derivations of direct recursions, data structure refinements, and generalization and embedding using new function symbols.

In refining specifications we distinguish the following four kinds of transformation steps:

- *Choose an equivalently axiomatized specification:* The class of possible implementations of a specification can be axiomatized by different sets of formulas. Minor manipulations of the specification may preserve the class of implementations but lead to an axiomatization that enables further transformation steps. Such steps can prepare major steps manifesting design decisions.

- *Enrichments:* The developer can enrich the specification by auxiliary function symbols or sorts. Enrichments prepare design decisions involving auxiliary function symbols and sorts.

- *Restricting possible implementations:* Such a step adds details to the specification and narrows the class of possible implementations. These steps are not invertible in the refinement relation, since the original specification and the refined specification are not equivalently axiomatized. The restriction steps are the most relevant transformation steps, since they represent genuine design decisions.

- *Embedding into a new specification:* A specification defines a class of possible implementations. If the defined implementations can be achieved by embedding them into super structures comprising the original structures as sub-structures, one can instead develop an implementation of the more general structures and use it as an implementation of the original specification. This embedding process forms a complex step in general. Data structure refinements embody such embedding steps.

In order to guide the refinement process a set of mechanizable property checks of specifications is sensible. The programmer can decide to refine the non-algorithmic specification parts or is informed about additional applicable transformation rules.

We are interested in the mechanization of the refinement steps. Therefore, we aim at correct transformation rules for specifications or parts of specifications. In the following chapters we will introduce various transformation rules. Chapter describes 6 basic transformation rules comprising several specification enrichments and term and equation manipulations. Chapter 7 considers fusion steps which transform function compositions into more efficient axiomatizations. Finally, we discuss data structure refinements in Chapter 8.

Chapter 6

Basic Transformation Steps

Basic transformation steps embody simple syntactic manipulations effecting small refinement steps. Specification enrichments and reductions support invent and verify steps. The manipulation of terms and equations realize fine grained transformations focusing on one axiom. In order to cope with inductions, a calculus on transformation nodes encapsulating induction hypotheses is presented. Various manipulations of terms and equations are introduced as rules of the calculus.

6.1 Specification enrichments and reductions

The transformation steps for enrichment and reduction satisfy the refinement relation. Enrichments and reductions are the basic refinement steps for the invent and verify approach [14]. Although we aim at providing methods for deriving an implementation by direct syntactic manipulations, we want to open the approach also for invent and verify steps. Moreover, enrichment steps are also required for transformational derivations such as introducing auxiliary functions.

6.1.1 Signature enrichments and reductions

During the refinement process additional function symbols and sorts may be required. Function symbols may serve as auxiliary functions refining original function symbols. Enrichments can be achieved by enlarging the family of function symbols and the set of sorts.

Let $\Sigma_1 = (S_1, F_1, C_1)$ be a subsignature of $\Sigma_2 = (S_2, F_2, C_2)$ and $C_{1,sc} = C_{2,sc}$, $C_{1,(s \to sc)} = C_{2,(s \to sc)}$ for all $sc \in S_1$. Then

$$(\Sigma_1, E) \xrightarrow{id} (\Sigma_2, E)$$

holds. The enrichment with new operations and sorts amounts to an extension of the signature and therefore is a refinement in any situation. The extension with constructors may lead to an enlargement of the model class and therefore does not form a refinement in general. In special cases, such enrichments also form correct refinements, see Subsection 8.4.3.

For auxiliary operations it is sensible to use specifications with hiding and insert the operation as hidden operations. The auxiliary operations can then be omitted if they are not used for the axiomatization of the visible operations.

Lemma 6.1.1 (Dropping hidden operations)
Let $(\Sigma = (S, F, C), E, \Sigma_v)$ be a specification with hiding and $f \in F \setminus (F_v \cup C)$ an algorithmic and terminating operation. If f does not occur in any equation of $E \setminus E_f$, then

$$(\Sigma, E, \Sigma_v) \twoheadrightarrow ((S, F \setminus \{f\}, C), E \setminus E_f, \Sigma_v)$$

holds.   □

The reduction of the constructor system is always possible, if the function symbol remains as operation (see Subsection 8.4.4).

6.1.2   Axiom enrichments and reductions

An enrichment of an axiom is a correct refinement step. The reduction of axioms requires a proof.

Enrichment   The properties of an operation can be enforced by adding axioms. Let E_{new} be a set of formulae then

$$(\Sigma, E) \twoheadrightarrow (\Sigma, E \cup E_{new}) .$$

The enrichment of axioms narrows the class of models of the specification which effects a design decision. The enrichment of axioms can result in an inconsistent specification, since the enriched properties and original properties may contradict. If an algorithmic specification can be derived from a specification, the specification turns out to be consistent.

Reduction   Let E_{th} be a set of closed (Σ, X)-formulae such that $E \vdash E_{th}$. Then

$$(\Sigma, E \cup E_{th}) \twoheadrightarrow (\Sigma, E)$$

holds. Clearly, it is also $(\Sigma, E) \twoheadrightarrow (\Sigma, E \cup E_{th})$, hence the two specifications are equivalently axiomatized. The reduction of equations changes the representation of the properties. The formulae in E_{th} are consequences of the axioms in E and are not necessary for the axiomatization. Hence, such formulae form theorems of (Σ, E).

The invent and verify approach alternates enrichment and reduction steps. The enrichment step adds new equations describing properties of the operations in a different form. The reduction step drops part of the axiomatization by proving that the eliminated equations are theorems of the specification.

The verification step can often be used to derive a new axiomatization by a deduction calculus.

6.2   Manipulations of terms and equations

In the following we will define a basic calculus for the refinement of algebraic specifications by transforming single axioms to a set of axioms which logically imply the original axiom. Besides the simplification of terms in an equation, the calculus comprises induction steps exploiting the generation constraints of constructor sorts. The calculus is similar to the calculus for conditional inductive theorem proving presented in [34], but is extended to be used for higher-order specifications and by inductions with semantic orders based on measure functions.

6.2.1   Requirements and foundations

The properties of the operations in a specification form the starting point for a derivation into an algorithmic form. This can be done by focusing on one axiom deriving a set of new equations that axiomatize the operation in an other manner. If the derivation steps preserve the property stated by the original axiom, we can exchange the original axiom by the resulting equations in the specification.

Besides the usual manipulations of terms and equations we need to exploit the generation property. This can be established by term induction [35] using a well-founded order on terms (see Subsection 5.3.1). We can formulate the term induction principle for an arbitrary reduction order on terms.

Definition 6.2.1 (Term induction)
Given a reduction order $\prec^{wf}$ on $T(\Sigma, X)$, a constructor sort $sc \in SC$ and a (Σ, X)-formula Φ with $Free(\Phi)_{sc} = \{x\}$, the *term induction* is given by the following rule:

$$\frac{\forall t_c \in T^{cons}(\Sigma, X)_{sc}(\forall t_y \in T^{cons}_{sc}(\Sigma, X)(t_y \prec^{wf}_{sc} t_c \Rightarrow \Phi\{x \mapsto t_y\})) \Rightarrow \Phi\{x \mapsto t_c\}}{\forall t \in T^{cons}(\Sigma, X) \ \Phi\{x \mapsto t\}}$$

$\square$

The term induction principle uses a *syntactic order*, since the application of the induction hypothesis is constrained by a condition which can be decided syntactically.

In some applications the usage of a *semantic order* is more sensible. A semantic order is based on a function symbol where each interpretation leads to a well-founded order. For using semantic orders we expect that the specification comprises the specifications *Nat* and *Bool*. The applicability of an induction hypothesis is decided with a *measure operation* mapping terms to natural numbers. The function symbol $lt : (nat, nat)bool$ describes a well-founded order on natural numbers in each model and hence it can serve as induction order along with the measure operation. The induction scheme using measure operations can be defined as follows.

Definition 6.2.2 (Measure induction)
Let $lt \in F_{(nat,nat)\rightarrow bool}$ be the less-than predicate, $m \in F_{sc\rightarrow nat}$ a measure operation, $sc \in SC$ a constructor sort and $\Phi \in \mathcal{F}(\Sigma, X)$ with $Free(\Phi)_{sc} = \{x\}$. Then the *measure induction* is the following proof rule:

$$\frac{\forall t_c \in T^{cons}(\Sigma, X)_{sc} \quad (\forall t_y \in T^{cons}(\Sigma, X)_{sc}(lt(m(t_y), m(t_c)) = true \Rightarrow \Phi\{x \mapsto t_y\})) \Rightarrow \Phi\{x \mapsto t_c\}}{\forall t \in T^{cons}(\Sigma, X)_{sc} \ \Phi\{x \mapsto t\}}$$

$\square$

Formulae in algebraic specifications have the form $\forall x : sc \ \Phi$. As a result of the generation constraint on constructor sorts we can apply the induction principles to such formulae since the carriers of constructor sorts can be generated by constructor terms.

In most cases the induction principle is used along with a complete case analysis on the structure of the terms. Thus, an induction step yields several formulae to be derived further. We express the usable induction hypotheses as a sequence of hypotheses. An induction hypothesis comprises an equation, the substitution accumulating former case analyses, and a syntactic order or a measure function for deciding the applicability of the hypothesis.

Definition 6.2.3 (Induction hypothesis)
Let $SY \subseteq (T(\Sigma, X) \times T(\Sigma, X))^{\mathbb{B}}$ be the set of reduction orders on $T(\Sigma, X)$. An *induction hypothesis* is a triple consisting of a formula $\varphi \in \mathcal{F}(\Sigma, X)$, a substitution and a reduction order or a *measure operation* $m \in F_{sc\rightarrow nat}$. The class of all hypothesis is defined by

$$Hyp = \mathcal{F}(\Sigma, X) \times SUBST(\Sigma, X) \times (SY \cup F_{(sc\rightarrow nat)}) .$$

$\square$

In an induction step we have to keep track of the usable induction hypotheses of an equation. We structure the deduction by using the notion of transformation nodes. Thus, we define a *transformation node* as a pair

$$(\Gamma \ \varphi)$$

where Γ is a sequence of induction hypotheses and φ is a (Σ, X)-formula. The *deduction calculus* consists of *deduction rules* showing the form

$$\frac{(\Gamma_1 \ \varphi_1), \dots, (\Gamma_n \ \varphi_n)}{(\Gamma \ \varphi)} .$$

If a transformation node $(\Gamma \ \varphi)$ can be derived by the deduction rules using the premises $(\Gamma_1 \ \varphi_1), \dots, (\Gamma_n \ \varphi_n)$ we write

$$(\Gamma_1 \ \varphi_1), \dots, (\Gamma_n \ \varphi_n) \Vdash (\Gamma \ \varphi) .$$

Using the calculus for refining equations we apply the calculus in opposite direction like backward proving the equation we start with. We begin with an equation $l = r \in E$ and the deduction node $(\langle\rangle \;\; l = r)$. Step by step the deduction rules are applied and result in a set of transformation nodes $(\Gamma_1 \;\; l_1 = r_1), \ldots, (\Gamma_n \;\; l_n = r_n)$ which are inserted into E instead of $l = r$ such that $(\Sigma, E) \twoheadrightarrow (\Sigma, (E \setminus \{l = r\}) \cup \{l_1 = r_1, \ldots, l_n = r_n\})$. Hence, the deduction is similar to proving $E \cup \{l_1 = r_1, \ldots, l_n = r_n\} \vdash l = r$, but the result of the deduction process are the achieved premises. One can say that the deduction of $l = r$ is like proving $l = r$ and inserting the necessary premises instead.

6.2.2 Term manipulations

The following term manipulations apply to the terms on the right-hand side of equations. Similarly, all manipulations can be performed on terms of the left-hand side of an equation. These derivation steps change the syntactic axiomatization only. The steps do not narrow the model class. However, they are important for achieving a syntactic representation where further design decisions are feasible.

Simplification The simplification of terms plays a major role in the derivations. Lemma 2.2.8 and properties of the conditional (see Subsection 2.1.4) give rise to small simplification steps.

$$\frac{(\Gamma \;\; t_l = t_g(t_f(t)))}{(\Gamma \;\; t_l = (t_g \circ t_f)(t))} \qquad \frac{(\Gamma \;\; t_l = @f\, t_1 \ldots t_n)}{(\Gamma \;\; t_l = f(t_1, \ldots, t_n))} \qquad \frac{(\Gamma \;\; t_l = t_i)}{(\Gamma \;\; t_l = \#i(t_1, \ldots, t_n))} \;\; (1 \leq i \leq n)$$

$$\frac{(\Gamma \;\; t_l = t_t)}{(\Gamma \;\; t_l = \text{if } true \text{ then } t_t \text{ else } t_e)} \qquad\qquad \frac{(\Gamma \;\; t_l = t_e)}{(\Gamma \;\; t_l = \text{if } false \text{ then } t_t \text{ else } t_e)}$$

These transformation steps reduce superfluous parts of the term construction in order to achieve simpler terms.

If-lifting Sometimes it is useful to lift a conditional outside of an application. This often enables further simplifications or rewrite steps on the terms of the *then-* and *else* branches.

$$\frac{(\Gamma \;\; t_l = \text{if } t_b \text{ then } t_f(t_t) \text{ else } t_f(t_e))}{(\Gamma \;\; t_l = t_f(\text{if } t_b \text{ then } t_t \text{ else } t_e))}$$

The same procedure is feasible for currying, tuple and function composition.

$$\frac{(\Gamma \;\; t_l = \text{if } t_b \text{ then } (t_1, \ldots t_{i-1}, t_t, t_{i+1} \ldots, t_n) \text{ else } (t_1, \ldots t_{i-1}, t_e, t_{i+1} \ldots, t_n))}{(\Gamma \;\; t_l = (t_1, \ldots t_{i-1}, \text{if } t_b \text{ then } t_t \text{ else } t_e, t_{i+1} \ldots, t_n))}$$

The rules for currying and function composition are similar.

Rewriting Assume that $l = r \in E$. If there is a position $p \in Pos(t_2)$ and a substitution σ such that $t_2|_p \cong l\sigma$, then we can replace the subterm $t_2|_p$ by $r\sigma$.

$$\frac{(\Gamma \;\; t_1 = t_2[r\sigma]_p)}{(\Gamma \;\; t_1 = t_2)} \;\; l = r \in E, t_2|_p \cong l\sigma$$

Similarly, an equation $l = r$ can also be applied as rewriting rule in right-to-left direction.

Application of induction hypothesis   For the application of induction hypotheses we have to distinguish between hypotheses emerged from term induction and those generated from measure inductions. In case of a term induction, we have given an induction hypothesis of the form $(l = r, \tau, \prec)$. If there is a position $p \in Pos(t_2)$ and a substitution σ such that $t_2|_p \mathrel{\widehat{=}} l\sigma$ and $l\sigma \prec l\tau$, we can replace the subterm $t_2|_p$ by $r\sigma$.

$$\frac{(\Gamma, (l = r, \tau, \prec)\ \ t_1 = t_2[r\sigma]_p)}{(\Gamma, (l = r, \tau, \prec)\ \ t_1 = t_2)}\ \ t_2|_p \mathrel{\widehat{=}} l\sigma, l\sigma \prec l\tau$$

Similarly, an equation $l = r$ can also be applied as rewriting rule in right-to-left direction. Note that in both directions we have to prove $l\sigma \prec l\tau$ in order to use one induction ordering only. For the application condition of an induction hypothesis emerged from a measure induction a proof obligation occurs.

$$\frac{(\Gamma, (l = r, \tau, m)\ \ t_1 = t_2[r\sigma]_p)}{(\Gamma, (l = r, \tau, m)\ \ t_1 = t_2)}\ \ t_2|_p \mathrel{\widehat{=}} l\sigma, lt(m(l\sigma), m(l\tau)) = true$$

The condition $lt(m(l\sigma), m(l\tau)) = true$ embodies a proof obligation which has to be shown by a proof calculus, for example a sequent calculus.

6.2.3   Equation manipulations

Equation manipulations transform both terms of an equation in one go. The induction step forms a powerful equation transformation capturing a case analysis along with the generation of an induction hypothesis.

Induction   Assume that $sc \in SC$ is a constructor sort and $x \in Var_{sc}(t_1)$ a constructor variable occurring in the term t_1. Let $\{t_{c,1}, \ldots, t_{c,n}\} \subseteq T_{sc}^{Cons}(\Sigma, X')$ be a complete case analysis on the constructor sort sc, where X' is a family of fresh variables.

For the usage of term induction we expect a reduction order $\prec$. The induction step introduces for each term of the complete case analysis a new equation substituting x by a constructor term of the case analysis. For each case a new induction hypothesis is provided:

$$\frac{\begin{array}{c}(\Gamma\tau_1, (t_1 = t_2, \tau_1, \prec)\ \ (t_1\tau_1 = t_2\tau_1)) \\ \vdots \\ (\Gamma\tau_n, (t_1 = t_2, \tau_n, \prec)\ \ (t_1\tau_n = t_2\tau_n))\end{array}}{(\Gamma\ \ t_1 = t_2)}\ \ x \in Var_{sc}, \tau_i = \{x \mapsto t_{c,i}\}\ \ (1 \le i \le n)$$

Similarly, the measure induction can be performed providing a measure operation m instead of a reduction ordering.

$$\frac{\begin{array}{c}(\Gamma\tau_1, (t_1 = t_2; \tau_1, m)\ \ (t_1\tau_1 = t_2\tau_1)) \\ \vdots \\ (\Gamma\tau_n, (t_1 = t_2; \tau_n, m)\ \ (t_1\tau_n = t_2\tau_n))\end{array}}{(\Gamma\ \ t_1 = t_2)}\ \ x \in Var_{sc}, \tau_i = \{x \mapsto t_{c,i}\}\ \ (1 \le i \le n)$$

In both cases we have to update the substitutions of the given hypothesis in order to enable the usage of the old hypothesis in resulting nodes:

$$\langle\rangle\tau \;=\; \langle\rangle$$
$$\Gamma,(l=r,\sigma,\prec)\tau \;=\; \Gamma\tau,(l=r,\tau\circ\sigma,\prec)$$
$$\Gamma,(l=r,\sigma,m)\tau \;=\; \Gamma\tau,(l=r,\tau\circ\sigma,m)$$

Although induction steps are not design decisions in the sense of narrowing the class of models, the choice of the complete case analysis is essential when proceeding with the transformation process.

Tuple unfold Let $s = (s_1,\dots,s_n) \in S^{\times,\rightarrow}$ be a tuple sort and $x \in Vars_s(t_1)$ a tuple variable occurring in t_1. If $x_i \in X_{s_i}$ are fresh variables, then a transformation node can be specialized by unfolding the tuple variable x:

$$\frac{(\Gamma\tau \;\; t_1\tau = t_2\tau)}{(\Gamma \;\; t_1 = t_2)} \quad \tau = \{x \mapsto (x_1,\dots,x_n)\}$$

This rule does not form a design decision but specializes the equation which possibly enables further transformation steps. In combination with the induction step, this offers the possibility of a wide range of case analyses of terms.

Decomposition If the outermost function symbols of both terms of an equation are equal, the outermost function symbol can be omitted which generates an equation of the arguments.

$$\frac{(\Gamma \;\; t_1 = t_2)}{(\Gamma \;\; f(t_1) = f(t_2))}$$

This step forms a real design decision, since the function symbol f can be seen as abstraction function; the equation $f(t_1) = f(t_2)$ only claims the equality on the abstract values of t_1, t_2.

Similarly, a tuple can be decomposed:

$$\frac{(\Gamma \;\; t_1 = t'_1),\dots,(\Gamma \;\; t_n = t'_n)}{(\Gamma \;\; (t_1,\dots,t_n) = (t'_1,\dots,t'_n))}$$

This step does not embody a design decision, since the equality on tuples implies the equality on the distinct elements.

Extensionality Let $s_1, s_2 \in S^{\times,\rightarrow}$, $t_f, t_g \in T(\Sigma,X)_{(s_1\rightarrow s_2)}$ and $x \in X_{s_1}$ be a fresh variable. Then the extensionality of functions leads to the rule

$$\frac{(\Gamma \;\; t_f(x) = t_g(x))}{(\Gamma \;\; t_f = t_g)} \; .$$

This step yields an equivalent axiomatization lifting the type of the equation to a simpler type.

Generalization Let $t_1, t_2, t_z \in T(\Sigma, X)$, $P_1 = \{p_{1,1},\dots,p_{1,m}\} \subseteq Pos(t_1)$ be the set of positions p of t_1 such that $t_1|_p \hat{=} t_z$ and $P_2 = \{p_{2,1},\dots,p_{2,n}\} \subseteq Pos(t_2)$ is the set of positions p of t_2 such that $t_2|_p \hat{=} t_z$. Clearly, the different occurrences of the term t_z do not overlap in the terms t_1 and t_2. Then, if $x \in X_s$ is a fresh variable, we have

$$\frac{(\Gamma \quad t_1[x]_{p_{1,1}} \ldots [x]_{p_{1,m}} = t_2[x]_{p_{2,1}} \ldots [x]_{p_{2,n}})}{(\Gamma \quad t_1 = t_2)} .$$

This derivation step forms a genuine design decision. It generalizes the elements for which the equality is valid. Thus the set of models are constrained to models showing the stated property for more elements.

6.2.4   Correctness of deduction calculus

In this subsection we will show the correctness of the deduction calculus wrt. the refinement relation. The proof is based on the correctness of each deduction rule. In order to use the induction hypotheses as equations, we will define the semantics of a sequence of hypotheses as the set of all valid instances.

Definition 6.2.4 (Semantics of induction hypothesis)
The semantics of an induction hypothesis is given by:

- $[(l = r, \sigma, \prec)] = \{l\tau = r\tau \mid l\tau \prec l\sigma, \tau$ is a constructor ground substitution$\}$

- $[(l = r, \sigma, m)] = \{l\tau = r\tau \mid \forall \mathcal{M} \in CGEN(\Sigma, E) :$
  $\mathcal{M} \models lt(m(l\tau), m(l\sigma)) = true, \tau$ is a constructor ground substitution$\}$

Moreover, the semantics of a sequence of hypotheses $[\Gamma]$ is given by the union over the semantics of each single hypothesis of Γ. $\square$

The correctness proof of the single deduction rules is based on a correct Gentzen-style sequent calculus [31, 38] for proving properties in first order predicate logic, thus

$$\text{If } E \vdash l = r, \text{ then for } \mathcal{M} \in MOD(\Sigma, E) \text{ it is } \mathcal{M} \models l = r .$$

Lemma 6.2.5 (Correctness of deduction rules)
For each deduction rule
$$\frac{(\Gamma_1 \quad \varphi_1), \ldots, (\Gamma_n \quad \varphi_n)}{(\Gamma \quad \varphi)}$$
of the calculus it is

$$(\Sigma, E \cup [\Gamma] \cup \varphi) \twoheadrightarrow (\Sigma, E \cup \{\varphi_1\} \cup \ldots \cup \{\varphi_n\}) .$$

Proof: For each rule show $[\Gamma], \varphi_1, \ldots, \varphi_n \vdash \varphi$. $\square$

The correctness of the single rules are direct consequences of predicate logic and Lemma 2.2.8. Finally, we can prove that the presented deduction calculus is correct.

Lemma 6.2.6 (⊩ refines specifications)
For each deduction

$$(\Gamma_1 \ \varphi_1), \ldots, (\Gamma_n \ \varphi_n) \Vdash (\langle\rangle \ \varphi)$$

of the calculus it is

$$CGEN(\Sigma, E \cup \{\varphi\}) \twoheadrightarrow CGEN(\Sigma, E \cup \{\varphi_1, \ldots, \varphi_n\}) .$$

Proof: Induction on the number of the deduction steps using Lemma 6.2.5. □

The correctness of the calculus allows to refine specifications by a sequence of term and equation manipulations applied to an axiom. Such transformation steps are implemented in the Lübeck Transformation System (see Section 10.2 and Subsection 11.3.1).

Chapter 7

Fusion Steps

Function composition supports structuring specifications but may lead to inefficient implementations. The fusion of a function with a catamorphism achieving again a catamorphism improves the efficiency. A set of function symbols represents a Σ-homomorphism if their axiomatization shows a certain syntactic shape. The composition of two Σ-homomorphisms again yields a Σ-homomorphism. The resulting Σ-homomorphism can be axiomatized by a couple of new axioms. This principle forms the basis for the fusion step manipulating a specification such that a function composition is fused. A generalized recursion scheme for so called paramorphisms can be handled in a similar way by tupling functions. An example demonstrates the fusion step for catamorphisms.

7.1 Requirements and motivation

Specifications define algebraic structures by the characteristic properties of their basic functions. More complex functions can be defined in a short and concise style by combining suitable basic or complex functions. In this way, function composition supports the problem-oriented structuring of complex tasks into simpler subtasks [10].

Given the *base operations* $f_1, \ldots, f_n$, $n \geq 2$, a *composed operation* h may be specified by the equation

$$h \;=\; f_n \circ \cdots \circ f_1 \,.$$

This axiomatization generally doesn't suit for an implementation, since the construction of the intermediate data structures emerging in between the base operations may lead to an inefficient implementation. Therefore, one heads for an axiomatization of the composed function symbol h which avoids intermediate data structures and merges as many neighbouring base operations as possible. If this procedure is done step by step fusing two neighbouring functions, the fusion problem can be reduced to the fusion of two operations:

$$h \;=\; g \circ f$$

A fusion step refines a specification $(\Sigma, E \cup \{h = g \circ f\})$ to a specification $(\Sigma, E \cup E_h)$ such that E_h specifies the composed operation h by a set of recursive equations not refering to the base operations f and g. If we additionally require that a fusion step does not impose implicit design decisions, we claim that

$$CGEN(\Sigma, E \cup \{h = g \circ f\}) \quad = \quad CGEN(\Sigma, E \cup E_h).$$

In this case a fusion step forms no design decision, but amounts to an important change of the axiomatization of the composed operation. A fusion step requires certain properties on the base operations and for mechanizing fusion steps the axioms describing the base functions must show a certain shape.

An important special case concerns the composition of a function with a catamorphism. This is a function traversing the data structure where the recursion follows the construction principle of the underlying data structure. For the implementation one heads for recursive function definitions that eliminate the intermediate data structures used in a function composition. If the operation g has certain properties, it is possible to construct a recursive axiomatization of h, which depends on a distributive property of g only.

Moreover, recursive algorithms can easily be compiled into efficient code, if the recursion follows the construction principle of the underlying data structure. Therefore, it is a major goal of program derivation to eliminate function compositions used on the specification level.

7.2   Fusion transformation for catamorphisms

The interpretations of the function symbols of a specification operate on the carrier sets of the corresponding sorts. Families of operations with indexed constructor sorts can be lifted to a Σ-homomorphism, if the involved operations fulfill certain properties. Such families of operations are called catamorphisms. The fusion theorem for catamorphisms claims that the function composition of two catamorphisms again forms a catamorphism.

7.2.1   Lifting operations to homomorphisms

In this subsection we assume that (Σ, E) is an algebraic specification as introduced in Definition 2.1.14 with $\Sigma = (S, F, C)$. Let $SR \subseteq SC$ be a subset of the constructor sorts and $\mathcal{A}, \mathcal{B}$ be Σ-algebras.

We will consider a family of SR-indexed functions $f_{sc} : sc^{\mathcal{A}} \to sc^{\mathcal{B}}$ and extend the family to all sorts. If the remaining carriers of basic sorts are equal in the algebras $\mathcal{A}$ and $\mathcal{B}$, the family can be propagated to S.

Definition 7.2.1 (Canonical extension)
Let $f : SR^{\mathcal{A}} \to SR^{\mathcal{B}}$ be an SR-indexed family of functions and $sb^{\mathcal{A}} = sb^{\mathcal{B}}$ for all $sb \in$

$S \setminus SR$. Furthermore, let $const_{s^B}$ be an element of $s^B \neq \emptyset$. The *canonical extension* $\langle f, SR \rangle : \mathcal{A} \to \mathcal{B}$ of the family f is an $S^{\times, \to}$-indexed family of mappings $h_s : s^A \to s^B$ with the following properties:

- The mapping for basic sorts $sb \in S$ is extended by the identity function:

$$h_{sb} = \begin{cases} f_{sb} & \text{if } sb \in SR \\ id_{sb^A} & \text{if } sb \notin SR \end{cases}$$

- The mapping for basic sorts can be propagated to derived sorts:

$$h_{(s_1,\ldots,s_n)}(a_1,\ldots,a_n) = (h_{s_1}(a_1),\ldots,h_{s_n}(a_n))$$

$$h_{(s_1 \to s_2)}(f)(a) = \begin{cases} h_{s_2}(f(v)) & \text{if there is } v \in s_1^A \text{ such that } h_{s_1}(v) = a \\ const_{s_2^B} & \text{otherwise} \end{cases}$$

If the context is clear we omit the family $SR = \{sc_1,\ldots,sc_n\}$ and denote the canonical extension of f by $\langle f_1,\ldots,f_n \rangle$. $\qquad\square$

In the following we will use interpretations of operations belonging to a specification (Σ, E) to construct a canonical extension. If the constructed algebra mapping forms a Σ_C-homomorphism (a Σ-homomorphism restricted to the constructor signature Σ_C) with a suitable target algebra, the family of operations is called a catamorphism.

Definition 7.2.2 (Catamorphism)
Given two sort morphisms $\alpha, \beta : S^{\times, \to} \to S^{\times, \to}$, let f be an SR-indexed family of operations, such that $f_{sc} \in F_{(\alpha(sc) \to \beta(sc))}$. The family f is called a *catamorphism*, if for all $\mathcal{M} \in CGEN(\Sigma, E)$ there are Σ_C-algebras $\mathcal{A}, \mathcal{B}$ such that $\mathcal{A} \overset{\alpha}{\subseteq} \mathcal{M}$ and $\mathcal{B} \overset{\beta}{\subseteq} \mathcal{M}$ and $\langle f^{\mathcal{M}}, SR \rangle : \mathcal{A} \to \mathcal{B}$ is a Σ_C-homomorphism. If the context is clear, we also call the involved operations $f_{sc} \in F_{(\alpha(sc) \to \beta(sc))}$ *catamorphisms*. $\qquad\square$

In Fig. 7.1 we illustrate Def. 7.2.2. The model $\mathcal{M}$ fixes the functions $f_i^{\mathcal{M}}$ mapping elements of the carriers $\alpha(sc_i)^{\mathcal{M}}$ to elements of the carriers $\beta(sc_i)^{\mathcal{M}}$. Let there be two Σ_C-algebras $\mathcal{A} \subseteq \mathcal{M}|_{\Sigma_C}$ and $\mathcal{B} \subseteq \mathcal{M}|_{\Sigma_C}$, which means that for all $1 \leq i \leq n$ it is $sc_i^{\mathcal{A}} \subseteq \alpha(sc_i)^{\mathcal{M}}$ and $sc_i^{\mathcal{B}} \subseteq \beta(sc_i)^{\mathcal{M}}$, respectively. If we can always find two Σ_C-algebras $\mathcal{A}$ and $\mathcal{B}$ such that the canonical extension of $f_1^{\mathcal{M}},\ldots,f_n^{\mathcal{M}}$ forms a Σ_C-homomorphism, we call the family of operations a catamorphism.

For the derivation of algorithmic operations one heads for catamorphisms with $\mathcal{A} = \mathcal{M}|_{\Sigma_C}$. In this case a constructive axiomatization can be found, if the interpretation of the involved constructors in $\mathcal{B}$ can be expressed by a term. Vice versa, if the axiomatization of the operations $f_1,\ldots,f_n$ has a certain syntactic form, such catamorphisms can be detected by an algorithm checking a sufficient syntactic criterion for catamorphisms.

Figure 7.1: Lifting operations to a homomorphism

7.2.2 The fusion theorem for catamorphisms

Many algorithms first traverse a recursive data structure and then process the result of the traversal. In the corresponding algorithmic scheme, the catamorphism is composed with a function. Under certain restrictions, the resulting composition function again forms a catamorphism. Then the evaluation of the result of the traversal can be integrated into the traversal.

Proposition 7.2.3 (Fusion theorem for catamorphisms)
Let (Σ, E) be a satisfiable algebraic specification, $\mathcal{M} \in CGEN(\Sigma = (S, F, C), E)$, $SR \subseteq SC$, α, β sort morphisms on S, h, g, f SR-indexed families of operations with $h_{sc} : sc \to \beta(sc)$, $g_{sc} : \alpha(sc) \to \beta(sc)$, $f_{sc} : sc \to \alpha(sc)$, $\mathcal{A} = \mathcal{M}|_{\Sigma_C}$ and $\mathcal{B} \in MOD(\Sigma_C, E_C)$ an embedded Σ_C-algebra of $\mathcal{M}$ via α such that $\langle f, SR \rangle : \mathcal{A} \to \mathcal{B}$ is a Σ_C-homomorphism and for all $sc \in SR$ it is $h_{sc} = (g_{sc} \circ f_{sc}) \in E$. If there is a Σ_C-algebra $\mathcal{Z} \in MOD(\Sigma_C, E_C)$, which is embedded into $\mathcal{M}$ via β, such that $(g_{sc}^{\mathcal{M}}|_{sc^{\mathcal{B}}}) : \mathcal{B} \to \mathcal{Z}$ is a catamorphism, then $h^{\mathcal{M}}$ is a catamorphism.

Proof: Since $h_{sc}^{\mathcal{M}} = g_{sc}^{\mathcal{M}} \circ f_{sc}^{\mathcal{M}}$, $f_{sc}^{\mathcal{M}} : sc^{\mathcal{M}} \to sc^{\mathcal{B}}$ and $g_{sc}^{\mathcal{M}}|_{sc^{\mathcal{B}}} : sc^{\mathcal{B}} \to sc^{\mathcal{Z}}$ we have $h_{sc}^{\mathcal{M}} : sc^{\mathcal{M}} \to sc^{\mathcal{Z}}$. Moreover, $\mathcal{Z}$ is embedded into $\mathcal{M}$. Finally,

$$\langle h^{\mathcal{M}}, SR \rangle = \langle g^{\mathcal{M}}, SR \rangle \circ \langle f^{\mathcal{M}}, SR \rangle : \mathcal{M} \to \mathcal{Z}$$

is a Σ_C-homomorphism since Σ_C-homomorphisms are closed under composition [62]. □

The fusion eliminates the intermediate data structure, which is described by $\mathcal{B}$, see Fig. 7.2. The algebras $\mathcal{A}, \mathcal{B}$ and $\mathcal{Z}$ are embedded in $\mathcal{M}|_{\Sigma_C}$, which means that for all

$sb \in S$ it is $sb^{\mathcal{A}} = sb^{\mathcal{M}}$, $sb^{\mathcal{B}} \subseteq \alpha(sb)^{\mathcal{M}}$ and $sb^{\mathcal{Z}} \subseteq \beta(sb)^{\mathcal{M}}$. The interpretations of the families f, g and h form algebra mappings. If f and g are catamorphisms, the algebra mapping h is a catamorphism, and the algebra $\mathcal{B}$ is superfluous for using h.

The fusion theorem lays a semantic basis for implementing the fusion step for catamorphisms. For performing a fusion step, we must find an appropriate Σ_C-algebra $\mathcal{Z}$ such that $h_{sc}^{\mathcal{M}} : sc^{\mathcal{M}} \to sc^{\mathcal{Z}}$ forms a catamorphism.

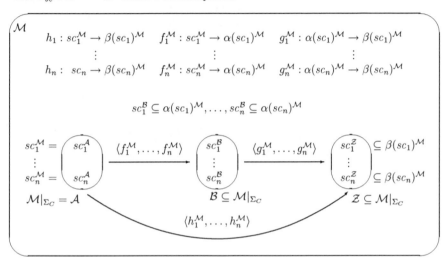

Figure 7.2: Fusion theorem for catamorphisms

7.3 Mechanizing the fusion step

In this section we head for sufficient syntactic criteria ensuring the soundness of the fusion step, and for algorithms detecting catamorphic operations. Moreover, we present a manipulation scheme for specifications embodying a fusion step. This includes the generation of new operations, new axioms and possibly proof obligations. The manipulations form a correct refinement step wrt. the refinement relation.

7.3.1 Detecting recursion structures for catamorphisms

The basis for detecting catamorphisms lays in the syntactic structure of the equations. The axioms of a specification can be grouped into constructive equations with the same outermost function symbol (see Def. 5.1.3). If the groups of equations defining a family of operations can be used to extract new interpretations of the constructors of the argument sorts, then the operations form a catamorphism.

For the following definitions we enumerate the finite set of constructors showing the same result sort and the involved sorts. Let in the following $(\Sigma = (S, F, C), E)$ be an algebraic specification. For $SR \subseteq SC$ let (c) be the SR-indexed family of non-empty sets of constructors such that $c_{sc} = \{c_{sc,1}, \ldots, c_{sc,n_{sc}}\}$ contains the constructors of result sort sc. Moreover, let $\alpha : S^{\times, \rightarrow} \rightarrow S^{\times, \rightarrow}$ be a sort morphisms, $k_{sc,i}$ the number of arguments of constructor $c_{sc,i}$ and $s_{sc,i,j}$ the sort of argument position j of constructor $c_{sc,i}$. The set E of equations is partitioned into mutually disjoint subsets E_f of those constructive equations showing the same outermost function symbol at the term on the left-hand side of the equation.

For detecting recursively axiomatized operations following the underlying data structure, we consider flat constructive equations.

Definition 7.3.1 (Flat constructive equation)
A set $E_{f_{sc}}$ of equations belonging to an operation f_{sc} of functionality $sc \rightarrow \alpha(sc)$ is called *flat constructive*, if all equations in $E_{f_{sc}}$ have the form

$$f_{sc}(c_{sc,i}(x_{i,1}, \ldots, x_{i,k_{sc,i}})) = t_{sc,i} . \qquad \square$$

For the remainder of this subsection we consider for fixed $SR \subseteq SC$ and $(f_{sc})_{sc \in SR}$ for each $sc \in SR$ the set $E_{f_{sc}}$.

$$f_{sc}(c_{sc,1}(x_{1,1}, \ldots, x_{1,k_{sc,1}})) = t_{sc,1}$$
$$\vdots$$
$$f_{sc}(c_{sc,n_{sc}}(x_{1,1}, \ldots, x_{1,k_{sc,n_{sc}}})) = t_{sc,n_{sc}}$$

For constructor sorts in SR we distinguish recursive and non-recursive argument positions of the constructors.

Definition 7.3.2 (Recursive sort, recursive argument position)
The sorts of SR are called *recursive sorts*. A *recursive argument position* of a function symbol $g \in F_{(s_1, \ldots, s_n) \rightarrow s}$ wrt. SR is an argument position i such that $s_i \in SR$ and a *recursive variable* is a variable of sort in SR. $\qquad \square$

For recursive axiomatizations of operations we are interested in recursive argument positions. These positions must be applied recursively by a catamorphism in order to yield an axiomatization of a catamorphism.

Definition 7.3.3 (Application following recursive sorts)
Let $SR \subseteq SC$, f be an SR-indexed family of operations and α a sort morphism such that $\alpha|_{S \setminus SR} = id_{S \setminus SR}$. The *application following recursive sorts* is an $S^{\times, \rightarrow}$-indexed family τ^f of functions $\tau^f_s : T(\Sigma, X)_s \rightarrow T(\Sigma, X)_{\alpha(s)}$ defined as follows:

$$\tau^f_s(t) = \begin{cases} f_s(t) & \text{if } s \in SR \\ t & \text{if } s \notin SR \end{cases}$$

$\qquad \square$

If in t_i all occurrences of recursive variables are directly applied by f, a context Ψ_i can be defined leaving gaps for all occurrences of $f(x_{i,j})$, if $x_{i,j}$ is recursive, and of $x_{i,j}$ otherwise.

Definition 7.3.4 (Recursion scheme, Recursion scheme instance)

Let $SR \subseteq SC$, $(f_{sc})_{sc \in SR}$ be an SR-indexed family of operations and α a sort morphism. A *recursion scheme of $sc \in SR$ and f* with a finite set of scheme variables $\{y_1 : \alpha(s_1), \dots, y_n : \alpha(s_n)\}$ is a term $\Psi \in T(\Sigma', \{y_1, \dots, y_n\})_{\alpha(sc)}$ with $\Sigma' = (S, F \setminus \{f_{sc} \mid sc \in SR\}, C)$.

A term $t \in T(\Sigma, \{x_1 : s_1, \dots, x_n : s_n\})_s$ is called a *recursion scheme instance* of sc and f if there is a recursion scheme Ψ of sc and f such that

$$\Psi[\{y_i \mapsto \tau_{s_i}^f(x_i) \mid 1 \leq i \leq n\}] \;\; \hat{=} \;\; t\,.$$

The interpretation $\Psi^{\mathcal{A}} : \alpha(s_1)^{\mathcal{A}} \times \cdots \times \alpha(s_n)^{\mathcal{A}} \to \alpha(sc)$ of a recursion scheme Ψ in a Σ-algebra $\mathcal{A}$ is given by

$$\Psi^{\mathcal{A}}(a_1, \dots, a_n) \;\; = \;\; \Psi_{v[y_1 \leftarrow a_1, \dots, y_n \leftarrow a_n]}^{\mathcal{A}}\,. \qquad \square$$

Recursion schemes give a syntactic classification of recursive axiomatizations traversing the data structure in top-down direction step by step.

Definition 7.3.5 (Top-down recursive)

A family f of SR-indexed operations is called *top-down recursive*, if for all $sc \in SR$ and all $1 \leq i \leq k_{sc,i}$ there is an equation $l = r \in E_{f_{sc}}$ such that

(C1) $l = r$ is flat constructive,

(C2) $l = r$ is left-linear,

(C3) r is a recursion scheme instance of sc and f. $\qquad \square$

The following proposition establishes a syntactic criterion for catamorphisms which can be checked by an efficient algorithm with complexity $O(|SR| \cdot n_{sc\ max} \cdot |t_{sc}|_{max})$, where $n_{sc\ max}$ is the maximum of all n_{sc} and $|t_{sc}|_{max}$ is the size of the greatest term of all $t_{sc,i}$.

Proposition 7.3.6 (Detection of Catamorphisms)

Let $SR \subseteq SC$ and f an SR-indexed family of operations. If the family f is *top-down recursive*, then f is a catamorphism.

Proof: Let $\mathcal{M} \in CGEN(\Sigma, E)$ and $\mathcal{B} \in MOD(\Sigma_C, E_C)$ such that $c_{sc,i}^{\mathcal{B}} = \Psi_{sc,i}^{\mathcal{M}}$,

$$sc^{\mathcal{B}} \;\; = \;\; \{f_{sc}^{\mathcal{M}}(c_{sc,i}^{\mathcal{M}}(u_1, \dots, u_{k_{sc,i}})) \mid u_k \in s_{sc,i,k}^{\mathcal{M}}, 1 \leq i \leq n, 1 \leq k \leq k_{sc,i}\} \subseteq s^{\mathcal{M}}$$

and $sb^{\mathcal{B}} = sb^{\mathcal{M}}$ for all $sb \in S$. The Σ_C-algebra $\mathcal{B}$ exists, since E_C is satisfied in $\mathcal{M}$ and therefore in $\mathcal{B}$, too.

Then $f_{sc}^{\mathcal{M}} : sc^{\mathcal{M}} \to sc^{\mathcal{B}}$ and $\langle f^{\mathcal{M}}, SR \rangle$ is a Σ_C-homomorphism since

$$\begin{aligned}
\langle f^{\mathcal{M}}, SR \rangle (c_i^{\mathcal{M}}(u_1, \dots, u_{n_i})) \;\; &= \;\; \Psi_{sc,i}^{\mathcal{M}}(\langle f^{\mathcal{M}}, SR \rangle(x_1), \dots, \langle f^{\mathcal{M}}, SR \rangle(x_{n_i})) \\
&= \;\; c_{sc,i}^{\mathcal{B}}(\langle f^{\mathcal{M}}, SR \rangle(x_1), \dots, \langle f^{\mathcal{M}}, SR \rangle(x_{n_i}))
\end{aligned}$$

for all $1 \leq i \leq n$. Because $\mathcal{M}$ is chosen arbitrarily, f is a catamorphism. $\qquad \square$

7.3.2 Generation of new axiomatization

The fusion theorem clarifies the semantic basis for fusing the composition of a function with a catamorphism. For mechanizing fusion as a transformation in a transformation system, we need a syntactic presentation of the fusion theorem.

After having detected a catamorphism and a family of sets of equations which define operations as the compositions of a function and a catamorphism, the fusion theorem can be applied. It introduces a new constructor algebra with certain properties. Again, we aim at a syntactical presentation of the new algebra by introducing so-called *combine operations* embodying the interpretation of all constructors. Additionally, new axioms are included, which define the operation in terms of the new combine operations. We claim that the enrichment of the specification constitutes a correct refinement step.

Proposition 7.3.7 (Fusion step)
Let $P = (\Sigma = (S, F, C), E)$ be a specification and h, g, f SR-indexed families of operations with $h_{sc} : sc \to \beta(sc)$, $g_{sc} : \alpha(sc) \to \beta(sc)$ and $f_{sc} : sc \to \alpha(sc)$. Let f be top-down recursive. Let the family $e_{sc} : h_{sc} = g_{sc} \circ f_{sc} \in E$ denote the composition of f_{sc} with an operation g_{sc}. Then the target specification $P' = (\Sigma', E')$ given by

$$\Sigma' = (S, F \cup \{cop_{sc,i} : (\beta(s_{sc,i,1}), \ldots, \beta(s_{sc,i,k_{sc,i}})) \to \beta(sc) \mid sc \in SR, 1 \le i \le n_{sc}\}, C)$$

$$E' = (E \setminus \{h_{sc} = g_{sc} \circ f_{sc} \mid sc \in SR\}) \cup E_h \cup E_{cop}$$

$$E_h = \{h_{sc}(c_{sc,i}(x_{i,1}, \ldots, x_{i,k_{sc,i}})) = cop_{sc,i}(\tau^h_{s_{sc,i,1}}(x_{i,1}), \ldots, \tau^h_{s_{sc,i,k_{sc,i}}}(x_{i,k_{sc,i}}))$$
$$\mid sc \in SR, 1 \le i \le n_{sc}\}, x_{i,j} : s_{i,j}$$

$$E_{cop} = \{g_{sc}(\Psi_{sc,i}[y_{sc,i,1}, \ldots, y_{sc,i,n_i}]) = cop_{sc,i}(\tau^g_{sc,i,1}(y_{sc,i,1}), \ldots, \tau^g_{sc,i,k_{sc,i}}(y_{i,k_{sc,i}}))$$
$$\mid sc \in SR, 1 \le i \le n_{sc}\}, y_{sc,i,j} : \alpha(s_{sc,i,j})$$

refines the specification P, and h is a catamorphism of P'.

Proof: We dropped the equations $h_{sc} = g_{sc} \circ f_{sc}$, and have to prove that they are implied by the new axiomatization:

$$\begin{aligned}
h_{sc}(c_{sc,i}(x_{sc,i,1}, \ldots, x_{sc,i,k_{sc,i}})) &= cop_{sc,i}(\tau^h_{sc,i,1}(x_{sc,i,1}), \ldots, \tau^h_{sc,i,n_i}(x_{sc,i,k_{sc,i}})) \\
&= cop_{sc,i}(\tau^{g \circ f}_{sc,i,1}(x_{sc,i,1}), \ldots, \tau^{g \circ f}_{sc,i,k_{sc,i}}(x_{sc,i,k_{sc,i}})) \\
&= g(\Psi_{sc,i}[\tau^f_{sc,i,1}(x_{sc,i,1}), \ldots, \tau^f_{sc,i,k_{sc,i}}(x_{sc,i,k_{sc,i}})]) \\
&= g(f(c_{sc,i}(x_{sc,i,1}, \ldots, x_{sc,i,k_{sc,i}}))) \\
&= (g \circ f)(c_{sc,i}(x_{sc,i,1}, \ldots, x_{sc,i,k_{sc,i}}))
\end{aligned}$$

Moreover, the new equations defining the operation h fulfill the criteria given in Prop. 7.3.6 and hence, h is a catamorphism. $\square$

The combine operations $cop_{sc,i}$ embody the interpretation of the constructors of sort sc in the Σ_C-algebra $\mathcal{Z}$ of Prop. 7.2.3. They are added to the signature, because they cannot be axiomatized completely. An algorithmic axiomatization would allow unfolding these operations in the equations E_h and thus make them superfluous. The properties given in E_{cop} can be used to derive an algorithmic description.

In Prop. 7.2.3 it is additionally required that the algebra $\mathcal{Z}$ fulfills the axioms of E_C. These equations can be seen as proof obligations stating that the interpretation of the combine operations have the properties of E_C.

7.3.3 Fusion for generalizations of catamorphisms

We generalize the top-down recursion scheme by allowing several families of operations to traverse the data structures. In this case a more general definition of recursion schemes is necessary.

Definition 7.3.8 (Para recursion scheme, Para recursion scheme instance)
Let $SR \subseteq SC$, f_i be SR-indexed families of operations, and α_i sort morphisms for $1 \leq i \leq m$. A *para recursion scheme* of $sc \in SR$ and $f_1, \ldots, f_m$ with a finite set of scheme variables $Y = \{y_{i,j} : \alpha_i(s_{i,j}) \mid 1 \leq i \leq m\}$ is a term $\Psi \in T(\Sigma', Y)_{\alpha(sc)}$ with $\Sigma' = (S, F \setminus \{f_{i,sc} \mid sc \in SR, 1 \leq i \leq m\}, C)$.

A term $t \in T(\Sigma, \{x_1 : s_1, \ldots, x_n : s_n\})_s$ is called a *recursion scheme instance* of sc and f if there is a recursion scheme Ψ of sc and f such that

$$\Psi[y_{i,j} \leftarrow \tau_{i,s_{i,j}}^{f_i}(x_i), 1 \leq i \leq n] \mathrel{\hat{=}} t. \qquad \square$$

In the para recursion schemes there may be several operations with the same argument sort involved whereas the top-down recursion scheme assumes only one operation for each operation. Hence the para recursion scheme is a generalization of the top-down recursion scheme. For the detection of such generalized recursion structure the following criterion can be used.

Definition 7.3.9 (Para top-down recursive, paramorphisms)
Let $SR \subseteq SC$, for $1 \leq i \leq m$ let f_i be SR-indexed families of operations. The families f_i are called *para top-down recursive* if for all $1 \leq i \leq m$ and $sc \in SR$ there is a family of equations $l = r \in E_{f_{i,sc}}$ such that

(C1) $l = r$ is flat constructive

(C2) $l = r$ is left-linear

(C3) r is a para recursion scheme instance of sc and $f_1, \ldots, f_m$.

The families f_i are called *paramorphisms*, if they are para top-down recursive. $\qquad \square$

This more general recursion scheme is similar to the top-down tree transducers of Zülöp and Vogler [36]. The top-down tree transducers are operating syntactically only. Therefore, the types can be omitted in this approach instead only arities are used. Moreover, non-free data structures can not be modeled with tree transducers.

The para top-down recursive families of operations can be transformed into a top down recursive family of operations using tupling.

Definition 7.3.10 (Tupling step)
With $\alpha(sc) = (\alpha_1(sc), \ldots, \alpha_m(sc))$ for all $sc \in SR$ we generate a new operation $f_{sc} : sc \to \alpha(sc)$ and new equations

$$E' = \left\{ \begin{array}{rcl} f_{sc}(x) & = & (f_{1,sc}(x), \ldots, f_{m,sc}(x)) \\ f_{i,sc}(x) & = & \#i(f_{sc}(x)) \end{array} \right\}$$

A case analysis on x yields a set of flat-constructive equations E''. The *tupling step* enriches a specification by the new function symbols f_{sc} and the equations E''.   □

The constructed SR-indexed family f is top-down recursive.

Proposition 7.3.11 (Tupling yields catamorphism)
The SR-indexed family f from Def. 7.3.10 is top down recursive.   □

The tupling step enables a fusion step with para recursion schemes by generating a top-down recursion scheme with a tuple result type.

7.4   An example fusion step

As an application we present an example fusion step for a simple function composition. We begin with a specification of an operation computing the sum of all nodes of a rose tree of natural numbers. The axiomatization is based on the auxiliary operations computing the list of elements of a rose tree and a summation of list elements. The composed function is axiomatized using the composition of the auxiliary functions. The result algebra and the Σ-homomorphism for a catamorphism is constructed and the fusion theorem is demonstrated by giving the concrete interpretations and target algebras in terms of a model of the specification. Finally, the fusion step is performed constructing the resulting specification including the combine operations and the proof obligations.

7.4.1   Rose trees

In this section we specify rose trees generated as a mutually recursive data structure. A rose tree consists of a natural number and a list of descendent rose trees. The list of rose trees is constructed by an empty list *notree*, a singleton tree *sgltree*, and the concatenation of two tree lists. We ensure the list properties by axioms for the associativity of the function symbol *cnctree* and neutrality wrt. *notree* .

The following specification defines rose trees along with lists of rose trees:

spec $SumElem = Nat +$
sorts $rtree = mktree(nat, rtlist),$
                $rtlist = notree \mid sgltree(rtree) \mid cnctree(rtlist, rtlist)$
vars $TK, TL, TR : rtlist, m, n : nat$
axioms
                $assoctree: \ cnctree(cnctree(TK, TL), TR) = cnctree(TK, cnctree(TL, TR)),$
                $neutrtree: \ cnctree(TL, notree) = TL = cnctree(notree, TL)$
end

If we additionally want to specify an operation computing the sum of all elements of a tree, we can separate the task into two simpler subtasks. We define it as composition of the auxiliary functions *sum* and *elements* using the intermediate data structure *list* . Hence, the specification *SumElem* is extended by:

sorts $list = nil \mid sglt(nat) \mid conc(list, list)$
ops $sumel : (rtree)nat$
vars $K, L, R : list, m, n : nat$
axioms
                $assoc: \ conc(conc(K, L), R) = conc(K, conc(L, R)),$
                $neutr: \ conc(L, nil) = L = conc(nil, L),$

            $sumel0: \ sumel = sum \circ elements$

The auxiliary operation *sum* computes the sum of a list, and the operation *elements* accumulates all elements of a tree in a list using the operation *toList* traversing the elements of lists of trees:

ops $sum : (list)nat,$
                $elements : (rtree)list,$
                $toList : (rtlist)list$

vars $K, L : list, n : nat, T : rtree, TK, TL : rtlist$
axioms $sum1 : sum(nil) = zero,$
                $sum2 : sum(sglt(n)) = n,$
                $sum3 : sum(conc(K, L)) = add(sum(K), sum(L)),$
            $elements1 : elements(mktree(a, TL)) = conc(sglt(a), toList(TL)),$
                $toList1 : toList(notree) = nil,$
                $toList2 : toList(sgltree(T)) = elements(T),$
                $toList3 : toList(cnctree(TK, TL)) = conc(toList(TK), toList(TL))$

The fusion transformation applied to the operation *sumel* should generate an equivalent axiomatization that does no longer refer to the auxiliary operations *sum* and *elements* . In this way the intermediate construction of the list of natural numbers can be avoided, compare Fig. 7.3 .

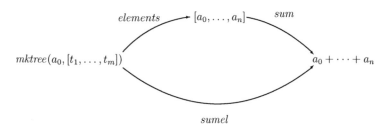

Figure 7.3: Fusion of *sum* and *elements*

In order to achieve such an axiomatization we will apply the fusion transformation of Prop. 7.3.7. This requires that the operation *elements* can be lifted to a $\Sigma_C^{SumElem}$-homomorphism. The operations *elements* and *toList* fulfill the properties $(C1) - (C3)$ (see Def. 7.3.5), i.e. they form a catamorphism as introduced in Def. 7.2.2. For each constructor of sort *rtree* there is a left-linear, flat constructive equation defining *elements*, and for each constructor of sort *rtlist* as well for the operation *toList*. Moreover, the condition $(C3)$ is fulfilled, since all recursive variables are applied by *elements* or *toList*. For example, in equation *toList3* the variables TK, TL of sort *rtlist* on the right-hand side of equation

$$toList3 : toList(cnctree(TK, TL)) = conc(toList(TK), toList(TL))$$

are applied by *elements* or *toList* recursively. Therefore, we can construct the recursion scheme

$$conc(y_1, y_2)$$

with the variables $y_1 : list, y_2 : list$. The right-hand side of equation *toList3* is an instance of this recursion scheme as demanded in $(C3)$.

7.4.2   Constructing the homomorphism

For the construction of the $\Sigma_C^{SumElem}$-homomorphism we set $SR = \{rtree, rtlist\}$. We will now construct a $\Sigma_C^{SumElem}$-algebra $\mathcal{B}$ and a $\Sigma_C^{SumElem}$-homomorphism φ from $\mathcal{A}$ to $\mathcal{B}$ such that φ is the canonical extension of *elements* and *toList*. Let $\mathcal{M} \in CGEN(SumElem)$ be a model of *SumElem* and $\mathcal{A} = \mathcal{M}|_{\Sigma_C}$. We construct the $\Sigma_C^{SumElem}$-algebra $\mathcal{B}$ based on the functions $elements^{\mathcal{M}}$ and $toList^{\mathcal{M}}$ as follows:

$$nat^{\mathcal{B}} = nat^{\mathcal{M}} \qquad zero^{\mathcal{B}} = zero^{\mathcal{M}} \qquad\qquad succ^{\mathcal{B}} = succ^{\mathcal{M}}$$

$$list^{\mathcal{B}} = list^{\mathcal{M}} \qquad nil^{\mathcal{B}} = nil^{\mathcal{M}} \qquad\qquad sglt^{\mathcal{B}} = sglt^{\mathcal{M}}$$
$$conc^{\mathcal{B}} = conc^{\mathcal{M}}$$

$$rtree^{\mathcal{B}} = list^{\mathcal{M}} \qquad mktree^{\mathcal{B}}(a, l) = conc^{\mathcal{M}}(sglt^{\mathcal{M}}(a), l)$$

$$rtlist^{\mathcal{B}} = list^{\mathcal{M}} \qquad notree^{\mathcal{B}} = nil^{\mathcal{M}} \qquad sgltree^{\mathcal{B}}(l) = l$$
$$cnctree^{\mathcal{B}} = conc^{\mathcal{M}}$$

By construction, the $\Sigma_C^{Listnat}$-algebra $\mathcal{B}$ satisfies $E_C^{SumElem}$, since $conc^{\mathcal{M}}$ is associative and $nil^{\mathcal{M}}$ is neutral with respect to $conc^{\mathcal{M}}$.

The family of functions $\varphi : \mathcal{A} \rightarrow \mathcal{B}$ is defined in accordance with axioms $elements1$, $toList1$, $toList2$ and $toList3$ as

$$
\begin{aligned}
\varphi_{nat}(a) &= id_{nat}(a) &&= a \\
\varphi_{list}(l) &= id_{list}(l) &&= l \\
\varphi_{rtree}(mktree^{\mathcal{A}}(a, tl)) &= mktree^{\mathcal{B}}(\varphi_{nat}(a), \varphi_{rtlist}(tl)) &&= conc^{\mathcal{M}}(sglt^{\mathcal{M}}(\varphi_{nat}(a)), \varphi_{rtlist}(l)) \\
\varphi_{rtlist}(notree^{\mathcal{A}}) &= notree^{\mathcal{B}} &&= nil^{\mathcal{M}} \\
\varphi_{rtlist}(sgltree^{\mathcal{A}}(t)) &= sgltree^{\mathcal{B}}(\varphi_{rtree}(t)) &&= \varphi_{rtree}(t) \\
\varphi_{rtlist}(cnctree^{\mathcal{A}}(tk, tl)) &= cnctree^{\mathcal{B}}(\varphi_{rtlist}(tk), \varphi_{rtlist}(tl)) &&= conc^{\mathcal{M}}(\varphi_{rtlist}(tk), \varphi_{rtlist}(tl))
\end{aligned}
$$

Therefore, φ forms a $\Sigma_C^{SumElem}$-homomorphism, and the SR-indexed family of operations $elements$ and $toList$ build a catamorphism.

7.4.3 Constructing the target algebra

We will now demonstrate the use of the fusion theorem. In order to apply the fusion theorem we are in need of additional operations to complete the second catamorphism involved in the fusion theorem.

$$
\begin{aligned}
sumel &= sum \circ elements \\
sumtrlist &= sumtl \circ toList
\end{aligned}
$$

Let $\mathcal{M} \in CGEN(SumElem)$. Then the Σ_C-algebra $\mathcal{B}$ is determined by the axioms $elements, toList1, toList2$ and $toList3$ defining the functions $elements^{\mathcal{M}}$ and $toList^{\mathcal{M}}$ as described in Subsection 7.4.2:

The fusion theorem (Prop. 7.2.3) requires a Σ_C-algebra $\mathcal{Z}$ such that the canonical extension

$$
\langle sum^{\mathcal{M}}|_{rtree^{\mathcal{B}}}, sumtl^{\mathcal{M}}|_{rtlist^{\mathcal{B}}} \rangle
$$

forms a $\Sigma_C^{SumElem}$-homomorphism from $\mathcal{B}$ to $\mathcal{Z}$. Thus, the following distributive properties must hold:

$$
\begin{aligned}
sum^{\mathcal{M}}(mktree^{\mathcal{B}}(a, l)) &= mktree^{\mathcal{Z}}(a, sum^{\mathcal{M}}(l)) \\
sumtl^{\mathcal{M}}(notree^{\mathcal{B}}) &= notree^{\mathcal{Z}} \\
sumtl^{\mathcal{M}}(sgltree^{\mathcal{B}}(l)) &= sgltree^{\mathcal{Z}}(sum^{\mathcal{M}}(l)) \\
sumtl^{\mathcal{M}}(cnctree^{\mathcal{B}}(k, l)) &= cnctree^{\mathcal{Z}}(sumtl^{\mathcal{M}}(k), sumtl^{\mathcal{M}}(l))
\end{aligned}
$$

If we choose $\mathcal{Z}$ such that we have $rtree^{\mathcal{Z}} = nat^{\mathcal{M}}$, $rtlist^{\mathcal{Z}} = nat^{\mathcal{M}}$, $mktree^{\mathcal{Z}} = add^{\mathcal{M}}$, $notree^{\mathcal{Z}} = zero^{\mathcal{M}}$, $sgltree^{\mathcal{Z}}(a) = a$, and $cnctree^{\mathcal{Z}} = add^{\mathcal{M}}$, then the above listed properties are fulfilled:

$$
\begin{aligned}
sum^{\mathcal{M}}(mktree^{\mathcal{B}}(a,l)) &= sum^{\mathcal{M}}(conc(sglt(a),l)) \\
&= add^{\mathcal{M}}(a, sum^{\mathcal{M}}(l)) \\
&= mktree^{\mathcal{Z}}(a, sum^{\mathcal{M}}(l)) \\
sumtl^{\mathcal{M}}(notree^{\mathcal{B}}) &= sumtl^{\mathcal{M}}(nil^{\mathcal{M}}) \\
&= zero^{\mathcal{M}} \\
&= notree^{\mathcal{Z}} \\
sumtl^{\mathcal{M}}(sgltree^{\mathcal{B}}(l)) &= sumtl^{\mathcal{M}}(l) \\
&= sgltree^{\mathcal{Z}}(sumtl(l)) \\
sumtl^{\mathcal{M}}(cnctree^{\mathcal{B}}(l,k)) &= sumtl^{\mathcal{M}}(conc^{\mathcal{M}}(l,k)) \\
&= add^{\mathcal{M}}(sumtl^{\mathcal{M}}(l), sumtl^{\mathcal{M}}(k)) \\
&= cnctree^{\mathcal{Z}}(sumtl^{\mathcal{M}}(l), sumtl^{\mathcal{M}}(k))
\end{aligned}
$$

Additionally, we have $\mathcal{Z} \in CGEN(\Sigma_C^{SumElem}, E_C^{SumElem})$, since

$$
\begin{aligned}
cnctree^{\mathcal{Z}}(cnctree(k,l),r) &= cnctree^{\mathcal{Z}}(k, cnctree^{\mathcal{Z}}(l,r)) \\
cnctree^{\mathcal{Z}}(l, notree^{\mathcal{Z}}) = \; l &= cnctree^{\mathcal{Z}}(notree^{\mathcal{Z}}, l) \, .
\end{aligned}
$$

The fusion theorem now claims that $sumel^{\mathcal{M}}$ and $sumtrlist^{\mathcal{M}}$ form a catamorphism, which implies the axioms

$$
\begin{aligned}
sumel^{\mathcal{M}}(mktree^{\mathcal{M}}(a,tl)) &= mktree^{\mathcal{Z}}(a, sumtrlist(tl)) \\
\\
sumtrlist^{\mathcal{M}}(notree^{\mathcal{M}}) &= notree^{\mathcal{Z}} \\
sumtrlist^{\mathcal{M}}(sgltree^{\mathcal{M}}(t)) &= sgltree^{\mathcal{Z}}(sumel(t)) \\
sumtrlist^{\mathcal{M}}(cnctree^{\mathcal{M}}(tl,tk)) &= cnctree^{\mathcal{Z}}(sumtrlist(tl), sumtrlist(tk)).
\end{aligned}
$$

This induces a new axiomatization of the operation $sumsq$ if the interpretations of the constructors of $list$ in $\mathcal{Z}$ can be expressed by terms of the signature.

In general the requested Σ_C-algebra $\mathcal{Z}$ can not be generated automatically by a transformation system. The extraction of the new interpretations of the constructors in $\mathcal{Z}$ in terms of the model $\mathcal{M}$ amounts to higher-order unification and is therefore undecidable. However, in many cases these interpretations can be generated by strategies. The Lübeck Transformation System provides a strategy that tries to find such interpretations by analyzing 'good term generalizations', see Subsection 11.4.2. If the strategy fails, manual transformations may complete the transformation step.

7.4.4   The fusion step

The fusion step manipulates specifications such that equations of the form $h = g \circ f$ are replaced by a catamorphic axiomatization of h. Therefore, combine operations are introduced denoting the interpretation of the constructors in the target algebra. Again we will demonstrate the result on our illustrating example.

The fusion step for $sumel = sum \circ elements$ leads to

$$\Sigma' \;=\; \Sigma_{Listnat} \cup \left\{ \begin{array}{lll} cop_{mktree} & : & (nat,nat)nat \\ cop_{notree} & : & nat, \\ cop_{sgltree} & : & (nat)nat, \\ cop_{cnctree} & : & (nat,nat)nat \end{array} \right\}$$

$$E_h \;=\; \left\{ \begin{array}{rcl} sumel(mktree(a,TL)) & = & cop_{mktree}(a,sumtrlist(TL)) \\ sumtrlist(notree) & = & cop_{notree} \\ sumtrlist(sgltree(t)) & = & cop_{sgltree}(sumel(t)) \\ sumtrlist(cnctree(TK,TL)) & = & cop_{cnctree}(sumtrlist(TK),sumtrlist(TL)) \end{array} \right\}$$

$$E_{cop} \;=\; \left\{ \begin{array}{rcl} sum(conc(sglt(a),L)) & = & cop_{mktree}(a,sumtl(l)) \\ sumtl(nil) & = & cop_{notree} \\ sumtl(l) & = & cop_{sgltree}(sum(l)) \\ sumtl(conc(L,K)) & = & cop_{cnctree}(sumtl(L),sumtl(K)) \end{array} \right\}$$

The equations in E_{cop} can now be used to derive the combine operation by applying axioms and using generalization:

$$\begin{array}{rcl} cop_{mktree} & = & add \\ cop_{notree} & = & zero \\ cop_{sgltree}(n) & = & n \\ cop_{cnctree} & = & add \end{array}$$

If the occurrences of the combine operations in E_h are unfolded, we get the following result:

$$\begin{array}{rcl} sumel(mktree(a,TL)) & = & add(a,sumtrlist(TL)) \\ sumtrlist(notree) & = & zero \\ sumtrlist(sgltree(t)) & = & sumel(t) \\ sumtrlist(cnctree(TK,TL)) & = & add(sumtrlist(TK),sumtrlist(TL)) \end{array}$$

Additionally, we have to prove the three application conditions emerged from the associativity and neutrality axioms of the specification *Listnat*:

$$add(n,zero) = n = add(zero,n)$$
$$add(add(m,n),k) = add(m,add(n,k))$$

Since the operation *add* is specified as usual and therefore satisfies these properties we omit the proof.

7.5   Concluding remarks on fusion steps

Fusion is a well-known technique for code optimization in functional languages [60]. The literature on fusion often employs this technique in terms of category theory using functors as description for free data types. Here, catamorphisms and paramorphisms consist of one function symbol only.

The work presented in this chapter extends the fusion theory for catamorphisms and paramorphisms to algebraic structures. We describe fusion by means of Σ-homomorphisms which integrates well into the theory of algebraic specifications. The involved function symbols can be axiomatized in a property-oriented style without requiring algorithmic functions. Moreover, our approach generalizes catamorphisms to systems of mutually recursive function symbols. As a major benefit the described approach also captures non-free data types constrained by constructor equations. As a consequence, the fusion step may generate further proof obligations resulting from the constructor equations of the source algebra.

A syntax based approach is given by Zülöp and Vogler [36]. They survey top-down tree transducer which are similar to paramorphisms. The composition of two top-down tree transducer can be fused into a new tree transducer. The approach is untyped and non-free data structures can not be modeled.

The fusion technique is used for the transformation of functional programs in several transformation systems. The HYLO system [65] applies the fusion theorem for hylomorphisms, a generalization of catamorphisms, to functional programs. The MAG system of de Moor [19] is a prototype system for automating the fusion on Haskell programs. Here the generation of the new combine operations is managed by a strategy for higher-order unification using so-called unbetasteps. The fusion step as described in this chapter is implemented in the Lübeck Transformation System [27]. Here the fusion step is performed in the setting of algebraic specifications (see Section 11.3.2).

Chapter 8

Data Structure Refinements

We describe a general semantic framework for data structure refinements and present several important refinement steps transforming entire specifications. A general method of data structure refinements is given by algebraic implementations. These steps embed a constructor sort into a derived sort using representation and abstraction function symbols inserted into the specification. For particular situations special data structure refinements are introduced. As simple cases we demonstrate constructor implementation, constructor introduction and enrichment and reduction of constructor systems.

8.1 Requirements and motivation

Data types with constructor generated sorts support the problem-oriented specification of data structures [46]. For an implementation one heads for data structures that allow an efficient implementation of the involved functions. Most programming languages provide efficient manipulations of standard data structures. Hence, in most cases data structures composed from standard data structures like natural numbers, lists, and arrays make an efficient implementation possible.

In the setting of algebraic specifications the problem-oriented description of data structures uses basic sorts. Data structure refinements implement a basic sort (the *abstract sort*) by a derived sort (the *implementation sort*). The axiomatization of the involved operations must be transformed taking the new representation of the data structure into account. We must guarantee that the behaviour of the operations after the refinement agrees with the behaviour on the abstract sort. Therefore, we constrain the refinement by a condition claiming that all models of the refined specification can be partitioned by a Σ-congruence such that there is a subalgebra of the corresponding quotient in the model class of the original specifications. This principle follows the refinement relation given in Definition 5.2.1.

In the following we will first address semantic aspects. The approach relies on a collection of representation and abstraction functions mapping elements of the abstract sort to elements of the implementation sort and vice versa. Based on the semantic treatment, we will define several data structure refinement steps: The algebraic implementation forms a general approach. By inserting the representation and the abstraction functions into the specification, the requirements and the application conditions can be expressed as newly generated axioms. The four simple data structure refinements cover particular situations where the explicit insertion of representation and abstraction functions is not required. The constructor implementation settles a representation by mapping each constructor term to a term of the implementation sort. This step embodies a short-cut of an algebraic implementation since the representation function is only given implicitly by the term mapping. This refinement is applicable only, if the axioms show a certain syntactic shape. The constructor introduction transforms a loose sort into a constructor sort by switching all relevant operations to constructors. Often the constructor introduction generates too many or too few constructors. Therefore, we provide data structure refinement steps that reduce or enrich the set of constructors.

8.2　Foundations of data structure refinements

Our semantic approach to data structure refinements refers to entire specifications and is based on representation and abstraction functions. A signature morphism is used to manifest implementation sorts and functions. These refinements can be described in different ways using solely representation functions, solely abstraction functions, or both representation and abstraction functions.

8.2.1　The general approach

A data structure refinement is settled by a signature morphism mapping abstract sorts to their implementation sorts and function symbols operating on abstract sorts to their implementation function symbols on the implementation sorts. Hence, a data structure refinement transforms an entire specification according to the signature morphism. Since the transformation must follow the refinement relation it must guarantee that the behaviour of the implementation functions operating on the implementation sorts agrees with the behaviour of the original function operation on the abstract sorts. In order to ensure this we relate the abstract and the implementation function symbols by auxiliary functions — representation and abstraction functions.

Fig. 8.1 illustrates the idea of representation and abstraction functions. The abstract sort sc is refined to the implementation sort se, and the abstract function symbol f_{old} is refined by the implementation function symbol f. The refinement of the data structure can be described by a representation function $repr : sc \rightarrow se$ mapping each element of the abstract sort to a corresponding element of the implementation sort. Vice versa an abstraction function $abstr : se \rightarrow sc$ maps elements of the implementation sort to elements of the abstract sort. These auxiliary functions can be used to relate the behaviour of the implementation function f using the commuting diagram. The relation can be established

$$sc \xrightarrow{\ f_{old}\ } sc$$

$$repr \left\downarrow\right\uparrow abstr \qquad repr \left\downarrow\right\uparrow abstr$$

$$se \xrightarrow{\ f\ } se$$

Figure 8.1: Data structure refinement

in different ways. For the higher-order approach additionally distributive properties for representation and abstraction functions on derived sorts are necessary.

In the following we will discuss important possibilities for modeling data structure refinements by representation and abstraction functions. The refinement of data structures will be described in terms of algebras of the corresponding signatures. If all algebras of the refined specification show certain properties that can be described by representation and abstraction functions we achieve a refinement.

In order to explicate this principle we assume in the following subsections that $(\Sigma_1 = (S_1, F_1, C_1), E_1)$ and $(\Sigma_2 = (S_2, F_2, C_2), E_2)$ are algebraic specifications, $\mathcal{A}$ is a Σ_1-algebra and $\mathcal{B}$ is a Σ_2-algebra. A signature morphism $\delta : \Sigma_1 \to \Sigma_2$ may determine the refinement of basic sorts in S_1 by derived sorts of S_2. Moreover, we call $\delta(sb)^{\mathcal{B}}$ the *implementation carrier* and $sb^{\mathcal{A}}$ the *abstract carrier*.

8.2.2 Simulation by data structure representations

We first discuss the so called L-simulation which uses representation functions only and requires that the interpretation of function symbols are mapped to the corresponding interpretation of the implementation function symbol.

We first describe an implementation relation on algebras. The algebra $\mathcal{B}$ implements each carrier set $sb^{\mathcal{A}}$ of a sort $sb \in S_1$ by a carrier $\delta(sb)^{\mathcal{B}}$ of the derived sort $\delta(sb) \in S_2^{\times, \to}$. This forms an embedding and can be established by an $S^{\times, \to}$-indexed family of functions mapping abstract elements to their representation. The family of functions must be compatible with forming tuples and applications; moreover the function symbols must be mapped according to δ.

Definition 8.2.1 (Representation functions, data structure representation)
An $S_1^{\times, \to}$-indexed family $repr^{\delta} : \mathcal{A} \to \mathcal{B}$ of mappings $(repr_s^{\delta} : s^{\mathcal{A}} \to \delta(s)^{\mathcal{B}})_{s \in S_1^{\times, \to}}$ is called a *family of representation functions*, if for all $n \geq 2$, $s_i \in S_1^{\times, \to}$, $a_i \in s_i^{\mathcal{A}}$ for $1 \leq i \leq n$, $s \in S_1^{\times, \to}$ and $g \in (s_1 \to s_2)^{\mathcal{A}}$

$$repr_{(s_1, \ldots, s_n)}^{\delta}(a_1, \ldots, a_n) = (repr_{s_1}^{\delta}(a_1), \ldots, repr_{s_n}^{\delta}(a_n))$$
$$repr_{(s_1 \to s_2)}^{\delta}(g)(repr_{s_1}^{\delta}(a_1)) = repr_{s_2}^{\delta}(g(a_1))$$

holds. If for all $f \in F_{1,s}$ additionally $repr_s^{\delta}(f^{\mathcal{A}}) = \delta(f)^{\mathcal{B}}$ holds, we call $repr^{\delta}$ a *data structure representation*. If for all $s \in S_1^{\times, \to}$ the function $repr_s^{\delta}$ is injective (surjective), the family $repr^{\delta}$ is called an *injective (surjective) family of representation functions*.

□

Using the images of the representation functions on the basic sorts, a data structure representation can be reduced to a Σ_1-homomorphism. This homomorphism is called the range homomorphism.

Definition 8.2.2 (Range algebra, range homomorphism)
Let $repr^\delta$ be a data structure representation as defined in 8.2.1. The *range algebra* $\mathcal{Z}^{repr}$ of $repr^\delta$ and the *range homomorphism* of $repr^\delta$ written $\varphi^{repr} : \mathcal{A} \to \mathcal{Z}^{repr}$ is defined by

$$
\begin{aligned}
sb^{\mathcal{Z}^{repr}} &= repr^\delta_{sb}(sb^{\mathcal{A}}) \text{ for all } sb \in S_1 \\
(s_1, \ldots, s_n)^{\mathcal{Z}^{repr}} &= s_1^{\mathcal{Z}^{repr}} \times \cdots \times s_n^{\mathcal{Z}^{repr}} \\
(s_1 \to s_2)^{\mathcal{Z}^{repr}} &= [s_1^{\mathcal{Z}^{repr}} \to s_2^{\mathcal{Z}^{repr}}] \\
f^{\mathcal{Z}^{repr}} &= \varphi_s^{repr}(f^{\mathcal{A}}) \text{ for all } s \in S^{\times, \to} \text{ and } f \in F_{1,s}
\end{aligned}
$$

and

$$
\begin{aligned}
\varphi_{sb}^{repr} &= repr^\delta_{sb} \text{ for all } sb \in S_1 \\
\varphi_{(s_1, \ldots, s_n)}^{repr}(a_1, \ldots, a_n) &= (\varphi_{s_1}^{repr}(a_1), \ldots, \varphi_{s_n}^{repr}(a_n)) \\
\varphi_{s_1 \to s_2}^{repr}(g)(\varphi_{s_1}^{repr}(a_1)) &= \varphi_{s_2}^{repr}(g(a_1))
\end{aligned}
$$

□

By construction the range homomorphism is surjective. Given a data structure representation $repr^\delta : \mathcal{A} \to \mathcal{B}$ the image of the range homomorphism $\varphi^{repr} : \mathcal{A} \to \mathcal{Z}^{repr}$ forms a subalgebra of $\mathcal{B}$.

Lemma 8.2.3 (L-simulation)
Let $repr^\delta : \mathcal{A} \to \mathcal{B}$ be a data structure representation. The image of the range homomorphism $\mathcal{Z}^{repr}$ is a subalgebra of $\mathcal{B}$ via δ.

Proof: We have to prove that $\mathcal{Z}^{repr}$ is an embedded algebra of $\mathcal{B}$, and that the interpretations of the function symbols correspond. The latter proof is performed by an induction on the construction principle of derived sorts.

- $sb^{\mathcal{Z}^{repr}} = repr^\delta_{sb}(sb^{\mathcal{A}}) \subseteq \delta(sb)^{\mathcal{B}}$ is a consequence of $repr^\delta_{sb} : sb^{\mathcal{A}} \to \delta(sb)^{\mathcal{B}}$.

- $f^{\mathcal{Z}^{repr}} \overset{\mathcal{Z}^{repr}}{\underset{s}{\approx}}{}^{\mathcal{B}} \delta(f)^{\mathcal{B}}$: We prove by structural induction on $S_1^{\times, \to}$ that for all $s \in S_1^{\times, \to}$ and $g \in s^{\mathcal{A}}$ it is $\varphi_s^{repr}(g) \overset{\mathcal{Z}^{repr}}{\underset{s}{\approx}}{}^{\mathcal{B}} repr^\delta_s(g)$:

  Basic sorts: Assume $s \in S_1$. Then $\varphi_s^{repr}(g) = repr^\delta_s(g)$ as introduced in Def. 8.2.2.

  Tuple sorts: Assume $s = (s_1, \ldots, s_n)$. Then we get by definition

$$
\begin{aligned}
\varphi_{(s_1, \ldots, s_n)}^{repr}(a_1, \ldots, a_1) &= (\varphi_{s_1}^{repr}(a_1), \ldots, \varphi_{s_n}^{repr}(a_n)) \text{ and} \\
repr^\delta_{(s_1, \ldots, s_n)}(a_1, \ldots, a_1) &= (repr^\delta_{s_1}(a_1), \ldots, repr^\delta_{s_n}(a_n))
\end{aligned}
$$

Since $\varphi_{s_i}^{repr}(a_i) \overset{\mathcal{Z}^{repr}}{\underset{s_i}{\approx}}{}^{\mathcal{B}} repr^\delta_{s_i}(a_i)$ holds by induction hypothesis, the claim is true for this case.

Function sorts: Assume $s = (s_1 \to s_2)$. Then let $a \in s_1^{\mathcal{Z}^{repr}}$. Since φ^{repr} is surjective there is $a' \in s_1^{\mathcal{A}}$ such that $a = \varphi_{s_1}^{repr}(a')$ and by induction hypothesis for s_1 we can assume that $a = \varphi_{s_1}^{repr}(a') \overset{\mathcal{Z}^{repr}}{\underset{s_1}{\succsim}}{}^{\mathcal{B}} repr_{s_1}^{\delta}(a') = b$. By induction hypothesis for s_2 we conclude

$$\varphi_{s_2}^{repr}(g(a')) \quad \overset{\mathcal{Z}^{repr}}{\underset{s_2}{\succsim}}{}^{\mathcal{B}} \quad repr_{s_2}^{\delta}(g(a')) \,.$$

By definition of φ^{repr} and $repr^{\delta}$ this implies

$$\varphi_{(s_1 \to s_2)}^{repr}(g)(\varphi^{repr}(a')) \quad \overset{\mathcal{Z}^{repr}}{\underset{s_2}{\succsim}}{}^{\mathcal{B}} \quad repr_{(s_1 \to s_2)}^{\delta}(g)(repr_{s_1}^{\delta}(a')) \,.$$

Finally, we get

$$\varphi_{(s_1 \to s_2)}^{repr}(g)(a) \quad \overset{\mathcal{Z}^{repr}}{\underset{s_2}{\succsim}}{}^{\mathcal{B}} \quad repr_{(s_1 \to s_2)}^{\delta}(g)(b)$$

which implies the claim. $\qquad\square$

Since φ^{repr} is a surjective homomorphism, $\mathcal{Z}^{repr} \in CGEN(\Sigma_1, E_1)$ holds. Moreover, $\mathcal{Z}^{repr}$ is a subalgebra of $\mathcal{B}$. We can now prove that a data structure refinement is correct, if there is a data structure representation.

Proposition 8.2.4 (L-data structure refinement)
If for all $\mathcal{B} \in CGEN(\Sigma_2, E_2)$ there is $\mathcal{A} \in CGEN(\Sigma_1, E_1)$ and a data structure representation $repr^{\delta} : \mathcal{A} \to \mathcal{B}$, we have $(\Sigma_1, E_1) \overset{\delta}{\rightarrowtail} (\Sigma_2, E_2)$.

Proof: Let $\mathcal{B} \in CGEN(\Sigma_2, E_2)$ and $\mathcal{A} \in CGEN(\Sigma_1, E_1)$ such that $repr^{\delta}$ is a data structure representation. We consider the image of the range homomorphism φ^{repr} : $\mathcal{A} \to \mathcal{Z}^{repr}$. The Σ_1-algebra $\mathcal{Z}^{repr}$ is a subalgebra of $\mathcal{B}$ via δ, see Lemma 8.2.3, and $\mathcal{Z}^{repr} \in CGEN(\Sigma_1, E_1)$, since surjective homomorphisms are property preserving, see Lemma 2.2.16. $\qquad\square$

If for all models of the original specification there is an injective data structure representation into a model of the refined specification, we call the data structure refinement injective.

Definition 8.2.5 (Injective (surjective) L-data structure refinement)

A data structure refinement $(\Sigma_1, E_1) \overset{\delta}{\rightarrowtail} (\Sigma_2, E_2)$ with $\delta : \Sigma_1 \to \Sigma_2$ is called an *injective (a surjective) data structure refinement* or *injective (surjective) embedding)* if for all $\mathcal{A} \in CGEN(\Sigma_1, E_1)$ there is $\mathcal{B} \in CGEN(\Sigma_2, E_2)$ such that there is an injective (surjective) family of representation functions $repr^{\delta} : \mathcal{A} \to \mathcal{B}$. $\qquad\square$

The injective data structure refinements embody pure embedding steps, whereas non-injective representations also contain a design decision identifying several elements with the same implementation value in $\mathcal{B}$. Therefore, injective representations are of special interest in order to distinguish the different kinds of refinement steps clearly.

Heading for mechanizable manipulations of specifications we present in Section 8.3 a transformation rule that makes use of Proposition 8.2.4.

8.2.3   Simulation by data structure abstractions

In this subsection we introduce simulations that are based on abstraction functions. Here, we assume that the abstraction of the interpretation of the implementation function symbols agrees with the interpretation of the original function symbol.

Again we will first explicate the implementation in terms of algebras. In the L^{-1}-simulation we describe the implementation by relating each element of the implementation sort to an element of the abstract sort using a family of abstraction functions.

Definition 8.2.6 (Abstraction functions, data structure abstraction)
An $\delta(S_1^{\times,\rightarrow})$-indexed family $abstr^\delta : \mathcal{B} \rightarrow \mathcal{A}$ of mappings $(abstr^\delta_{\delta(s)} : \delta(s)^\mathcal{B} \rightarrow s^\mathcal{A})_{s \in S_1^{\times,\rightarrow}}$ is called a *family of abstraction functions*, if for all $n \geq 2$, $s_i \in S_1^{\times,\rightarrow}$ and $b_i \in \delta(s_i)^\mathcal{B}$ for $1 \leq i \leq n$ and $g \in \delta(s_1 \rightarrow s_2)^\mathcal{B}$ we have:

$$abstr^\delta_{(\delta(s_1),\dots,\delta(s_n))}(b_1,\dots,b_n) = (abstr^\delta_{\delta(s_1)}(b_1),\dots,abstr^\delta_{\delta(s_n)}(b_n))$$
$$abstr^\delta_{(\delta(s_1)\rightarrow\delta(s_2))}(g)(abstr^\delta_{\delta(s_1)}(b_1)) = abstr^\delta_{\delta(s_2)}(g(b_1))$$

If for all $f \in F_{1,s}$ additionally $abstr^\delta_{\delta(s)}(\delta(f)^\mathcal{B}) = f^\mathcal{A}$ holds, we call $abstr^\delta$ a *data structure abstraction*.   □

The properties of the data structure abstraction ensure that the Σ_1-algebra $\mathcal{A}$ is congruent to $\mathcal{B}$ via δ.

Lemma 8.2.7 (L^{-1}-simulation)
Let $\mathcal{A}$ be a Σ_1-algebra and $\mathcal{B}$ a Σ_2-algebra. If there is a data structure abstraction $abstr^\delta : \mathcal{B} \rightarrow \mathcal{A}$, then there is a Σ_2-congruence $\approx^\mathcal{B}$ such that $\mathcal{A} = \mathcal{B}/_{\approx^\mathcal{B}}$.

Proof: We construct $\approx^\mathcal{B}$ such that $a \approx^\mathcal{B}_s b \Leftrightarrow abstr^\delta_s(a) = abstr^\delta_s(b)$ for all $s \in \delta(S_1^{\times,\rightarrow})$, and $a \approx^\mathcal{B}_s a$ for all $s \in S_2^{\times,\rightarrow} \setminus \delta(S_1^{\times,\rightarrow})$, and furthermore $\approx^\mathcal{B}$ is compatible with tupling and application:

$$(a_1,\dots,a_n) \approx^\mathcal{B}_{(s_1,\dots,s_n)} (b_1,\dots,b_n) \Leftrightarrow a_1 \approx^\mathcal{B}_{s_1} b_1 \wedge \cdots \wedge a_n \approx^\mathcal{B}_{s_n} b_n$$
$$f \approx^\mathcal{B}_{(s_1\rightarrow s_2)} g \Leftrightarrow \text{if for all } b_1, b_2 \text{ it is } b_1 \approx^\mathcal{B}_{s_1} b_2, \text{ then } f(b_1) \approx^\mathcal{B}_{s_2} g(b_2).$$

Such a congruence exists because $abstr^\delta$ is compatible with tupling and application:

Tuple sorts: Let $(s_1,\dots,s_n) \in S_1^{\times,\rightarrow}$. Then we have

$$abstr^\delta_{(\delta(s_1),\dots,\delta(s_n))}(a_1,\dots,a_n) = abstr^\delta_{(\delta(s_1),\dots,\delta(s_n))}(b_1,\dots,b_n)$$
$$\Leftrightarrow (abstr^\delta_{\delta(s_1)}(a_1),\dots,abstr^\delta_{\delta(s_n)}(a_n)) = (abstr^\delta_{\delta(s_1)}(b_1),\dots,abstr^\delta_{\delta(s_n)}(b_n))$$
$$\Leftrightarrow abstr^\delta_{\delta(s_1)}(a_1) = abstr^\delta_{\delta(s_1)}(b_1) \wedge \cdots \wedge abstr^\delta_{\delta(s_n)}(a_n) = abstr^\delta_{\delta(s_n)}(b_n)$$
$$\Leftrightarrow a_1 \approx^\mathcal{B}_{\delta(s_1)} b_1 \wedge \cdots \wedge a_n \approx^\mathcal{B}_{\delta(s_n)} b_n$$
$$\Leftrightarrow (a_1,\dots,a_n) \approx^\mathcal{B}_{(\delta(s_1),\dots,\delta(s_n))} (b_1,\dots,b_n).$$

Function sorts: Let $(s_1 \to s_2) \in S_1^{\times, \to}$. Then we have

$$abstr^{\delta}_{(\delta(s_1) \to \delta(s_2))}(f) = abstr^{\delta}_{(\delta(s_1) \to \delta(s_2))}(g)$$

$\Leftrightarrow$ If for all $a_1, a_2 \in s_1^{A}$ it is $a_1 = a_2$, then
$$abstr^{\delta}_{(\delta(s_1) \to \delta(s_2))}(f)(a_1) = abstr^{\delta}_{(\delta(s_1) \to \delta(s_2))}(g)(a_2).$$

$\Rightarrow$ If for all $b_1, b_2 \in \delta(s_1)^{B}$ it is $abstr^{\delta}_{\delta(s_1)}(b_1) = abstr^{\delta}_{\delta(s_1)}(b_2)$, then
$$abstr^{\delta}_{(\delta(s_1) \to \delta(s_2))}(f)(abstr^{\delta}_{\delta(s_1)}(b_1)) = abstr^{\delta}_{(\delta(s_1) \to \delta(s_2))}(g)(abstr^{\delta}_{\delta(s_1)}(b_2)).$$

$\Leftrightarrow$ If for all $b_1, b_2 \in \delta(s_1)^{B}$ it is $abstr^{\delta}_{\delta(s_1)}(b_1) = abstr^{\delta}_{\delta(s_1)}(b_2)$, then
$$abstr^{\delta}_{\delta(s_2)}(f(b_1)) = abstr^{\delta}_{\delta(s_2)}(g(b_2)).$$

$\Leftrightarrow$ If for all $b_1, b_2 \in \delta(s_1)^{B}$ it is $b_1 \approx^{B}_{\delta(s_1)} b_2$, then $f(b_1) \approx^{B}_{(\delta(s_1) \to \delta(s_2))} g(b_2)$.

Since all elements of the carriers of B that are mapped to the same element in B are equivalent in $\approx^{B}$, we have $A = B/_{\approx^{B}}$. $\qquad\square$

The lemma forms the basis for refinements described by data structure abstractions.

Proposition 8.2.8 (L^{-1}-data structure refinement)
If for all $B \in CGEN(\Sigma_2, E_2)$ there is $A \in CGEN(\Sigma_1, E_1)$ and a data structure abstraction $abstr^{\delta} : B \to A$, we have $(\Sigma_1, E_1) \overset{\delta}{\twoheadrightarrow} (\Sigma_2, E_2)$. $\qquad\square$

In some situations a family of abstraction functions can be used along with a family of representation functions in order to achieve a simulation that describes the implementation function symbols in a direct way. This kind of simulation is called U^{-1}-simulation.

Proposition 8.2.9 (U^{-1}-data structure refinement)
If $repr^{\delta} : A \to B$ is a family of representation functions and $abstr^{\delta} : B \to A$ a family of abstraction functions such that

$$\begin{aligned}
\delta(f)^{B} &= repr^{\delta}_s \circ f^{A} \circ abstr^{\delta}_{\delta(s)} & (U_1) \\
abstr^{\delta}_{\delta(s)} \circ repr^{\delta}_s(a) &= a & (U_2)
\end{aligned}$$

holds, we have $(\Sigma_1, E_1) \overset{\delta}{\twoheadrightarrow} (\Sigma_2, E_2)$.

Proof: As a consequence of (U_1) it is

$$abstr^{\delta}_{\delta(s)} \circ \delta(f)^{B} = repr^{\delta}_s \circ f^{A} \circ abstr^{\delta}_{\delta(s)}$$

With (U_2) we obtain $abstr^{\delta}_{\delta(s)} \circ \delta(f)^{B} = f^{A} \circ abstr^{\delta}_{\delta(s)}$. With Prop. 8.2.8 it follows $(\Sigma_1, E_1) \overset{\delta}{\twoheadrightarrow} (\Sigma_2, E_2)$. $\qquad\square$

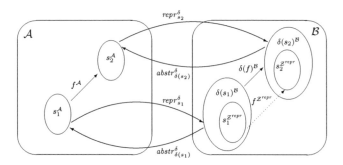

Figure 8.2: Data structure embedding with representation and abstraction functions

Several other simulations can be constructed which can all be reduced to L- and L^{-1}-simulations. We refer to [20] for a more detailed discussion on using simulations with representation and abstraction functions.

In Section 8.3 we will demonstrate how the L^{-1} and U^{-1} data structure refinements can be used for a mechanizable data structure transformation.

In Fig. 8.2.3 we illustrate the overall scheme of a data structure refinement described sofar. The Σ_1-algebra $\mathcal{A}$ is embedded into the Σ_2-algebra $\mathcal{B}$ by a family of representation functions $repr^\delta$. The Σ_1-algebra $\mathcal{Z}^{repr}$ is the image of the range homomorphism of $repr^\delta$ and forms a subalgebra of $\mathcal{B}$. In the L-simulation the interpretation of the function symbol f in $\mathcal{Z}^{repr}$ must correspond to $\delta(f)^\mathcal{B}$. The family of abstraction functions $abstr^\delta$ maps elements from $\delta(s_1)^\mathcal{B}$ and $\delta(s_2)^\mathcal{B}$ to the corresponding interpretation of s_1 and s_2 in $\mathcal{A}$. Elements of $\delta(s_1)^\mathcal{B}$ that are mapped to the same element $a \in s_1^\mathcal{A}$ embody equivalent implementations of a.

In this section we have discussed the refinement of data structures from a semantic point of view. Heading for mechanizing the refinement of data structures we will introduce in the following sections syntactic manipulation schemes, i.e. transformation rules, on entire specifications that realize the described data structure refinements. The correctness proofs of these rules will make use of the results of this section.

8.3   Algebraic implementations

The principle of algebraic implementation forms a general approach of refining data structures. In this approach the described foundations for simulating the implementation functions are directly transfered into the specification using new function symbols for the representation and abstraction functions. The application conditions of the simulations are assured by explicitly inserting the necessary properties as axioms.

8.3.1 Refinement rules for algebraic implementations

In the following we will describe the specification modifications and enrichments necessary for general data structure refinements. We introduce three transformation rules for their different simulations and establish the correctness.

The idea of algebraic implementations centers on the explicit enrichment of function symbols for the representation functions and abstraction functions. The interpretations of these function symbols in the corresponding models form the representation and abstraction functions required for a data structure refinement as described in the last section. In order to guarantee the conditions of the propositions, axioms are inserted in the specifications.

Let (Σ_1, E_1) be an algebraic specification, Σ_2 a signature and $\delta : \Sigma_1 \to \Sigma_2$ a signature morphism. In this subsection we assume without loss of generality that the signatures Σ_1 and Σ_2 are disjoint and *repr* and *abstr* do not occur as function symbols in Σ_1 and Σ_2. The signature Σ_2 comprises the implementation sorts and the implementation function symbols operating on the implementation sorts instead of the abstract sorts. The algebraic implementation forms the union of the two disjoint signatures, inserts function symbols for the representation and abstraction functions and adds axioms guaranteeing the required properties of representation and abstraction functions.

Definition 8.3.1 (L-algebraic implementation)
Let (Σ_1, E_1) be an algebraic specification and $\delta : \Sigma_1 \to \Sigma_2$ a signature morphism. The L-*algebraic implementation via* δ results in a specification (Σ_3, E_3) such that $\Sigma_3 = (S_3, F_3, C_3)$ and

$$S_3 \;=\; S_1 \cup S_2$$

$$F_3 \;=\; F_1 \stackrel{+}{\cup} F_2 \stackrel{+}{\cup} \left(repr_s : s \to \delta(s)\right)_{s \in S_1^{\times, \to}}$$

$$C_3 \;=\; C_1 \stackrel{+}{\cup} C_2$$

$$E_3 \;=\; E_1 \cup$$

$$\bigcup_{s_1,\ldots,s_n,s \in S_1^{\times,\to}} \left\{ \begin{array}{rcl} repr_s(f) &=& \delta(f) \text{ for all } f \in F_{1,s}, \\ repr_{(s_1,\ldots,s_n)}(a_1,\ldots,a_n) &=& (repr_{s_1}(a_1),\ldots,repr_{s_n}(a_n)), \\ repr_{(s_1 \to s_2)}(g)(repr_{s_1}(a)) &=& repr_{s_2}(g(a)) \end{array} \right\}.$$

□

We find for each model $\mathcal{B}$ of the implementation specification a model $\mathcal{A} = \mathcal{B}|_{\Sigma_1}$ of the abstract specification (Σ_1, E_1) such that $repr^{\mathcal{B}}$ forms a family of representation functions.

Lemma 8.3.2 (Correctness of L-algebraic implementation)
Let $\delta : \Sigma_1 \to \Sigma_2$ be a signature morphism, (Σ_1, E_1) an algebraic specification and (Σ_3, E_3) the L-algebraic implementation via δ of (Σ_1, E_1). Then $(\Sigma_1, E_1) \overset{\delta}{\twoheadrightarrow} (\Sigma_3, E_3)$ holds.

Proof: Let $\mathcal{B} \in CGEN(\Sigma_3, E_3)$. Clearly, $\mathcal{A} = \mathcal{B}|_{\Sigma_1} \in CGEN(\Sigma_1, E_1)$. Moreover, the family $(repr_s^{\mathcal{B}})_{s \in S_1^{\times,\to}}$ forms a data structure representation since the required properties are inserted as axioms in E_3. With Prop. 8.2.4 the claim follows.   □

Similarly, for achieving an L^{-1}-algebraic implementation we insert abstraction function symbols with the relevant axioms.

Definition 8.3.3 (L^{-1}-algebraic implementation)
Let (Σ_1, E_1) be an algebraic specification and $\delta : \Sigma_1 \to \Sigma_2$ a signature morphism. The L^{-1}-*algebraic implementation via* δ results in a specification (Σ_3, E_3) such that $\Sigma_3 = (S_3, F_3, C_3)$ and

$$S_3 \;=\; S_1 \cup S_2$$

$$F_3 \;=\; F_1 \overset{+}{\cup} F_2 \overset{+}{\cup} \left(abstr_{\delta(s)} : \delta(s) \to s\right)_{s \in S_1^{\times,\to}}$$

$$C_3 \;=\; C_1 \overset{+}{\cup} C_2$$

$$E_3 \;=\; E_1 \cup$$

$$\bigcup_{s_1,\ldots,s_n,s \in S_1^{\times,\to}} \left\{ \begin{array}{rcl} (abstr_{\delta(s)}(\delta(f)) &=& f \text{ for all } f \in F_{1,s}, \\ abstr_{(\delta(s_1),\ldots,\delta(s_n))}(x_1,\ldots,x_n) &=& \\ && (abstr_{\delta(s_1)}(x_1),\ldots,abstr_{\delta(s_n)}(x_n)), \\ abstr_{(\delta(s_1)\to\delta(s_2))}(g)(abstr_{\delta(s_1)}(x)) &=& abstr_{\delta(s_2)}(g(x)) \end{array} \right\} .$$

□

The L^{-1} algebraic implementation follows the refinement relation.

Lemma 8.3.4 (Correctness of L^{-1}-algebraic implementation)
Let $\delta : \Sigma_1 \to \Sigma_2$ be a signature morphism, (Σ_1, E_1) an algebraic specification and (Σ_3, E_3) the L^{-1}-algebraic implementation via δ of (Σ_1, E_1). Then $(\Sigma_1, E_1) \overset{\delta}{\twoheadrightarrow} (\Sigma_3, E_3)$ holds.   □

The proof is a consequence of Prop. 8.2.8. As in Lemma 8.3.2 the corresponding abstraction functions are the interpretations of the inserted functions symbols.

Using both representation and abstraction functions for a U^{-1}-simulation yields a further enlargement of the specification. For the sake of brevity we will omit the transformation rule here. The rule inserts, similar to the L- and L^{-1}-algebraic implementation, representation and abstraction function symbols along with the corresponding distributive equations and, additionally, the equations of the U^{-1}-simulation.

Heading for a direct algorithmic axiomatization of the implementation function symbols, the U^{-1}-algebraic implementation is superior to the L^{-1} approach because it defines the new function symbol by $\delta(f) = repr \circ f \circ abstr$. However, in the L^{-1}-algebraic implementation the new function symbols are not fixed on non-embedded elements of the new sort. Hence, the L^{-1}-algebraic implementation leaves a maximum of freedom on the behaviour of the new function symbols on non-embedded elements of the new sort.

Heading for the mechanization of the discussed transformation rules a reduction to finite enlargement of the specifications is necessary. The constructions of (Σ_3, E_3) can be minimized by only inserting the operations $repr_s$ and $abstr_s$ of those sorts which occur in the derived sorts s with $F_{1,s} \neq \emptyset$. Since the specification (Σ_1, E_1) and the signature Σ_2 are finite, the minimized construction (Σ_3, E_3) is also finite.

The inserted equation of the transformation rules for algebraic implementations can serve as starting point of a derivation by further refinement steps aiming at an algorithmic axiomatization of the implementation function symbols. Clearly, this is only possible if the auxiliary function symbols for representation and abstraction have been sufficiently axiomatized. If the auxiliary functions symbols are specified completely by a set of constructive equations the derivation can be mechanized easily and the Lübeck Transformation System provides strategies trying to derive an algorithmic axiomatization automatically, see Subsection 11.4.3.

8.3.2   Procedure of data structure refinements

The procedure of an algebraic implementation comprises the following steps.

Preparation   In this step the developer may enrich the signature or the axioms of the specification in order to include all relevant signature elements and properties.

Generation of new specification   Following the constructions of algebraic implementations a specification (Σ_3, E_3) is constructed where the original signature is merged with the range of a signature morphism $\delta : \Sigma_1 \to \Sigma_2$ and the new axioms are inserted. Unless there are proper higher-order function symbols, it is possible to simplify the generated axioms such that only one abstraction and/or one representation function symbol for each $sc \in SC$ with $\delta(sc) \neq sc$ is used, namely $repr_{sc}$ and $abstr_{\delta(sc)}$. The distributive properties of the representation and abstraction functions are used to simplify the axioms. The representation functions $repr$ and the abstraction functions $abstr$ are just inserted in the signature, there are no axioms defining algorithmically their behaviour. This gives a maximum of freedom for the data structure refinement. The generated new specification forms a frame for a refinement of the involved data structures. The specification is enlarged in order to ensure the correctness of the refinement step.

Precision of embedding   The developer can now insert a definition of the representation and/or the abstraction function. This will fix the data structure refinement uniquely and the derivation of the operations can be started.

Derivation of operations   For practical use one heads for algorithmic axiomatizations of the new function symbols operating on the implementation sorts. The axiomatization resulting from an algebraic implementation is based on the representation and abstraction function symbols defining the behaviour in terms of the old function symbols which operate on the abstract sorts. By using basic refinement steps the developer can derive an algorithmic axiomatization of the new function symbols or may use further design decisions determining the behaviour of the new function symbols.

The described procedure for an algebraic implementation is supported by the Lübeck Transformation System (see Subsection 11.3.3). The system automatically generates the new specification and provides strategies for automatically deriving algorithmic axiomatizations of the new function symbols.

The algebraic implementation is a general approach of refining data structures. The transformation enlarges the specification in order to express the refinement within the theory. This overhead can be omitted, if the specification shows a certain syntactic structure or the data structure refinement forms a special case.

8.4 Simple data structure refinements

In this section we introduce four simple techniques for data structure refinements. For each case a syntactic manipulation scheme for a transformation step is given and the correctness is proved by the existence of a family of representation functions.

The constructor implementation simplifies the algebraic implementation by omitting the function symbols for the representation and abstractions functions and the corresponding axioms of the application conditions. This is possible only, if the representation functions can be given by a translation of the constructor terms and the syntactic structure of the axiomatizations implies the application conditions. The constructor introduction establishes a first generation constraint on loose sorts. The set of constructors of a constructor sort can be enriched or reduced, if the specification shows a certain syntactic structure.

8.4.1 Constructor implementation

We propose a data structure refinement by translating constructor terms of the abstract sort into terms of the implementation sort. The translation can be given by a set of equations. We prove the correctness by falling back on Prop. 8.2.4 and constructing the representation function.

A term translation maps terms of a signature to terms of another signature respecting substitutions.

Definition 8.4.1 (Term translation)
Let (Σ_1, X), (Σ_2, Y) be bases and $\delta : \Sigma_1 \to \Sigma_2$ a signature morphism. A *term translation* respecting δ is an $S_1^{\times,\to}$-indexed family of mappings $\kappa_s : T(\Sigma_1, X)_s \to T(\Sigma_2, Y)_{\delta(s)}$ such that

- $X_s = Y_{\delta(s)}$ and $Var_{\delta(s)}(\kappa(t)) \subseteq Var_s(t)$,

- $\kappa(x) = x$ for all $x \in X_s$,

- κ is compatible with substitutions: $\kappa_{sc}(t\sigma) = \kappa_{sc}(t)(\{x \mapsto \kappa(\sigma(x)) \mid x \in X\})$. $\quad\square$

A term translation can be constructed by a family of equations defining a translation for each constructor.

Definition 8.4.2 (Constructor translation, canonical term translation)
Let (Σ_1, X), (Σ_2, Y) be bases and $\delta : \Sigma_1 \to \Sigma_2$ a signature morphism. Furthermore let $SC_1' \subseteq SC_1$ be a subset of the constructor sorts of S_1 and $C_1' \subseteq C_1$ the subfamily of all constructors with result sort in SC_1'.

a) The C_1'-indexed family of equations $(t_c = t_c')_{c \in C_1'}$ with $t_c, t_c' \in T(\Sigma_2, Y)$ is called a *constructor translation*, if for all $c \in C_1'$ with result sort $sc \in SC_1'$ we have:

- $t_c \,\hat{=}\, \delta(c)$ in case $c \in C_{1,sc}'$ and $t_c \,\hat{=}\, \delta(c)(x)$ for $c \in C_{s_1 \to sc}'$ and $x \in Y_{s_1}$
- $t_c' \in T_{\delta(sc)}(\Sigma_2, Y)$.

b) A constructor translation $(t_c = t_c')_{c \in C_1'}$ can be extended to the *canonical term translation* $\kappa : T(\Sigma_1, X) \to T(\Sigma_2, Y)$ as defined inductively by

$$\text{(i)} \quad \kappa_s(x) = x \text{ for } x \in X_s \qquad\qquad\qquad\qquad\qquad\qquad \text{(variable)}$$

$$\text{(ii)} \quad \kappa_s(f) = \begin{cases} t_c' & \text{if } f = c \in C_{1,sc}' \\ \delta(f) & \text{otherwise} \end{cases} \qquad\qquad \text{(function symbol)}$$

$$\text{(iii)} \quad \kappa_{(s_1 \to \dots \to s_n \to s)}(@f) = @(\kappa_{(s_1, \dots, s_n) \to s_n}(f)) \qquad \text{(currying)}$$

$$\text{(iv)} \quad \kappa_{(s_1, \dots, s_n)}(t_1, \dots, t_n) = (\kappa_{s_1}(t_1), \dots, \kappa_{s_n}(t_n)) \qquad \text{(tuple)}$$

$$\text{(v)} \quad \kappa_{s_2}(t_f(t_a)) = \begin{cases} t_c'[x \leftarrow \kappa_{s_1}(t_a)] & \text{if } t_f = c \in C_{1,s_1 \to sc}' \\ \kappa_{(s_1 \to s_2)}(t_f)(\kappa_{s_1}(t_a)) & \text{otherwise} \end{cases} \quad \text{(application)}$$

$$\text{(vi)} \quad \kappa_{(s_1 \to s_3)}(t_g \circ t_f) = \kappa_{(s_1 \to s_3)}(t_g) \circ \kappa_{(s_1 \to s_2)}(t_f) \qquad \text{(function composition)}$$

$\quad\square$

The constructor implementation requires a signature morphism and a constructor translation. The constructor translation effects a term translation. The term translation is applied to the axioms of the original specification achieving the axioms of the refined specification. Additionally, the equations of the constructor translation are added to the axioms of the refined specification.

Definition 8.4.3 (Constructor implementation)
Let $(\Sigma_1 = (S_1, F_1, C_1), E_1)$ be an algebraic specification, $SC_1' \subseteq SC_1$ a subset of the constructor sorts of S_1 and $C_1' \subseteq C_1$ the subfamily of all constructors with result sort in

SC'_1. Furthermore, let $\delta : \Sigma_1 \to \Sigma_2$ be a signature morphism, such that $C_2 \cap \delta(C'_1) = \emptyset$, and $(t_c = t'_c)_{c \in C'_1}$ a constructor translation. The *constructor implementation* results in a specification (Σ_2, E_2) such that

$$E_2 \;\; = \;\; \{\kappa(t_1) = \kappa(t_2) \mid t_1 = t_2 \in E_1\} \cup \bigcup_{c \in C'_1} \{t_c = t'_c\}$$

where κ is the canonical term translation of the constructor implementation $(t_c = t'_c)_{c \in C_1}$.

$\square$

The correctness of the constructor implementation is proved by the notion of data structure embeddings using Prop. 8.2.4. The constructor implementation is correct, if all operations of the original specification are defined by a complete set of constructive equations. The proof constructs an L-simulation based on the constructor implementation.

Proposition 8.4.4 (Correctness of constructor implementation)
For the constructor implementation from Def. 8.4.3 $(\Sigma_1, E_1) \twoheadrightarrow (\Sigma_2, E_2)$ holds.

Proof: Let $\mathcal{B} \in CGEN(\Sigma_2, E_2)$. There is $\mathcal{A} \in CGEN(\Sigma_1, E_1)$ with $sb^{\mathcal{A}} = \delta(sb)^{\mathcal{B}}$ for non-constructor basic sorts and

$$sc^{\mathcal{A}} \;\; = \;\; \text{the smallest subset of } sc^{\mathcal{B}} \text{ such that}$$
$$sc^{\mathcal{A}} \text{ is generated by } C_1 \text{ with}$$
$$c^{\mathcal{A}} \;\; = \;\; \kappa(c)^{\mathcal{B}} \text{ for all } c \in C_{1,sc}$$
$$c^{\mathcal{A}}(a) \;\; = \;\; \kappa(c(z))^{\mathcal{B}}_{[z \leftarrow b]} \text{ with } a \; {}^{\mathcal{A}}\!\asymp^{\mathcal{B}}_{s_1} b \text{ for all } c \in C_{1,s_1 \to sc}$$

for constructor sorts. Since all function symbols are specified completely by E_1 the subalgebra condition holds, i.e. $\mathcal{A}$ is a subalgebra of $\mathcal{B}$ via δ. By Prop. 8.2.4 it suffices to construct a family of representation functions. Let κ be the canonical term translation of $(t_c = t'_c)_{c \in C_1}$. For all loose sorts $sb \in S_1$ and all constructor sorts $sc \in S_1$ we define the data structure representation as follows:

$$
\begin{aligned}
repr^\delta_{sb}(a) &= a & &\text{for all loose sorts } sb \in S_1 \\
repr^\delta_{sc}(c) &= \kappa_{sc}(c)^{\mathcal{B}} & &\text{for all } c \in C_{1,sc} \\
repr^\delta_{sc}(c(a)) &= \kappa_{sc}(c(z))^{\mathcal{B}}_{[z \leftarrow repr^\delta_{s_1}(a)]}(repr^\delta_{s_1}(a)) & &\text{for all } c \in C_{s_1 \to sc}
\end{aligned}
$$

The properties for representations functions (see Def. 8.2.1) complete the definition of the data structure representation. As a consequence the claim holds.

$\square$

The condition for completely specified operations in (Σ_1, E_1) is a far-reaching restriction. If the terms of t'_c are constructor terms and form a complete case analysis in the implementation sorts, the embedding is surjective and the condition can be omitted. Injective embeddings by constructor implementation are difficult to detect because this depends not only on an injective term translation but also on the existence of free interpretations of the involved data types, which is in general not a consequence of the absence of data structure constraints. In Subsection 8.5.1 an example constructor implementation is described revisiting these problems.

8.4.2 Introduction of generation constraint

This step transforms a loose sort into a constructor sort by changing the constructor affiliation of some operations. This step achieves a first implementable data type definition for loose sorts.

First we define the transformation rule.

Definition 8.4.5 (Constructor introduction)
Let $\Sigma_1 = (S_1, F_1, C_1)$ be a signature and (Σ_1, E_1) an algebraic specification. Furthermore let $SB \subseteq S_1$ be a set of loose sorts and $C_1' \subseteq F_1$ be an $S_1^{\times, \rightarrow}$-indexed family of operations with result type in SB. Then the *constructor introduction* yields the specification (Σ_2, E_2) with $\Sigma_2 = (S_1, F_1, C_1 \cup C_1')$ and $E_2 = E_1$. □

This transformation changes the constructor affiliation of operations with a loose result sort. As a consequence the former loose sorts become constructor sorts.

Proposition 8.4.6 (Correctness of constructor introduction)
For the constructor introduction from Def. 8.4.5 $(\Sigma_1, E_1) \twoheadrightarrow (\Sigma_2, E_2)$ holds.

Proof: With Prop. 8.2.4 it suffices to show that there is a family of representation functions. Let $\mathcal{B} \in CGEN(\Sigma_2, E_2)$. Since $E_1 = E_2$ it is $\mathcal{B} \in CGEN(\Sigma_1, E_1)$ and with $repr_s = id_s$ the claim follows immediately. □

The constructor implementation forms a proper design decision since the models of the specification are confined to models where the former loose sorts are generated. An example constructor introduction is described in Subsection 8.5.1.

8.4.3 Enrichment of constructor system

We introduce data structure refinements by enriching the constructor system and prove the correctness.

The constructors of a constructor sort form a generation constraint confining the carrier sets to reachable elements. The additional enriched constructors build new elements and therefore the refined specification defines super-algebras wrt. the models of the original specification. Hence, constructor enrichments can be seen as embedding steps. The constructor enrichment transformation changes the constructor affiliation of a set of function symbols.

Definition 8.4.7 (Constructor enrichment)
Let $\Sigma_1 = (S_1, F_1, C_1)$ be a signature, (Σ_1, E_1) an algebraic specification and $C_1' \subseteq F_1$ a family of operations with a constructor result sort. Furthermore, let all $f \in F_s \setminus C_s$ be specified completely by axioms in E_1. Then a *constructor enrichment* results in an algebraic specification (Σ_2, E_2) where $\Sigma_2 = (S_1, F_1, C_1 \cup C_1')$ and $E_2 = E_1$. □

The difference between constructor introduction and constructor enrichment is that, the constructor enrichment extends the constructor system of constructor sorts that already have a generation constraint, whereas constructor introduction adds new constructors for previously loose sorts. Hence, constructor enrichments form injective embeddings whereas constructor introductions embody design decisions reducing the semantics to constructor generated models.

The restriction of the step to specifications with completely specified operations is necessary for the satisfaction of the subalgebra condition. The operations have to be settled in a unique way in order to guarantee that elements constructed by the original constructor system are mapped to original values again (see Fig. 8.2.3). This is a far-reaching restriction since for all operations an algorithmic axiomatization is required. But the development has to guarantee that operations must fulfill the properties of the original specification. This comprises that the return values of operations invoked with original values can be constructed by the original constructor system. This can only be guaranteed if the behaviour of the operations is completely settled for the original sorts.

The correctness of constructor enrichment steps is proved by constructing the representation functions.

Proposition 8.4.8 (Correctness of constructor enrichment)
For the constructor enrichment of Def. 8.4.7 $(\Sigma_1, E_1) \rightarrowtail (\Sigma_2, E_2)$ holds.

Proof: Let $\mathcal{B} \in CGEN(\Sigma_2, E_2)$ and $\mathcal{A}$ be a Σ_2-algebra such that

$$\begin{aligned} sb^{\mathcal{A}} &= sb^{\mathcal{B}} \text{ for all loose sorts of } S_2 \\ sc^{\mathcal{A}} &= \text{ the smallest subset of } sc^{\mathcal{B}} \text{ such that} \\ &\quad\ sc^{\mathcal{A}} \text{ is generated by } C_2 \text{ for all } sc \in SC_2 \,. \end{aligned}$$

Clearly, $\mathcal{A}$ is constructor generated and hence $\mathcal{A} \in CGEN(\Sigma_1, E_1)$. With $\delta = id$ and $repr_{sb} = id$ such that $repr$ additionally fulfills the properties of a data structure representation, it follows $(\Sigma_1, E_1) \rightarrowtail (\Sigma_2, E_2)$ with Prop. 8.2.4 . Such representation functions exists since all operations are completely specified. $\square$

If we assure that the operations keep the subalgebra condition, the enrichment of constructors is a correct refinement step. This condition can be checked by a sufficient syntactic criterion. The representation functions for the basic sorts agree with the identity function and the constructor enrichment is an injective embedding.

8.4.4   Reduction of constructor system

We introduce a refinement step for the reduction of the constructor system and prove the correctness. Special cases, which can be detected by sufficient syntactic criteria form an injective embedding.

The constructor reduction drops a subset of the constructors by changing their constructor affiliation. The function symbols have to remain in the signature in order to keep the interface complete.

Definition 8.4.9 (Constructor reduction)
Let $\Sigma_1 = (S_1, F_1, C_1)$ be a signature, (Σ_1, E_1) an algebraic specification and $C_1' \subset C_1$ a sub family of constructors. The *constructor reduction* yields the specification (Σ_2, E_2) with $\Sigma_2 = (S_1, F_1, C_1 \setminus C_1')$ and $E_2 = E_1$. □

This step reduces the number of models in general and therefore forms a design decision. Since the generation constraint of (Σ_1, E_1) is a consequence of the generation constraint of (Σ_2, E_2), the constructor reduction transformation forms a correct refinement step.

Proposition 8.4.10 (Correctness of constructor reduction)
For the constructor reduction from Def. 8.4.9 $(\Sigma_1, E_1) \twoheadrightarrow (\Sigma_2, E_2)$ holds.

Proof: Let $\mathcal{B} \in CGEN(\Sigma_2, E_2)$ and $\mathcal{A} = \mathcal{B}$. Clearly, $\mathcal{A} \in MOD(\Sigma_1, E_1)$ since $E_1 = E_2$. Moreover, it is for all constructor sorts $sc \in S_1$

$$sc^{\mathcal{A}} = \text{the smallest set such that}$$
$$sc^{\mathcal{A}} \text{ is generated by } C_1$$

since C_1 is a superset of C_2. Hence $\mathcal{A} \in CGEN(\Sigma_1, E_1)$. If we set $repr_{sb} = id_{sb}$ for all basic sorts extended to $S_1^{\times, \rightarrow}$ by the properties of a data structure representation and $\delta = id$, we obtain the claim with Prop. 8.2.4. □

If for all $c \in C_1'$ there is an algorithmic and terminating set of axioms specifying c completely wrt. the other constructors, the constructor reduction is injective.

Proposition 8.4.11 (Injective reduction)
If for all $c \in C'$ there is an algorithmic and terminating set of axioms $E_c \subseteq E_1$ specifying c completely wrt. $C_1 \setminus C_1'$, the reduction embedding is injective □

In the above described case the refinement yields an equivalently axiomatized specification, as because of the set E_c the constructor c does not contribute to the construction of the elements of the carrier. Each element can be reduced to a construction without c. Moreover, the reduction changes the constructor affiliation of the function symbols of C_1' to an operation. The set of axioms E_c defines c algorithmically which keeps the specification consistent and algorithmic. We survey an injective constructor reduction in Subsection 8.5.1.

8.5 Examples for the refinement of data structures

We illustrate the refinement of data structures by two examples. In the first example we consider the refinement of sets of natural numbers by three simple data structure refinements. The loose sort *set* is first refined by a constructor introduction followed by a constructor reduction. Finally, sets are implemented as arrays with element type *bool* using a constructor implementation. The second example shows an algebraic implementation for representing stacks as pairs of stack pointer and array.

In order to keep the examples simple and self-contained, we do not use the parameterized standard specifications of Chapter 4. Rather we use non-parameterized specifications comprising all essential parts in one specification.

8.5.1   Sets of natural numbers

The specification *FinSet* (see Fig. 8.3) describes sets of natural numbers along with a member operation and the set union.

$$
\begin{array}{ll}
\textbf{spec} & \textit{FinSet} = \textit{Nat}; \\
\textbf{sorts} & \textit{set} \\
\textbf{ops} & \textit{emptset} : \textit{set}, \\
& \textit{addElem} : (\textit{nat}, \textit{set})\textit{set}, \\
& \quad \textit{union} : (\textit{set}, \textit{set})\textit{set}, \\
& \quad \textit{member} : (\textit{nat}, \textit{set})\textit{bool} \\
\textbf{axioms} & \\
& \textit{union}_{comm} : \textit{union}(r, s) = \textit{union}(s, r), \\
& \textit{union}_{ass} : \textit{union}(\textit{union}(r, s), t) = \textit{union}(r, \textit{union}(s, t)), \\
& \textit{union}1 : \textit{union}(s, \textit{emptset}) = s, \\
& \textit{union}2 : \textit{union}(s, \textit{addElem}(a, t)) = \textit{addElem}(a, \textit{union}(s, t)), \\
& \textit{member}1 : \textit{member}(x, \textit{emptset}) = \textit{false}, \\
& \textit{member}2 : \textit{member}(x, \textit{addElem}(a, s)) = \textit{or}(\textit{eqNat}(x, a), \textit{member}(x, s)) \\
\textbf{end} &
\end{array}
$$

Figure 8.3: Specification of sets of natural numbers

As *set* is a loose sort, the specification is not algorithmic. In order to achieve an algorithmic axiomatization, we add a generation constraint by constructor introduction. A first approach to find a constructor system is to take all function symbols with result sort *set*. According to Def. 8.4.5 we apply a constructor introduction with $C_1' = \{\textit{emptset}, \textit{addElem}, \textit{union}\}$ and achieve the specification shown in Fig. 8.4.

In order to minimize the constructor system we head for an injective data structure embedding keeping the freedom for possible implementations. As the function symbol *union* is specified completely and terminating by the axioms *union*1 and *union*2, the elimination of the constructor *union* forms an injective embedding. By a reduction of the constructor system we obtain a refined specification illustrated in Fig. 8.5.

Now the sort *set* is defined by two constructors *emptset* embodying the empty set and *addElem* inserting an element to a given set. Although the specification is algorithmic, the implementation of sets as data type may prevent an efficient implementation of the involved functions. An implementation using arrays is more desirable. We will embed the

---

spec $FinSet = Nat;$
sorts $set = emptset \mid addElem(nat, set) \mid union(set, set)$
ops $member: (nat, set)bool$
axioms

$union_{comm}:$ $union(r, s) = union(s, r),$
$union_{ass}:$ $union(union(r, s), t) = union(r, union(s, t)),$
$union1:$ $union(s, emptset) = s,$
$union2:$ $union(s, addElem(a, t)) = addElem(a, union(s, t)),$
$member1:$ $member(x, emptset) = false,$
$member2:$ $member(x, addElem(a, s)) = or(eqNat(x, a), member(x, s))$

end

Figure 8.4: Introduction of generation constraint

sort *set* into arrays with element sort *bool* as defined in Fig. 8.6 (compare also Subsection 4.2.5).

The specification name *BoolArray* is added to the importing of the specification *FinSet*.

We will use a constructor implementation to refine the data structure. Therefore, we define the constructor translation as follows:

$$emptset \;\; = \;\; init$$
$$addElem(x, r) \;\; = \;\; put(r, x, true)$$

The canonical term translation replaces all occurrences of the constructors by their implementation and keeps the remaining term structures. We translate the signature elements by the identity signature morphism.

In other cases it may be sensible to rename sorts and function symbols for a constructor implementation. Fig. 8.7 presents the result after constructor implementation.

---

spec $FinSet = Nat;$
sorts $set = emptset \mid addElem(nat, set)$
ops $member: (nat, set)bool,$
            $union: (set, set)set$
axioms

$union_{comm}:$ $union(r, s) = union(s, r),$
$union_{ass}:$ $union(union(r, s), t) = union(r, union(s, t)),$
$union1:$ $union(s, emptset) = s,$
$union2:$ $union(s, addElem(a, t)) = addElem(a, union(s, t)),$
$member1:$ $member(x, emptset) = false,$
$member2:$ $member(x, addElem(a, s)) = or(eqNat(x, a), member(x, s))$

end

Figure 8.5: Reduction of constructor system

---

spec $BoolArray = Nat$;
sorts $array = init \mid put(array, nat, bool)$
ops $lookup:$ $(nat, array)elem$
axioms

$\quad\quad\quad put1:$ $put(put(a, m, c), n, e) =$ **if** $eqNat(m, n)$ **then** $put(a, n, e)$
$\quad\quad\quad\quad\quad\quad$ **else** $put(put(a, n, e), m, c),$
$\quad\quad\quad lookup1:$ $lookup(n, put(a, m, e)) =$ **if** $eqNat(n, m)$ **then** e **else** $lookup(n, a),$
end

Figure 8.6: Specification of Boolean arrays

Since each constructor is implemented by a constructor term, we achieve again constructive equations. Other constructor implementations may require some further derivation steps in order to yield constructive equations if constructors are implemented by non-constructor terms.

Clearly, the constructor implementation forms a proper embedding since there are boolean arrays that do not form an implementation of a set of natural numbers. Hence the embedding is not surjective. Consequently, the embedding just determines the behaviour of the operations for arrays that emerged from constructor terms of sort set. The behaviour for arrays constructed by $put(x, s, false)$ is not specified. As a consequence, the function symbols $member$ and $union$ are not specified completely. By settling the function symbols for the case $put(x, s, false)$ the user makes design decisions. The following two

---

spec $FinSet = Nat + BoolArray$;
sorts $set = array$
ops $member:$ $(nat, set)bool,$
$\quad\quad\quad\quad union:$ $(set, set)set,$
$\quad\quad\quad\quad emptset:$ $set,$
$\quad\quad\quad\quad addElem:$ $(nat, set)set$
axioms

$\quad\quad\quad union_{comm}:$ $union(r, s) = union(s, r),$
$\quad\quad\quad union_{ass}:$ $union(union(r, s), t) = union(r, union(s, t)),$
$\quad\quad\quad union1:$ $union(s, init) = s,$
$\quad\quad\quad union2:$ $union(s, put(t, m, true)) = put(union(s, t), m, true),$
$\quad\quad\quad member1:$ $member(x, init) = false,$
$\quad\quad\quad member2:$ $member(x, put(s, m, true)) = or(eqNat(x, m), member(x, s)),$
$\quad\quad\quad emptset1:$ $emptset = init,$
$\quad\quad\quad addElem1:$ $addElem(m, s) = put(s, m, true)$
end

Figure 8.7: Constructor implementation

enrichments are possible completing the function symbol *member*:

a) $member3 : member(x, put(a, s, false)) = member(x, s)$,
b) $member3 : member(x, put(a, s, false)) = and(not(eqNat(x, a)), member(x, s))$

Version *a)* ignores updates of the array with *false* whereas *b)* respects such updates as implicit deletions. Similarly, the function symbol *union* can be completed in manifold ways.

The restriction of constructor implementations to specifications with completely specified operations is essential in this case. Assume the axiom *union1* is missing before the data structure refinement. After the data structure refinement then an axiom

$$union1 : union(s, init) = put(zero, s, false)$$

can be inserted. Now the original interface of the specification *FinSet* can be used to construct irregular sets not constructed by *emptset* and *addElem*. This violates the interface faithfulness since irregular sets can emerge by properly using the interface of the specification *FinSet*. Technically such cases are excluded by the subalgebra condition.

8.5.2 An algebraic implementation for stacks

As second example we consider stacks. A specification for stacks is refined to an implementation of stacks by arrays using an L^{-1}-simulation.

Stacks are specified in the usual way as a data type constructed by the constructors *empty* and *push*, see Fig. 8.8.

$$
\boxed{
\begin{array}{lll}
\textbf{spec} & Stack = Bool; \\
\textbf{sorts} & elem, \\
& stack = empty \mid push(elem, stack) \\
\textbf{ops} & error: & elem, \\
& pop: & (stack)stack, \\
& top: & (stack)elem \\
\textbf{axioms} & \\
& top1: & top(empty) = error, \\
& top2: & top(push(e, s)) = e, \\
& pop1: & pop(empty) = empty, \\
& pop2: & pop(push(e, s)) = s \\
\textbf{end} &
\end{array}
}
$$

Figure 8.8: Specification of stacks

The specification contains the usual operations *top* and *pop* on stacks.

The data structure refinement presented in this subsection is an algebraic implementation using an L^{-1}-simulation. It refines the data type *stack* of the specification *Stack* to a specification implementing stacks as pairs ($nat, array$) of a stack-pointer and an array with entries of sort $elem$. We specify arrays similar to Subsection 4.2.5, but without parameterization and provide an element sort $elem$ instead, see Fig. 8.9).

> **spec** $ElemArray = Nat;$
> **sorts** $elem,$
> $\qquad array = init \mid put(array, nat, elem)$
> **ops** $\quad lookup: \; (nat, array)elem$
> **axioms**
> $\qquad put1: \; put(put(a, m, c), n, e) = \textbf{if } eqNat(m, n) \textbf{ then } put(a, n, e)$
> $\qquad\qquad\qquad\qquad\qquad\qquad\qquad\qquad \textbf{else } put(put(a, n, e), m, c),$
> $\qquad lookup1: \; lookup(n, put(a, m, e)) = \textbf{if } eqNat(n, m) \textbf{ then } e \textbf{ else } lookup(n, a),$
> **end**

Figure 8.9: Specification of arrays

The process of the data structure refinement follows the procedure introduced in Subsection 8.3.2.

Preparation   For preparing the data structure refinement we enrich the specification *Stack* by the importing *ElemArray*.

Generation of new specification   For the application of an algebraic implementation we must provide a signature morphism mapping each signature element to an implementation. Here, we demonstrate the L^{-1}-simulation. The construction of Def. 8.3.3 requires that the original signature and the range signature of the signature morphism are disjoint. In order to use the standard names of a stack as implementation we first rename the original signature elements of *Stack*. This is done by a signature morphism postfixing all signature elements with *old*. The signature morphism δ belonging to the data structure refinement is defined by:

$$
\begin{aligned}
\delta(stack_{old}) &= stack = (nat, init) \\
\delta(empty_{old}) &= empty \\
\delta(push_{old}) &= push \\
\delta(top_{old}) &= top \\
\delta(pop_{old}) &= pop
\end{aligned}
$$

The construction of Def. 8.3.3 then yields the signature illustrated in Fig. 8.10. For the axioms, see Fig. 8.11, we present a simplified form using only one abstraction operation for the implementation sort *stack*. This suffices because the required properties of an L^{-1}-simulation can be used to simplify the construction such that only one abstraction function is necessary. The other operations of the family of abstraction functions can be omitted.

The new operations and constants *top*, *pop*, and *push* resulting from the signature morphism δ are described in terms of the abstraction operation and the corresponding original operation. Finally, the old axioms remain in the specification after applying the signature

$$
\begin{array}{ll}
\textbf{spec} & StackByArray = Nat + ElemArray; \\
\textbf{sorts} & elem, \\
& stack_{old} = empty_{old} \mid push_{old}(elem, stack_{old}), \\
& stack = (nat, array) \\
\hline
\textbf{ops} & abstr: \quad (stack)stack_{old}, \\
& pop: \quad (stack)stack, \\
& empty: \quad stack, \\
& push: \quad (elem, stack)stack, \\
\hline
& error: \quad elem, \\
& top_{old}: \quad (stack_{old})elem, \\
& pop_{old}: \quad (stack_{old})stack_{old}
\end{array}
$$

Figure 8.10: Signature of new specification

morphism to the function symbols. The former constructors of *stack* remain as operations in the refined specification in order to retain the complete interface of stacks. The specification is not algorithmic and requires some treatment of further refinement steps for an algorithmic form.

Precision of embedding The first step for the derivation of an algorithmic form is to establish the data structure refinement by axiomatizing the abstraction function. This step forms a design decision since it settles the mapping between elements of the implementation sort *stack* and the abstract sort $stack_{old}$:

$$
\begin{array}{lll}
abstr1 & : & abstr(zero, a) = empty_{old} \\
abstr2 & : & abstr(succ(n), a) = push_{old}(lookup(succ(n), a), abstr(n, a))
\end{array}
$$

The abstraction maps each pair of zero and any array to the empty stack, and uses the constructor $push_{old}$ for mapping a non-empty stack to an old stack. Here, the operation *lookup* encapsulates the essential part of the abstraction. The representation of a non-empty stack is constructed by the new push operation *push*.

Derivation of operations For most operations the new algorithmic axiomatization can be derived by a few basic transformation steps. Here, we will demonstrate the derivation

$$
\begin{array}{l}
top: top(s) = top_{old}(abstr(s)) \\
pop: abstr(pop(s)) = pop_{old}(abstr(s)) \\
empty: abstr(empty) = empty_{old} \\
push: abstr(push(e, s)) = push_{old}(e, abstr(s)) \\
\hline
top1: top_{old}(empty_{old}) = error \\
top2: top_{old}(push_{old}(e, s)) = e \\
pop1: pop_{old}(empty_{old}) = empty_{old} \\
pop2: pop_{old}(push_{old}(e, s)) = s
\end{array}
$$

Figure 8.11: Axioms of new specification

of the operation *pop* as example. We start with the equation

$$abstr(pop(s)) \;=\; pop_{old}(abstr(s))$$

and first do a complete case analysis on s according to the definition of *abstr* :

$$\left\{ \begin{array}{rcl} abstr(pop(zero,a)) & = & pop_{old}(abstr(zero,a)) \,, \\ abstr(pop(succ(n),a)) & = & pop_{old}(abstr(succ(n),a)) \end{array} \right\}$$

Unfolding *abstr* results in

$$\left\{ \begin{array}{rcl} abstr(pop(zero,a)) & = & pop_{old}(empty_{old}) \,, \\ abstr(pop(succ(n),a)) & = & pop_{old}(push_{old}(lookup(succ(n),a), abstr(n,a))) \end{array} \right\}$$

By axioms *pop*1 and *pop*2 we get

$$\left\{ \begin{array}{rcl} abstr(pop(zero,a)) & = & empty_{old} \,, \\ abstr(pop(succ(n),a)) & = & abstr(n,a) \end{array} \right\}$$

Using axiom *abstr*1 transforms the equations to

$$\left\{ \begin{array}{rcl} abstr(pop(zero,a)) & = & abstr(zero,a) \,, \\ abstr(pop(succ(n),a)) & = & abstr(n,a) \end{array} \right\}$$

These equations describe the behaviour of *pop* not completely. The abstraction of the result of $pop(succ(n),a)$ for arbitrary n and a must agree with the abstraction of (n,a). There are several pairs of a natural number and an array that fulfill this constraint. The simplest solution is the pair (n,a) itself. Therefore, we apply a decomposition step and achieve

$$\left\{ \begin{array}{rcl} pop(zero,a) & = & (zero,a) \,, \\ pop(succ(n),a) & = & (n,a) \end{array} \right\}$$

Similarly, the other operations can be transformed into an algorithmic form.

In order to simplify the refinement and to thin out the specification, the operations $abstr$, top_{old} and pop_{old} can be hidden since they only serve as starting point for deriving the new operations on the implementation of stacks. Consequently, these operations can be dropped after obtaining an algorithmic axiomatization of the implementation function symbols.

8.6   Concluding remarks on refining data structures

In this chapter we have given the theoretical foundations for data structure refinements based on representation and abstraction functions. We discussed five refinement steps that can be played back to the introduced theory. The algebraic implementation is a general refinement lifting the foundations into the specification. The price for the generality of the approach lays in the overhead of additional function symbols and axioms. The constructor implementation avoids this overhead by omitting function symbols for representation and abstraction functions. In contrast to algebraic implementations, the constructor implementation requires an algorithmic structure of the original specifications. In summary the constructor implementation forms an easily applicable and mechanizable way of refining data structure. The far-reaching restrictions, however, limits the range of possible applications. In order to refine loose sorts we provide a refinement step for introducing a generation constraint for a loose sort. The generation constraint can be refined by enriching or reducing the family of constructors.

The idea of describing the correctness of data structure embeddings by representation and abstraction functions was first given by Hoare [46]. Our approach extends this idea to higher-order algebraic specifications with loose semantics. Algebraic implementations for the first-order case have been discussed implicitly by Broy [15, 16], but there are no explicit transformation rules for specifications given. The transformation rules introduced in this chapter can be mechanized and application conditions can be assured by sufficient syntactic criteria. The Lübeck Transformation System provides transformation steps for these data structure refinements [26]. Non-algebraic model oriented data structure refinements are surveyed in detail in [20].

Chapter 9

A Case Study for a Compositional Derivation

We illustrate the approach proposed in Chapter 5 for the compositional development of software systems by focusing on a booking optimizer for holiday trips using XML -based request handling.

The problem definition consists of an informal description and a system specification of the booking optimizer. A composite system specification is obtained by glueing pre-defined specifications with new specification elements. The initial specification is stepwise refined into an efficient algorithmic specification which can easily be implemented in a functional programming language. We structure the development process of the overall specification using derivations of sub specifications.

9.1 Problem definition

We present a composite specification of a booking optimizer for holiday trips. After presenting an informal description the formal specification of the system is structured into three parts. The user interface defines the interaction with the system from the client's point of view. Combinations of products can be arranged and a collection of combinations can be sent as XML document to a request handler. The second part contains the specification of the request handler including optimization and deletion of unavailable products. In the last part the evaluation of product combinations is specified.

9.1.1 Problem description

A booking contains a set of products like a flight, a hotel room and a rented car. A combination of products consists of a complete booking required for a holiday trip.

We assume the set of products to be partitioned into different kinds. The booking optimizer must provide a user interface allowing to generate requests of product combinations.

119

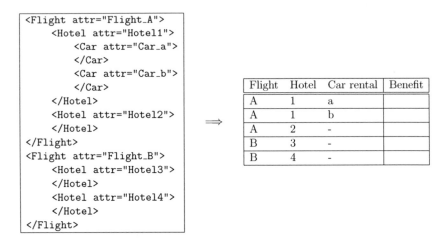

Figure 9.1: Example for a product combination

A customer of the booking system may define a request by the user interface. The generated XML document is then sent to a request handler for evaluation. The result of the evaluation comprises a product combination of maximum benefit. Fig. 9.1 shows an XML document on the left which determines the entries in the table on the right. We are interested in the combination showing a maximum benefit.

The benefit depends on a weight function, which associates with each product a natural number. The benefit of a product combination is equal to the sum of weights of the composed products.

9.1.2   Compositional requirements specification

The requirements specification makes use of the pre-defined specifications in Chapter 4. We construct a composite system specification by glueing these specifications together using new auxiliary functions and function composition. We follow a top-down design wrt. to the import graph: We first specify the user interface which forms the root specification of the development graph. This specification imports the specification of the request handler evaluating the product combination of maximum benefit. The request handler depends on a specification that evaluates collections of products, which is specified last.

The initial development graph of the overall system specification is illustrated in Fig. 9.2. Here the import graph is illustrated by simple arrows and a dotted arrow denotes a parameter specification. The system specification is constructed out of several standard

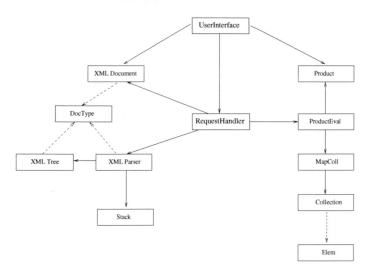

Figure 9.2: Development graph of problem definition

specifications for XML handling and standard data structures. The specifications introduce new function symbols and additional axioms for glueing the standard components together achieving the desired functionality.

User interface The front-end is given by the possible user inputs. The user navigates through a tree-like structure of input masks defining different products. We model products by two sorts *product* and *kind* with an equality predicate and an operation *getKind* delivering the kind of a product:

spec $Product = Nat + (Elem)[elem/kind, eqEl/eqKind]$;
sorts $product$
ops $getKind : (product)kind$
$\quad\quad eqProd : (product, product)bool$
end

The product combinations can be arranged by several operations simulating activity components of graphical user interfaces, e.g. buttons and pop-up menus. The corresponding constructors and function symbols are defined in the specification *UserInterface*, see Fig. 9.3.

The elements of sort *inputState* reflect a state during arranging product combinations. The operation *new* starts a new arrangement by settling a first product that is a member of all product combinations defined later on. With the operation *addAlt* a new product is added to an existing product combination or an alternative product combination is generated. After completing a mask for a product including all alternatives the user may

---

spec *UserInterface = XMLDoc[Product* **fit** *tag/kind, eqTag/eqKind, attr/product]+*
    RessourceRetriever;
sorts *inputState*
ops   *new* : (*kind, product*)*inputState,*
         addAlt : (*inputState, kind, product*)*inputState,*
         accept : (*inputState, kind*)*inputState,*
           undo : (*inputState*)*inputState,*
       sendReq : (*inputState*)*result*
axioms
         undo1 : *undo*(*new*(*k, p*)) = *new*(*k, p*),
         undo2 : *undo*(*addAlt*(*s, k, p*)) = *s,*
         undo3 : *undo*(*accept*(*s, k*)) = *s*
end

Figure 9.3: User interface of the system

accept the definition. The operation *undo* deletes the last included alternative, provided
it exists.

The system behaviour is defined from the users point of view by the operation *sendReq* :

$$sendReq = (handleRequest \circ mkXMLStream)$$

The function symbol *mkXMLStream* : (*inputState*)*xmldoc* is an auxiliary operation transforming the input to an XML -document for transmission via the web. The function
symbol is added to the specification *UserInterface* along with the following axioms:

mkXMLStream1 : *mkXMLStream*(*new*(*k, p*)) = *insert*(*btag*(*k, p*), *EoF*)
mkXMLStream2 : *mkXMLStream*(*addAlt*(*s, k, p*)) = *appTag*(*mkXMLStream*(*s*), *btag*(*k, p*))
mkXMLStream3 : *mkXMLStream*(*accept*(*s, k*)) = *appTag*(*mkXMLStream*(*s*), *etag*(*k*))

The specification *UserInterface* embodies the client of the booking system that sends
requests to a server for evaluating a product combination of maximum benefit. The
connection to the server is modeled by the function *handleRequest* which will be declared
in the specification *RessourceRetriever* .

Request handling We will use the given XML components of Section 4.3 to specify the
problem on the server side. Additional function symbols and axioms glue the components
together achieving a composite specification of the problem. Here, function composition
will play a major role as structuring principle.

The request handler accepts XML documents as input and outputs as result a collection
of products with the corresponding benefit.

spec *Result = SP* **as** *Collection[Product* **fit** *elem/product, eqEl/eqProd];*
sorts   *result* = (*nat, SP.coll*)
ops *maxRes* : (*result, result*)*result*
end

We will specify the problem using a top-down procedure of a user request. We split the task into two sub tasks: A function *parse* transforms the XML document into an XML tree, and an operation *getBestAlt* which traverses the XML tree computes a product combination of maximum benefit.

$handleRequest1 : handleRequest = (getBestAlt \circ parse)$

The function *parse* is taken from the specification *XMLParser* introduced in Section 4.3.

The function *getBestAlt* splits again into three subtasks. We first compute the list of all possible combinations of products described by an XML tree. Each combination corresponds to a path from the root to a leaf in the tree. Then we apply a function *getResultOfAlt* to all possible product combinations computing the pair of the benefit of the combination along with the solution itself. In a last step the function *maxResList* extracts a combination with a maximum benefit.

$getBestAlt1 : getBestAlt = maxResList \circ (@M.map\ getResultOfAlt) \circ getAlt$

The list of product combinations from an XML tree is generated by the operations

$getAlt : (XMLTree)PLS.list$
$getAltL : (XMLTreeList)PLS.list$
$addToAll : (product, PLS.list)PLS.list.$

The sort *PLS.list* denotes lists of product combinations. The auxiliary operations have a clear purpose and can be axiomatized by a couple of straightforward equations. The following axioms describes the generation of lists of product combinations from XML tress:

$getAlt1 : getAlt(Leaf(p,v)) = newColl(v),$
$getAlt2 : getAlt(CTree(p,v,xtl)) = addToAll(v, getAltL(xtl))$

$getAltL1 : getAltL(noTree) = PLS.nil$
$getAltL2 : getAltL(appTree(xt,xtl)) = PLS.conc(getAlt(xt), getAltL(xtl))$

$addToAll1 : addToAll(p, PLS.nil) = PLS.nil$
$addToAll2 : addToAll(p, PLS.cons(s,l)) = PLS.cons(SC.addElem(p,s), addToAll(p,l))$

The mutually recursive structure of the construction of product combinations is a consequence of the mutually recursive data structure definition of XML trees.

A product combination is evaluated by the operation *getResultOfAlt* : $(SP.coll)result$ achieving a pair of the corresponding benefit and the combination itself. The axiomatization of this operation requires an operation *getValOfColl* computing the benefit of one product combination.

$getResultOfAlt1 : getResultOfAlt(s) = (getValOfColl(s), s)$

The product evaluation with the operation *getValOfColl* is defered to the next subsubsection.

A result of maximum benefit is computed by the operation *maxResList* which is based on the standard operation *maxRes* of the specification *Result* delivering the maximum of two results:

spec *RessourceRetriever* =
   Nat + *ProductEval* +
   XMLTree[*Product* **fit** *val/product, tag/product, eqTag/eqProd*] +
   XMLParser[*Product* **fit** *val/product, tag/product, eqTag/eqProd*] +
   (*RL* **as** *List*[*Result* **fit** *T/result*] +
   (*M* **as** *Map*[(*SP* **as** *Collection*[*Product* **fit** *elem/product, eqEl/eqProd*]) **fit** *T1/SP.coll*]
   [{**sorts** *result*} **fit** *T2/result*])[*L1.* * */PLS.*, *L2.* * */RL.**]);
ops   *getAlt* : (*XMLTree*)*PLS.list*,
       getAltL : (*XMLTreeList*)*PLS.list*,
   getResultOfAlt : (*SP.coll*)*result*,
     getBestAlt : (*XMLTree*)*result*,
    maxResList : (*RL.list*)*result*,
      addToAll : (*product, PLS.list*)*PLS.list*,
   handleRequest : (*TL.list*)*result*

Figure 9.4: The server side of the booking optimizer

$maxResList1 : maxResList(RL.nil) = (zero, clear)$
$maxResList2 : maxResList(RL.cons(r, RL.nil)) = r$
$maxResList3 : maxResList(RL.cons(r, RL.cons(s, rl))) =$
$$maxResList(RL.cons(maxRes(r, s), rl))$$

The operation *maxResList* traverses the list and keeps the intermediate result, i.e. the maximum of the traversed list as first element of the argument list.

The computation of a combination with maximum benefit may be expensive for large XML trees. If a certain product must not occur in a solution it can be deleted in forehand. In order to manage such situations we introduce a function symbol which deletes all combinations containing a certain product. We specify this function symbol in a non-algorithmic manner by using again the auxiliary function symbol *getAlt* and a function symbol *filter* : (*product, PLS.list*)*PLS.list* deleting all product combinations that contain the product. The function symbol *delAlt* : (*product, XMLTree*)*XMLTree* is axiomatized by the following equation:

$delAlt1 : getAlt(delAlt(t, xt)) = filter(t, getAlt(xt))$

The auxiliary function *filter* required for the deletion can be defined easily by the following equations:

$filter1 : filter(t, PLS.nil) = PLS.nil$
$filter2 : filter(t, PLS.cons(s, l)) =$ **if** $SC.contains(t, s)$ **then** $filter(t, l)$
                       else $PLS.cons(s, filter(t, l))$

The complete specification of the request handling then consists of a specification expression making use of predefined and new specifications (see Fig. 9.4).

Evaluation of product combinations For specifying the product evaluation we first apply the operation *getVal* to all products of a collection, and then the auxiliary operation *sum* adds the elements of the collection of natural numbers. The specification *ProductEval* is illustrated in Fig. 9.5 .

spec	$ProductEval = Nat +$
	$(MPN \textbf{ as } MapColl[Product \textbf{ fit } T1/product, eq1/eqProd]$
	$[Nat \textbf{ fit } T2/nat, eq2/eqNat])[S1.*/SP.*, S2.*/SN.*] ;$
ops	$getVal : (product)nat$
	$getValOfColl : (SP.coll)nat$
	$sum : (SN.coll)nat$
vars	$s : SP.coll, t, u : SN.coll, n : nat, p : product$
axioms	
	$getValOfColl1 : getValOfColl = sum \circ (@map\ getVal)$
	$sum1 : sum(SN.empty) = zero$
	$sum2 : sum(SN.single(n)) = n$
	$sum3 : sum(SN.union(t, u)) = add(sum(t), sum(u))$
hide	sum
end	

Figure 9.5: Specification of product evaluation

Since the auxiliary operation *sum* is hidden, it is not exported to specifications using *ProductEval* .

The transformation steps described in the sequel of this chapter aim at an efficient algorithmic axiomatization of the client and server system.

9.2 Improving the XML parser

The XML parser makes use of the data structure *stack* . As demonstrated in Subsection 8.5.2, the stack specification can be refined by an algebraic implementation such that a stack is represented by a pair of a stack pointer and an array using the specification *Array* . The resulting specification is illustrated in Fig. 9.6 .

We get an implementation of *XMLParser* by replacing the imported specification *Stack* by the refined specification *StackByArray* . The resulting specification is not algorithmic since the set of equations

$dropTree1 : dropTree(empty, xl) = xl$

$dropTree2 : dropTree(push(a, s), TL.cons(btag(t), xl)) =$
$$dropTree(push(t, push(a, s)), dropTrL(xl))$$

$dropTree3 : dropTree(push(a, s), TL.cons(etag(t), xl)) =$
$$\textbf{if } eqTag(a, t) \textbf{ then } dropTree(s, xl) \textbf{ else } TL.nil$$

$dropTree4 : dropTree(push(a, s), TL.cons(stag(v), xl)) = dropTree(push(a, s), xl)$

spec *StackByArray*
sorts $stack_{old} = empty_{old} \mid push_{old}(elem, stack_{old})$
$\quad\quad\quad stack = (nat, array)$
ops $\quad\quad pop: (stack)stack,$
$\quad\quad isempty: (stack)bool,$
$\quad\quad\quad top: (stack)elem,$
$\quad\quad empty: stack,$
$\quad\quad\quad push: (elem, stack)stack$
vars $a: array, m: nat, e: elem$
axioms
$\quad\quad pop1: pop(zero, a) = (zero, init),$
$\quad\quad pop2: pop(succ(m), a) = (m, a),$
$\quad isempty1: isempty(zero, a) = true,$
$\quad isempty2: isempty(succ(m), a) = false,$
$\quad\quad top2: top(succ(m), a) = lookup(succ(m), a),$
$\quad\quad empty1: empty = (zero, init),$
$\quad\quad push1: push(e, (m, a)) = (succ(m), put(succ(m), e, a))$
end

Figure 9.6: Specification of stacks implemented by arrays

is not constructive, because *push* is no more a constructor. For this implementation we have to revise the specification *XMLParser*. We first transform the equations into a form using only the full term $push(a, s)$ and not a or s itself in the right-hand terms of the equations. This leads to a new version of the axioms (see Fig. 9.7).

$dropTree1: dropTree(empty, xl) = xl$
$dropTree2: dropTree(push(a, s), TL.cons(btag(t), xl)) =$
$\quad\quad\quad\quad$ **if** $isempty(push(a, s))$ **then** $dropTree(push(t, push(a, s)), dropTrL(xl))$
$\quad\quad\quad\quad$ **else** $TL.cons(btag(t), xl)$
$dropTree3: dropTree(push(a, s), TL.cons(etag(t), xl)) =$
$\quad\quad\quad\quad$ **if** $isempty(push(a, s))$ **then**
$\quad\quad\quad\quad\quad\quad$ **if** $eqTag(top(push(a, s)), t)$ **then** $dropTree(pop(push(a, s)), xl)$
$\quad\quad\quad\quad\quad\quad$ **else** $TL.nil$
$\quad\quad\quad\quad$ **else** $TL.cons(etag(t), xl)$
$dropTree4: dropTree(push(a, s), TL.cons(stag(v), xl)) =$
$\quad\quad\quad\quad$ **if** $isempty(push(a, s)$ **then** $dropTree(push(a, s), xl)$
$\quad\quad\quad\quad$ **else** $TL.cons(stag(v), xl))$

Figure 9.7: Step 1 for revising the **XML** parser

By generalizing the term $push(a, s)$ we obtain an axiomatization which is not using *empty* and *push* in the first argument of left-hand terms of the equations and hence yield constructive equations as shown in Fig. 9.8.

$dropTree1 : dropTree(empty, xl) = xl$

$dropTree2 : dropTree(s, TL.cons(btag(t), xl)) =$
$\qquad$ **if** $isempty(s)$ **then** $dropTree(push(t, s), dropTrL(xl))$
$\qquad$ **else** $TL.cons(btag(t), xl)$

$dropTree3 : dropTree(s, TL.cons(etag(t), xl)) =$
$\qquad$ **if** $isempty(s)$ **then**
$\qquad\qquad$ **if** $eqTag(top(s), t)$ **then** $dropTree(pop(s), xl)$
$\qquad\qquad$ **else** $TL.nil$
$\qquad$ **else** $TL.cons(etag(t), xl))$

$dropTree4 : dropTree(s, TL.cons(stag(v), xl)) =$
$\qquad$ **if** $isempty(s)$ **then** $dropTree(s, xl)$ **else** $TL.cons(stag(v), xl))$

Figure 9.8: Step 2 for revising the XML parser

Finally, we can eliminate the axiom *dropTree1* which is after the generalization covered by the rest of the axioms. Now the imported specification *Stack* can be exchanged by the refined specification *StackByArray* achieving again an algorithmic specification.

9.3 Refining the product evaluation

The evaluation of a collection of products is specified in a rather abstract way exploiting the functional *map* and the auxiliary operation *sum*. In this section we will change the axiomatization by using the fusion step for catamorphisms of Section 7.3. Furthermore, we will implement collections using lists and exchange the imported specification for collections by the implementation of lists.

9.3.1 Simplifying the product evaluation

The application of the fusion theorem yields a new combine operation for the constructor *union*; the non-recursive constructors are handled in a direct way (see Fig. 9.9).

Since the two operations $cop1_{union}$ and *sum* are hidden and not used anymore for the axiomatization of other operations, we can omit them. Moreover, we can drop the proof obligations $getValOfColl1_{ass}$, $getValOfColl1_{comm}$ and $getValOfColl1_{neutr}$ by proving that they are consequences of the specification *Nat*. Finally, we arrive at a simple specification with one function symbol and three axioms describing the function symbol in an algorithmic way. The final specification is illustrated in Fig. 9.10.

The fusion step illustrates, how the structured specification of functions by function compositions can be transformed in an efficient algorithmic solution.

spec $ProductEval =$
        MPN **as** $MapColl[Product$ **fit** $elem/product, eqEl/eqProd]$
                $[Nat$ **fit** $elem2/nat, eqEl2/eqNat])[S1.*/SC.*, S2.*/SN.*];$
ops $getValOfColl : (SP.coll)nat$
                $sum : (SN.coll)nat$
                $cop1_{union} : (nat, nat)nat$
vars $r, s : SP.coll, t, u : SN.coll, n, m, n_1, n_2, n_3 : nat, p : product$
axioms
            $cop1_{union}1 : cop1_{union}(m, n) = add(m, n)$
      $getValOfColl1_{empty} : getValOfColl(SP.empty) = zero$
      $getValOfColl1_{single} : getValOfColl(SP.single(p)) = getVal(p)$
      $getValOfColl1_{union} : getValOfColl(SP.union(r, s)) =$
                                    $add(getValOfColl(r), getValOfColl(s))$
                $sum1 : sum(SN.empty) = zero$
                $sum2 : sum(SN.single(n)) = n$
                $sum3 : sum(SN.union(t, u)) = add(sum(t), sum(u))$
        $getValOfColl1_{ass} : add(add(n_1, n_2), n_3) = add(n_1, add(n_2, n_3))$
      $getValOfColl1_{comm} : add(n_1, n_2) = add(n_2, n_1)$
      $getValOfColl1_{neutr} : add(n, zero) = n = add(zero, n)$
hide $sum, cop1_{union}$
end

Figure 9.9: Refining the product evaluation by fusion

9.3.2   Implementing collections

The data structure *coll* of the specification *Collection* is implemented by lists. With the constructor implementation

$$clear \quad \rightarrow \quad nil$$
$$newColl(x) \quad \rightarrow \quad cons(x, nil)$$
$$addAll(b, c) \quad \rightarrow \quad conc(b, c)$$

we achieve a new implementation for collections. We apply the constructor implementation to the specification *Collection* replacing constructor terms by their implementation (see Fig. 9.11).

As the specification *CollByList* does not show an algorithmic shape anymore, we perform some simple transformation steps to equation *contains2* in order to generalize it to nonempty lists:

$$contains2 : contains(x, cons(y, p)) = or(eqEl(x, y), contains(x, p))$$

Moreover, we simplify the equation *addElem1* by rewriting steps and drop the axioms $ass, neutr1$ and $neutr2$, which can easily be derived from the axioms $conc1$ and $conc2$

---

spec *ProductEval* =
    MPN **as** *MapColl[Product* **fit** *elem/product, eqEl/eqProd]*
                  [Nat **fit** *elem2/nat, eqEl2/eqNat])[S1. * /SC.*, S2. * /SN.*]*;
ops   *getValOfColl : (SP.coll)nat*
axioms
    getValOfColl1$_{empty}$: getValOfColl(SP.empty) = zero
    getValOfColl1$_{single}$: getValOfColl(SP.single(p)) = getVal(p)
    getValOfColl1$_{union}$: getValOfColl(SP.union(r, s)) =
                                  add(getValOfColl(r), getValOfColl(s))
end

Figure 9.10: Simplified product evaluation

of the specification *List* . Finally, we drop *contains3* which is a consequence of *contains1* and *contains2*. The specification illustrated in Fig. 9.12 shows the derived algorithmic implementation of collections by lists.

We choose a new name for the refined specification which becomes part of the development graph.

---

spec *CollByList*
sorts   *coll = list*
ops   *contains :* *(elem, coll)bool*
        addElem : *(elem, coll)coll*
           clear : *coll*
        newColl : *(elem)coll*
         addAll : *(coll, coll)coll*
axioms
             ass : *conc(conc(s, p), q) = conc(s, conc(p, q))*
         neutr1 : *conc(nil, p) = p*
         neutr2 : *conc(p, nil) = p*
     contains1 : *contains(x, nil) = false*
     contains2 : *contains(x, cons(y, nil)) = eqEl(x, y)*
     contains3 : *contains(x, conc(s, p)) = or(contains(x, s), contains(x, p))*
     addElem1 : *addElem(x, s) = conc(cons(x, nil), s)*
           cl1 : *clear = nil*
         nC1 : *newColl(x) = cons(x, nil)*
        addA1 : *addAll(s, p) = conc(s, p)*
end

Figure 9.11: Implementation of collections by lists

```
spec  CollByList
sorts      coll = list
ops    contains :  (elem, coll)bool
       addElem :  (elem, coll)coll
          clear :  coll
       newColl :  (elem)coll
        addAll :  (coll, coll)coll
axioms
       contains1 :  contains(x, nil) = false
       contains2 :  contains(x, cons(y, nil)) = eqEl(x, y)
       addElem1 :  addElem(x, s) = conc(cons(x, nil), s)

            cl1 :  clear = nil
            nC1 :  newColl(x) = cons(x, nil)
           addA1 :  addAll(s, p) = conc(s, p)
end
```

Figure 9.12: Specification for collections implemented by lists

9.3.3   Revising the product evaluation

In Figure 9.13 we illustrate the situation after refining the system specifications by implementing *Stack* by *StackByArray*, revising the specification *XMLParser*, refining *ProductEval* and implementing *Collection* by *CollByList*. The data structure refinement of *Collection* yields a new specification *CollByList*. The refinement relation is denoted by an arrow with a bold head. For the fusion step in *ProductEval* no new specification is generated; instead the old specification is replaced by the refined specification.

In the specification *ProductEval* we import collections via the specification *MapColl*. Since we do not use the operation *map* anymore after the fusion step, we exchange the import of the specification *MapColl* by the import of the specification *Collection*:

    spec *ProductEval* = *Nat* +
        SP **as** *Collection*[*Product* **fit** $T1/product, eq1/eqProd$] ;

Now, we can exchange the import of *Collection* by the refinement *CollByList* simply by redirecting the import-arrow along the refinement relation.

    spec *ProductEval* = *Nat* +
        SP **as** *CollByList*[*Product* **fit** $T1/product, eq1/eqProd$] ;

This affects a change of the syntactic properties of *ProductEval*, since the function symbols *empty*, *newColl* and *addAll* do not belong to the constructors anymore. Hence, the specification is not algorithmic. The implementation of the former constructors can be used to exchange them by their implementations in the respective axioms:

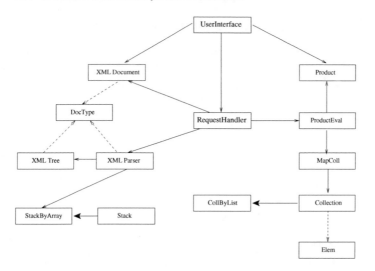

Figure 9.13: Development graph with refined specifications

$getValOfColl1 : getValOfColl(nil) = zero$
$getValOfColl2 : getValOfColl(cons(p, nil)) = getVal(p)$
$getValOfColl3 : getValOfColl(conc(s_1, s_2)) = add(getValOfColl(s_1), getValOfColl(s_2))$

The axioms can be transformed into an algorithmic shape using rewriting, generalization and dropping the axiom $getValOfColl3$:

$getValOfColl1 : getValOfColl(nil) = zero$
$getValOfColl2 : getValOfColl(cons(p, s)) = add(getVal(p), getValOfColl(s))$

This completes the refinement of the product evaluation. We have now achieved a more efficient implementation of the specification $ProductEval$.

9.4 Refining the request handler

The request handler evaluates the product combination of maximum benefit. In order to yield an efficient algorithmic implementation of this part of the system the specification is refined in various ways. We will refine the specification first by deriving a tail-recursive axiomatization of the maximum function. Moreover, we apply two fusion steps in order to eliminate the auxiliary data structures of the function composition used for the definition of $getBestAlt$. Finally, we derive an algorithmic implementation of the function symbol $delAlt$.

9.4.1   Improving the maximum computation

For efficiency reasons we transform linear recursions into tail recursions. Hence we will introduce a new function symbol $maxR$ computing the maximum result of a list of results. We begin with the embedding:

$$maxR(mr, L) \quad = \quad maxResList(cons(mr, L))$$

By a complete case analysis on L according to the operation $maxResList$ we achieve two cases:

$maxR1 : maxR(mr, nil) = maxResList(cons(mr, nil))$
$maxR2 : maxR(mr, cons(s, rl)) = maxResList(cons(mr, cons(s, rl)))$

Several refinement steps lead to a repetitive axiomatization of $maxR$:

$maxR1 : maxR(mr, nil) = mr$
$maxR2 : maxR(mr, cons(s, rl)) = maxR(maxRes(mr, s), rl)$

Inserting the specialization

$$maxResList(L) \quad = \quad maxRes((zero, clear), maxResList(L)) = maxR((zero, clear), L)$$

we can exchange the axiomatization of $handleRequest$ by the axiom

$$getBestAlt \quad = \quad (@maxR(zero, clear)) \circ (@M.map getResultOfAlt) \circ getAlt \,.$$

The improvement of the maximum computation again yields a more efficient implementation.

9.4.2   Splitting composition chains

Function composition supports the structured high level specification of systems, but for implementation function compositions often lead to overhead of constructing and eliminating intermediate data structures. In order to smoothen the result of such a specification fusion of neighbouring function applications is sensible. Heading for fusion steps of two involved functions, we have to split a composition chain of several functions into compositions where only two functions are involved. Of course, this requires additional auxiliary function symbols for expressing the parts of the composition.

The function composition of the axiomatization of the operation $getBestAlt$ can be split into two axioms. Therefore, a new function symbol $getPossList$: $(XMLTree)RL.list$ is introduced. The axiomatization comprises two axioms.

$getBestAlt : getBestAlt(xt) = ((@maxR(zero, clear)) \circ getPossList)(xt)$
$getPossList : getPossList = (@map\ getResultOfAlt) \circ getAlt$

This prepares two fusion steps on the new axioms which is described in the next two subsections.

9.4.3 Fusing result and alternatives computation

The sorts *XMLTree* and *XMLTreeList* are mutually recursive and as a consequence the computation of all alternatives of a tree is defined mutually recursively by the two function symbols *getAlt* and *getAltL*. Hence, a fusion step also requires two function symbols and two axioms describing the behaviour of the function symbols by function compositions. Therefore, we extend the specification by a new function symbol *getPossListL* and a new axiom. The fusion step then takes the two axioms

$$getPossList = (@map\ getResultOfAlt) \circ getAlt$$
$$getPossListL = (@map\ getResultOfAlt) \circ getAltL$$

and generates a new axiomatization showing the shape of a catamorphism

$$getPossList(Leaf(k,p)) = cons((getVal(p), newColl(p)), nil)$$
$$getPossList(CTree(k,p,xl)) = cop_{CTree}(p, getPossListL(xl))$$
$$getPossListL(noTree) = nil$$
$$getPossListL(appTree(t,xl)) = cop_{appTree}(getPossList(t), getPossListL(xl))$$

The new combine operations cop_{CTree} and $cop_{appTree}$ must satisfy the following conditions:

$$(map\ getResultOfAlt)(addToAll(p,L)) = cop_{CTree}(p, (map\ getResultOfAlt)(L))$$
$$(map\ getResultOfAlt)(conc(L,K)) =$$
$$cop_{appTree}((map\ getResultOfAlt)(L), (map\ getResultOfAlt)(K))$$

These conditions serve as starting point for the derivation of an algorithmic implementation of the combine operations. For the sake of simplicity, we first focus on a derivation for $cop_{appTree}$. We add a new axiom to the specification which will later be proved and dropped. The property states that the *map* function symbol distributes with the concatenation on lists:

$$@map\ f\ (conc(L,K)) = conc(@map\ f\ L, @map\ f\ K)$$

This formula is a consequence of the constructive axiomatization of *map* and *conc*. Applying the new axiom and swapping the left and right-hand side of the condition for $cop_{appTree}$ yields

$$cop_{appTree}((@map\ getResultOfAlt)(L), (@map\ getResultOfAlt)(K)) =$$
$$conc((@map\ getResultOfAlt)(L), (@map\ getResultOfAlt)(K))$$

A generalization of the terms $@map\ getResultOfAlt\ L$ and $@map\ getResultOfAlt\ K$ leads to the desired algorithmic axiomatization which can be summarized by $cop_{appTree} = conc$.

For the derivation of the combine operation cop_{CTree} more effort has to be spent. Here a case analysis on the variable L is necessary. The derivation results in an algorithmic description of cop_{CTree}:

$$cop_{CTree}(p, nil) = nil$$
$$cop_{CTree}(p, cons((n,r), rl)) = cons((add(getVal(p), n), addElem(p,r)), cop_{CTree}(p, rl))$$

In contrast to other fusion examples here the combine operation cannot be eliminated from the axiomatization of the synthesized function symbol.

9.4.4   Fusing result and maximum computation

We proceed with the second fusion step. Again, we will enrich the specification by a new function symbol $getBestAltL : (XMLTreeList)result$ in order to cope with the mutually recursive data structures $XMLTree$ and $XMLTreeList$:

$$getBestAlt = (@maxR(zero, clear)) \circ getPossList$$
$$getBestAltL = (@maxR(zero, clear)) \circ getPossListL$$

We apply the fusion transformation and achieve the following equations:

$$getBestAlt(Leaf(k, p)) = (getVal(p), newColl(p))$$
$$getBestAlt(CTree(k, p, xl)) = cop2_{CTree}(k, p, getBestAltL(xl))$$
$$getBestAltL(noTree) = (zero, clear)$$
$$getBestAltL(appTree(t, xl)) = cop2_{appTree}(getBestAlt(t), getBestAltL(xl))$$

The fusion transformation generates two axioms for the new combine operations $cop2_{CTree}$ and $cop2_{appTree}$:

$$maxR(mr, cop_{CTree}(k, p, L)) = cop2_{CTree}(k, p, maxR(mr, L))$$
$$maxR(mr, conc(L, K)) = cop2_{appTree}(maxR(mr, L), maxR(mr, K))$$

After some transformation steps we obtain an algorithmic axiomatization of the combine operations.

$$cop2_{CTree}(k, p, (n, nil)) = (zero, clear)$$
$$cop2_{CTree}(k, p, (n, cons(y, r))) = (getVal(p) + n, addElem(p, cons(y, r)))$$

This derivations exploits the monotonicity of the function symbol add, since the comparison of different product combinations is transfered to the comparison of the disjunct sub-combinations.

Expanding the combine operations in the new axiomatization of $getBestAlt$ and $getBestAltL$ yields the following axiomatization:

$$getBestAlt(Leaf(k, p)) = (getVal(p), newColl(p))$$
$$getBestAlt(CTree(k, p, xl)) = cop2_{CTree}(k, p, getBestAltL(xl))$$

$$getBestAltL(noTree) = (zero, clear)$$
$$getBestAltL(appTree(t, xl)) = maxRes(getBestAlt(t), getBestAltL(xl))$$

$$cop2_{CTree}(k, p, (n, nil)) = (zero, clear)$$
$$cop2_{CTree}(k, p, (n, cons(y, r))) = (add(getVal(p), n), addElem(p, cons(y, r))).$$

These equations form a more elaborated and efficient algorithm of finding the product combination with maximum benefit. Clearly, the best alternative along with the benefit of the alternative is computed bottom-up in the XML tree. This avoids the construction of the intermediate data structures i.e. lists of product combinations and lists of results.

9.4.5 Deriving an implementation for deletion

For the deletion of a product in a product combination we derive an algorithmic description of *delAlt*.

We start with the equation of the system specification

$$getAlt(delAlt(x, xt)) = filter(x, getAlt(xt)).$$

Since the data structures *XMLTree* and *XMLTreeList* are mutually recursive we additionally insert a function symbol *delAltL* and the axiom

$$getAltL(delAltL(x, xl)) = filter(x, getAltL(xl))$$

describing the deletion of a product in a list of XML trees similarly to the deletion in an XML tree. The derivation is based on a case analysis on xt and xl.

$$
\begin{aligned}
getAlt(delAlt(x, Leaf(k, p))) &= filter(x, getAlt(Leaf(k, p))) \\
&= filter(x, newColl(p)) \\
&= \textbf{if } eqProd(x, p) \textbf{ then } clear \textbf{ else } newColl(p) \\
&= getAlt(\textbf{if } eqProd(x, p) \textbf{ then } CTree(k, p, noTree) \\
&\qquad\qquad \textbf{else } Leaf(k, p))
\end{aligned}
$$

A decomposition step yields

$$delAlt(x, Leaf(k, p)) = \textbf{if } eqProd(x, p) \textbf{ then } CTree(k, p, noTree) \textbf{ else } Leaf(k, p)$$

Similarly, the case $xt = CTree(k, p, xl)$ can be derived. The essential idea of these derivations is to shift the function symbol *getAlt* on the right-hand side to the outermost position using various distributive properties. In both cases the final step drops the outermost function symbol *getAlt* on both sides of the equation by a decomposition step. This results in a new axiomatization of *delAlt*:

$$
\begin{aligned}
delAlt(x, Leaf(k, p)) &= \textbf{if } eqProd(x, p) \textbf{ then } CTree(k, p, noTree) \textbf{ else } Leaf(k, p) \\
delAlt(x, CTree(k, p, xl)) &= \textbf{if } eqProd(x, p) \textbf{ then } CTree(k, p, noTree) \\
&\qquad\qquad \textbf{else } CTree(k, p, delAltL(x, xl))
\end{aligned}
$$

Similarly, the equation for *delAltL* can be refined to

$$
\begin{aligned}
delAltL(x, noTree) &= noTree \\
delAltL(x, appTree(t, xl)) &= appTree(delAlt(x, t), delAltL(x, xl)).
\end{aligned}
$$

As a consequence of the implicit specification of *delAlt*, the solution is strongly related to the recursion structure of *getAlt* and *getAltL*. The specification leaves the freedom to structure the XML tree after the deletion. The design decision in this derivation appears in the decomposition step and in the strategy for shifting the function symbol *getAlt* to the outermost position.

9.5   Refining the user interface

We refine the user interface by introducing a generation constraint and implementing the input state by an XML document.

We first achieve a simple data structure for the input by introduction of a generation constraint (see Subsection 8.4.2):

$$inputState \ = \ new \mid addAlt(inputState, tag, product)$$
$$\mid accept(inputState, tag) \mid undo(inputState)$$

Since the function symbol *undo* is completely specified and all axioms are constructive and terminating, we can omit *undo* as constructor (see Subsection 8.4.4). This yields

$$inputState \ = \ new \mid addAlt(inputState, tag, product) \mid accept(inputState, tag) \,.$$

We can then refine the data structure by using XML documents. The sort *inputState* is implemented by the sort *XMLDoc* using the following constructor translation:

$$
\begin{aligned}
new(k, p) &\ \rightarrow\ insert(btag(k, p), EoF) \\
addAlt(s, k, p) &\ \rightarrow\ insert(btag(k, p), s) \\
accept(s, k) &\ \rightarrow\ insert(etag(k), s)
\end{aligned}
$$

The input is now represented by a list of XML tags. The order of the tags is reversed wrt. the order of the resulting XML document for transmission to the request handler. The adapted operation *mkXMLStream* then simply reverts the list of tags. As a result we achieve an algorithmic specification for the user interface.

9.6   Concluding remarks on the case study

The developed client and server provide a framework where the specification *Product* has to be implemented for concrete applications. If it is implemented by an algorithmic specification, the structured specification *UserInterface* is algorithmic as well. Hence it can easily be implemented in a functional programming language and compiled to an application. The framework can be generalized by parameterizing the weights of the products, the corresponding order, a smallest weight and the combine operation for weights. This requires additional properties stating that the smallest weight is neutral with regard to the combine operation and that the combine operation is associative.

The transformations required for the overall derivations were performed with the Lübeck Transformation System. Strategies and analysis procedures overtake most of the mechanical tasks of the derivation. Many application conditions for transformation steps can be verified automatically. In the following Chapter 10 and 11 we will give an overview of the system features and illustrate how the Lübeck Transformation System assists the user in developing software.

Part III

The Lübeck Transformation System
LTS

Chapter 10

Overview of LTS

This chapter presents an overview of the Lübeck Transformation System [28]. We begin with a description of the system summarizing its characteristic features and the history. Then we focus on the treatment of specifications by the system. The specifications loaded into the system show a characteristic life cycle. The major functionalities for passing through system states of the life cycle are illustrated. Finally, we explicate the design principles of LTS and survey the implementation.

10.1 System description

LTS is a transformation system for the stepwise refinement of algebraic specifications. The system description summarizes the characteristic features and outlines briefly the development of LTS.

10.1.1 Characteristic features

The Lübeck Transformation System handles algebraic specifications with higher-order sorts having a constructor generated loose semantics. The syntax is similar to the notation used in Chapter 4. The user refines specifications by invoking transformation commands.

The transformations head for algorithmic specifications which can be compiled into Standard ML code. The system uses analysis algorithms for syntactic criteria of desirable or critical properties defined in 5.3.1. In this way the status of the development is continously visible to the user (see Section 11.2.1). Moreover, guidance for possible continuing transformation steps is provided using further analysis algorithms and heuristics (see Subsection 11.2.4). As LTS is completely implemented in Standard ML, the top level environment of SML serves as user interface.

LTS is a prototype system which has been developed at the Institute of Software Technology and Programming Languages at the University of Lübeck. For the design of the

kernel system, the emphasis was laid on clear semantic concepts supporting sound transformation rules which preserve the behavioural properties of the initial specification.

10.1.2   History of the system

The development of the system started in 1998 aiming at a platform for investigating
wide-spanning transformation steps. The initial version was limited to first order sorts
and function symbols; it implemented only a simple structuring concept for specifications.
The refinement machinery was restricted to equation and term manipulations. In order
to increase the power of transformation steps strategies have been integrated later on,
enabling user defined transformation steps based on the implemented atomic transformations on terms and equations. Soon it became evident that transformations focusing
on terms and equations along with strategies do not suffice to mechanize wide-spanning
refinement steps. As a consequence, a transformation machinery for entire specifications
was implemented. This allows to exploit properties of a broader context and to manipulate several specification parts in one go. As a result of several case studies, a lack of
expressibility of the specification language was discovered. In response, the system then
was extended by higher order sorts and function symbols in order to provide concepts
of advanced functional programming. Moreover, the structuring concepts were adapted
to the essential concepts of CASL [64]; this design step opens the system for component
based developments. Finally, development graphs and their manipulations have been
implemented.

10.2   Life cycle of specifications during refinement

Specifications show a characteristic life cycle when they are transformed with LTS . After
a specification has been loaded, it resides in the system ready for transformation. Transformations can be performed either in the specification mode treating entire specifications
or in the fine tuning mode performing a sequence of equation and term manipulations.
After one or more refinement steps the transformed specification can be checked in replacing the original specification. The life cycle of a specification residing in the system
is illustrated in Fig. 10.1 .

10.2.1   Analyzing specifications

After parsing and context checking, the specification is analyzed with regard to desirable
or critical properties. These results assist the programmer in making further design
decisions, in revising previous transformation steps, or in detecting contradictions in the
axiomatization. During its life cycle, LTS analyzes a specification completely when it is
loaded into the system, and incrementally, after it has been transformed. The analysis
process comprises the properties defined in Subsections 5.3.1 and 5.1.2 . The major results

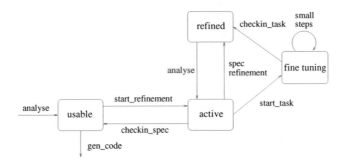

Figure 10.1: Life cycle of a specification in the system

of the analysis phase are displayed along with the specification on the screen. Unsolvable critical pairs possibly revealing contradictory axioms can be queried by an extra command.

10.2.2 Refining specifications

Specifications can be refined by the transformations introduced in Chapters 6, 7 and 8; all transfomations described in this thesis are implemented in the Lübeck Transformation System.

The user selects one of the loaded specifications and starts a refinement process. The selected specification becomes active, and the system enters the specification mode. This mode allows refinements addressing the entire specification like specification enrichments and reductions (see Section 6.1), fusion steps (see Section 7.3) or data structure refinements (see Section 8.4 and 8.3). Moreover, manipulations of the development graph (see Subsection 5.3.2) like exchanging imports can be performed in this mode.

Besides the specification mode, a specification can also be transformed in fine tuning mode. Here, a single axiom is picked as start axiom for a sequence of equation and term manipulations as introduced in Section 6.2. The start axiom is embedded into a transformation node encapsulating additional information about its status and applicable induction hypotheses. The internal state of the fine tuning mode comprises a stack of transformation nodes. Each transformation step is applied to the top transformation node. When carrying out the transformations, it is replaced by one or more resulting transformation nodes possibly enriched by additionally applicable hypotheses. In order to apply refinement steps to transformation nodes beneath the top transformation node, commands for reorganizing the stack are available. Moreover, the system provides a strategy language of LCF style [71] for combining atomic fine tuning transformations to powerful transformation steps. A sequence of refinements in fine tuning mode leads to a couple of new equations logically implying the start axiom. The refinement of the overall specification consists in replacing the start axiom by the generated axioms.

After a refinement step, i.e. a refinement in the specification mode or a sequence of equation manipulations in fine tuning mode, the specification is analyzed to update its semantic properties.

10.2.3   Updating the development graph

When the user decides to finish the transformation process, the refined specification can be inserted into the collection of loaded specifications replacing the original specification. Alternatively, the refined specification can first be renamed and then inserted into the collection of loaded specifications. This keeps the original specification and adds a refinement edge to the development graph. When a specification is detected to be algorithmic, it can be compiled into Standard ML code (see Section 11.5).

10.3   Implementation of LTS

We summarize the requirements on the basic design principles and illustrate the system architecture.

10.3.1   Design principles

The Lübeck Transformation System was designed with emphasis on flexible modification and extension. Therefore LTS is completely implemented in the functional programming language Standard ML 97 using Moscow ML 2.0. The system also runs under SML/NJ 110.0.

During system start a collection of prelude specifications like Boolean values, natural numbers and lists are loaded. An autostart file is executed containing the user preferences and user-specific rule catalogues. After the system start, specifications can be loaded and manipulated by invoking transformation commands implemented as SML functions.

The fine tuning commands reside in different modules which are mutually independent and can be loaded as needed. Each command is implemented by a transformation function which applies the single step strategy associated with it. The transformation function uses the transformation node on top of the stack as an implicit argument. Further arguments are supplied as parameters when invoking the transformation function. In this way the system can be customized using different collections of refinement modules.

The functions performing the refinement steps serve as commands of an abstract machine providing correctness preserving manipulations of specifications and equations. The commands can be structured into strategies which represent programs of the abstract machine. Hence, deriving a software system is similar to writing a program for the abstract transformation machine.

10.3.2   System architecture

In the sequel, we describe the architecture of the system, survey the status, and explain important implementation decisions.

The approximately 12 000 lines of code are structured into 21 modules. The system is roughly composed of eight software layers, compare Fig. 10.2. Apart from the graphical user interface the layers are completely implemented.

The abstract syntax layer comprises the data structures used for representing the specification language and the transformations. Various node types of the abstract syntax tree like axioms, function symbols and specifications contain a list of attributes recording properties inferred in the analysis phase. Further attributes can easily be implemented on demand.

The next layer provides auxiliary functions for basic manipulations of specifications and for querying parts of specifications. Here operations on signatures and specifications are provided, for example merging signatures and applying signature morphisms to specifications.

The next three layers of the system architecture are separated into two parts. Whereas the right part consists of three modules for parsing, context checking and code generation, the left part contains the manipulation and analysis part of the system. More general the right part contains all modules which are relevant for a pure compiler functionality while the left part embodies the abstract transformation machine.

The parser is a bottom-up-parser built by the lex and yacc tools [44]; it is used for loading new specifications. The context check module contains all functions for context checking, in particular type checking. The code generator translates constructor sorts into SML data types and groups of constructive equations into SML function declarations using pattern matching. Moreover, the output is structured into SML structures.

The abstract transformation machine is split into three layers which reflect three abstraction levels of manipulations: terms and equations, transformation nodes and entire specifications.

The term and equation layer provides functions for simplifying, currying and uncurrying terms, matching, rewriting, replacement of sub terms and unification modulo the curry/uncurry relation. For rewriting and replacement the three strategies left-most innermost, left-most outermost and occurrence-based are provided. Most algorithms are variants of the algorithms found in the text books [3, 4]. The system automatically curries and uncurries a term during matching and unification. These functions form the foundation for the next layer.

The layer for tackling transformation nodes provides functions for the manipulation of terms and equations explained in Section 6.2. These functions are separated into mutually independent modules such that the collection of needed modules can be loaded. This enables an application dependent usage of the manipulation functions by choosing the relevant modules. In this way, the system can be tailored to particular application fields,

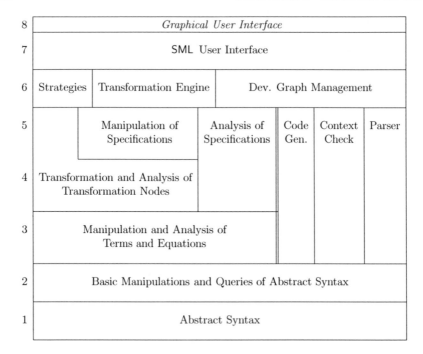

Figure 10.2: System architecture of LTS

for example stream processing functions [29] or high level parallel programming [30]. Parts of this layer are passed up to layer 6 in order to make the provided functions available for the construction of strategies.

The specification analysis module provides all necessary functions for the analysis of specifications. A specification is analyzed whenever it is loaded or refined. In this way, the user is continuously informed about its semantic properties allowing profound design decisions. The semantic properties of a specification found during analysis are also used for verifying the applicability conditions in various specification refinement steps. This module is directly based on the manipulation and analysis module for terms and equations.

The layer for manipulating specifications encapsulates all the functions and data structures used for the refinement of specifications. Specification enrichments and reductions, fusion steps, data structure refinements and import replacements are handled in this module. Some transformations are based on the manipulation of transformations nodes.

The next layer captures the construction of strategies and comprise the state relevant parts of the system. Besides the I/O handling of the parser, all functions in layers 1 to 5 are purely functional. Layer 6 manages the state of the development graph and the transformation process.

The strategy module is completely based on the layers 4 and 5; it performs all manipulations for specifications and equations using these layers. Moreover, basic manupulation commands can be combined into powerful transformation steps. The bottom layers 1 to 5 can therefore be seen as kernel architecture of the system.

The transformation engine consists of functions and data structures encapsulating the state of the refinement process. Here a refinement can be started and stopped, the active specification can be refined, a fine tuning process can be started and strategies can be executed. Each refinement step can be annulled by an undo function.

The module for the management of the development graph provides functions and data structures for handling the development graph. LTS can only handle one development graph at a time and each specification which is loaded is inserted into the graph. At the end of a refinement process a new refinement edge can be added to the development graph.

On top of layer 6 the user interface is located. The user interface provides functions for loading, refining and code generation of specifications. In order to allow comfortable user inputs, the user interface uses a combinator parser for parsing specification parts which serve as arguments for functions.

A possibility of connecting foreign user interfaces to LTS is provided by an XML communication via Unix files. The system reads commands coded as XML files, performs the functions and writes the new state of the transformation as an XML string into an output file which can be used by the user interface.

10.4   Concluding remarks on LTS

The Lübeck Transformation System provides some features that are superior to that of other transformation systems. LTS can deal with higher-order algebraic specifications. Thus, it also supports advanced concepts of functional programming. Yet, the specification language allowing arbitrary equations is more expressive than pure functional programs. The chosen compromise between algebraic specifications and functional programming concepts offers a coherent framework for both property oriented specifications and high level algorithms. LTS combines the semantic analysis of higher-order theories with a transformation engine allowing the assistance of design decisions. This combination leads to a better integration of computer inferred information and user guidance. The distinction between specification transformations and fine tuning steps clearly separates the concerns in a hierarchical way. The transformation of entire specifications affecting several axioms and operations renders wide-spanning transformation steps possible.

In the next chapter we will describe in more detail how the system supports the development of software systems.

Chapter 11

Supporting Software Development by LTS

In this chapter we will illustrate the mechanical support for software development provided by LTS in more detail. We first explicate the system states of LTS, i.e. the fine tuning mode and the specification mode. We proceed with an overview of the analysis process. Here, we explain how the results of the analysis algorithms can guide and assist the user in various situations of the development. Then we survey how specifications can be refined using commands of LTS. This comprises fine tuning transformations as well as transformations in the specification mode, fusion steps and data structure refinements. The pre-integrated strategies are introduced in the following section. Finally, we will sketch the code generation for algorithmic specifications. In Appendix C we provide a user manual for LTS.

11.1 System states

The state of the transformation system consists of the development graph containing all loaded specifications, one active specification and a stack of transformation nodes. If there is no active specification the system is in the state 'ready'. A transformation process can be started by activating one named specification of the development graph. A fine tuning process can then be initiated focusing further fine tuning commands on one equation. The equation is set on top of the stack of transformation nodes. Each transformation node contains an equation along with applicable induction hypotheses as introduced in 6.2.1. The stack of transformation nodes encapsulates the state of the fine tuning mode. At the end of a fine tuning process the original equation is replaced in the active specification by the newly emerged equations on the stack of transformation nodes.

The Lübeck Transformation System supports two distinct working modes. The *specification mode* provides elementary and complex refinement steps affecting the entire specification. The refinement steps comprise elementary steps (see Section 6.1) and complex

steps (see Chapters 7 and 8). The *fine tuning mode* allows the transformation of single
equations using various logic and algebraic rules (see Section 6.2). The different modes
can be reached by invoking special commands.

The entire fine tuning process can be seen as one refinement step in the specification
mode. In fact, complex transformation steps of the specification mode like data structure
refinements or transformation strategies use automatically performed sequences of fine
tuning steps. In contrast to (semi-)automated steps, the fine tuning process entirely relies
on user interaction.

11.2   Guidance and assistance by analysis algorithms

The Lübeck Transformation System assists the user by checking various properties of the
specification to be transformed. The analysis of a specification might reveal its inconsistency or discover an under specification. As a major benefit, the analysis can detect useful
properties that guide the user in selecting the next transformation step. The properties
refer to the different constituents of specifications, viz. single equations, single operations
or entire sub-specifications.

We describe how the results of the analysis process can be used to support the application
of refinement steps and the discovery of inconsistencies. Finally, we consider user guidance
during the fine tuning steps exploiting the results of analysis algorithms.

11.2.1   Analysis process

The analysis process consists of several algorithms that implement sufficient syntactic
criteria for desirable or critical semantic properties of specifications or specification constituents. Most of the properties are defined in Subsections 5.1.2 and 5.3.1 . The analysis
process for a specification is started after loading a specification and whenever a refinement
step has been performed on the specification. In that way it is all the time guaranteed
that the actual semantic properties are available. The user can lookup the properties
by special commands writing specifications along with their semantic properties on the
screen.

11.2.2   Assistance for refinement steps

Based on the results of the analysis process, some pre-conditions for refinement steps can
be deduced automatically.

- For a fusion step for catamorphisms (see Section 7.3) it is presupposed that the inner
  function symbol of the function composition is top down recursive, i.e. it forms a
  catamorphism.

- When eliminating constructors of a constructor sort (see Subsection 8.4.4) it must be assured that the dropped constructors are constructive and complete wrt. the other constructors and all contributing axioms are terminating.

- The enrichment of a constructor system (see Subsection 8.4.3) requires that all function symbols are specified completely.

- Function symbols that are specified completely suggest a case analysis usable for inductions.

- For eliminating hidden function symbols (see Subsection 6.1.1) we must assure that the dropped function symbol is algorithmic and does not appear in any other axiom than the contributing axioms.

11.2.3 Discovering inconsistencies

Sometimes the axioms of a specification may imply properties that are not intended to hold, or even worse that exclude models of imported specifications. Then the specification is not persistent (see Def. 3.2.9). For example, non-terminating recursive equations can imply the equivalence of *true* and *false* in all models. Such inconsistencies can be immanent in the requirements specifications from the beginning or creep into consistent specifications by refinement steps.

The detection of inconsistencies in specifications is undecidable, but there are good syntactic criteria to detect contradictory axiomatizations. If such an axiomatization is found, a closer look at the reason is recommended. In the following we will describe three kinds of hints to inconsistencies.

An unjoinable critical pair may indicate an inconsistency of the specification. Critical pairs emerge from two different possible ways of evaluating the normal form of a term wrt. to the associated rewrite system of the specification. Unjoinable critical pairs therefore suggest the manifold definition of one term which may cause a contradiction. This problem often occurs in conjunction with non-free data structures. The set of unjoinable critical pairs of a specification is displayed in LTS with the command show_cps(specname) .

Another reason for inconsistencies may occur from non-terminating equations. For example, if we enrich the specification *Nat* (see Section 4.1) by an operation $f : (nat)nat$ and by the equation

$$f(m) = succ(f(m)) \,,$$

then in all models there are elements $a \in nat^{\mathcal{M}}$ such that $a = succ^{\mathcal{M}}(a)$. Therefore this equation excludes the standard interpretation of the sort *nat* as the set of natural numbers.

The termination of the directed equations is undecidable; hence LTS uses a sufficient syntactic criterion for termination. If termination is not detected by the system, a closer look is appropriate.

Finally, we refer to equations that are not left-linear or violate the variable condition. Such equations often reveal oversights in specifying the system. Moreover, function symbols that are not specified completely may point to missing axioms in the specifications.

11.2.4   Guidance for the fine tuning mode

In the fine tuning mode the transformation process focuses on equations. In most situations we head for the derivation of constructive equations that show a certain shape on the right side. Here LTS guides the user by proposing sensible next transformation steps. After invoking the command hint LTS prints several proposals for following steps on the screen.

If the focused equation is not constructive, syntactic criteria suggest sensible generalization steps or decomposition steps that make progress towards a constructive equation still fulfilling the variable condition.

By matching algorithms it is found out whether further rewrite steps or applications of an induction hypothesis are possible. If rewriting (simplification) is not possible the system tries to find out by unification whether further case analyses are sensible to make further rewrite rules or induction hypotheses applicable. If further case analyses are not sensible the system suggests the enrichment of the specification by new axioms which enable the desired simplifications.

11.3   Performing refinement steps

We illustrate how the refinement steps introduced in Chapters 6, 7 and 8 can be performed by LTS. Moreover, we point out extensions that reduce the bureaucratic expense of refining specifications and describe how LTS mechanizes complex transformation steps.

The refinement steps are implemented by SML functions to be invoked by the user. In general the functions operate on the active specification. Functions for fine tuning steps operate on the stack of transformation nodes.

11.3.1   Fine tuning steps

When starting a fine tuning process, a transformation node is generated containing the selected equation along with its status, a set of induction hypotheses and a substitution. In the beginning the latter two are empty. The new transformation node is pushed onto the top of the initially empty stack of transformation nodes. The transformation node on top of the stack can now be refined by invoking particular commands like rewriting (application of other axioms), complete case analysis (induction), application of induction hypotheses, generalization and decomposition.

Alternatively, the transformation node on top of the stack can be postponed. Then it is moved to the bottom of the stack, and the next transformation node becomes active.

Each command may generate several new transformation nodes, specialize the current substitution, and add induction hypotheses accompanied by an induction order. Frequently used syntactic orders like the lexicographic path order or the multiset order are built in. Semantic orders can be user-defined by a measure function mapping the elements of the induction sort into the standard sort nat. The application of the induction hypothesis forms a conditional transformation; before using the induction hypothesis, the application condition must be verified.

Assume that the current transformation node has a substitution σ and an induction hypothesis $l = r$ with the syntactic order $\prec^{wf}$. The substitution reflects the history of the case analyses introduced on the current transformation node so far; the induction hypothesis was generated by a former induction step. If the induction hypothesis can be applied to a subterm t of the current transformation node with matching $l[\tau] \;\hat{=}\; t$, then LTS attempts to prove automatically the application condition $l[\tau] \prec^{wf} l[\sigma]$ of the induction hypothesis. If $\prec^{wf}$ is a semantic order with measure operation mes, and the induction variable is va, then the application condition lt(mes(τ(va)),mes(σ(va)))=true has to be proved.

After several fine tuning steps, the user can replace the start equation by the derived equations residing on the transformation stack. Checking in the derived equations, concludes the fine tuning process of the start equation.

The entire fine tuning process can be seen as one large refinement step in the specification mode. In fact, complex transformation steps of the specification mode like fusion and fold/unfold use automatically performed sequences of fine tuning steps. In contrast to (semi-)automated steps, the fine tuning process entirely relies on user interaction.

11.3.2   Fusion steps

In this section we explain, how LTS supports fusion steps. Moreover, we introduce extensions to the presented principle and explicate the handling of fusing composition chains.

Performing the fusion step with LTS   The fusion step of Prop. 7.3.7 can be applied to an axiom of the active specification. The system checks first whether the fusion pattern $h = (g \circ f)$ matches the axiom. If the function f has been detected to be a catamorphism, the active specification is enriched according to Prop. 7.3.7. The original axiom is removed since the equations of E_h substitute it. The new equations of E_h and E_{cop} reside in tasks, because they will be transformed in most cases after a fusion step in order to derive algorithmic combine operations. The new combine operations can be transformed into an algorithmic version and the occurrences of the combine operations in the new axiomatization of h can be unfolded. As a result the definition of the new catamorphism is independent of the new combine operations.

Extensions   In Subsection 7.3.1 we have described the detection of catamorphisms and homomorphisms and the fusion theorem for unary function symbols only. In practice, many catamorphisms arise which can be built by fixing one variable of multiary functions to a constant. The member function for collections, for example, has two arguments:

```
contains1 :   contains(m,clear)   =  false,
contains2 :   contains(m,newColl(n))   =   eqEl(m,n),
contains3 :   contains(m,maddAll(L,K))  = or(contains(m,L),contains(m,K))
```

The operation `contains` does not form a catamorphism in the sense of Prop. 7.3.6. However, the functions `@contains mc` for a fixed constant `mc` embody catamorphisms as defined in 7.2.1. LTS detects and applies the fusion theorem with these generalized catamorphisms as well. Similarly, an n-ary catamorphism can be built by the fusion step if an n-ary operation is defined by the composition of another operation and a catamorphism. Here the additional parameters are passed as constants through the fusion step.

Fusion of composition chains   In order to cope with chains of function compositions like

$$h = f_1 \circ f_2 \circ \cdots \circ f_n \, ,$$

LTS provides transformation steps to partition the composition into two composition chains. With $1 \leq i < j \leq n$ this introduces a new function symbol g and two equations

$$\begin{aligned} g &= f_i \circ \cdots \circ f_j \\ h &= f_1 \circ \cdots \circ f_{i-1} \circ g \circ f_{j+1} \circ \cdots \circ f_n \end{aligned}$$

replacing the original axiom. Multiple partitions produce a set of $(n-1)$ equations each of which comprises only one function composition. Such axioms can then be handled by the fusion step.

11.3.3   Data structure refinements

We describe how LTS supports the refinement of data structures as presented in Sections 8.3 and 8.4. In principle the proposed refinement steps are implemented in a straight forward way. Strategies support the completion of such transformations aiming at an algorithmic axiomatization.

Algebraic implementation

An algebraic implementation can be performed with LTS by a sequence of interactive steps comprising the derivation of the implemented function symbols. The application conditions are not checked by the analysis algorithms; instead they are inserted as axioms into the specification constituting further proof obligations.

The procedure of an algebraic implementation in LTS comprises the following steps.

Preparation   In this step the user may enrich the signature and the axioms of the specification in order to establish all relevant signature elements and properties.

Generation of new specification The generation of an algebraic implementation can be started by several commands representing L, L^{-1} and U^{-1} simulations. The commands expect as parameters the abstract sort along with the implementation sort and a new name for the generated specification. After invoking the command for a data structure refinement, LTS acts automatically. According to the manipulation schemes of algebraic implementations (see Subsection 8.3.1) it copies and renames the actual specification, transforms the signature and inserts new axioms for application conditions and new operations. Unless there are higher-order function symbols, it is possible to simplify the generated axioms such that only one abstraction and one representation function symbol are needed. The properties of representation and abstraction functions described in Definitions 8.2.1 and 8.2.6 are used to simplify the axioms. Only the representation function symbol and the abstraction function symbol are inserted in the signature; there are no axioms defining algorithmically the behaviour which gives a maximum of freedom for the embedding. Finally, LTS inserts an edge into the development graph to record the refinement relation between the old an the new specification. This information can be used to exchange the old specification imported in another specification by a refined specification.

Precision of embedding The user can now insert an algorithmic definition of the representation and the abstraction function. This will fix the embedding uniquely, and the system is prepared for the derivation of the new operations.

Automatic derivation of operations For the development of the implemented function symbols LTS provides a strategy for automatically deriving an algorithmic definition of the operations.

Manual completion If the strategies do not succeed, the user can manually complete the derivation.

Other data structure refinements

Other data structure refinements can be performed by simply invoking the corresponding functions.

Constructor implementation A constructor implementation according to Subsection 8.4.1 is realized by one transformation command. The constructor implementation requires three arguments, viz. the abstract sort, the implementation sort and a list of equations. The list of equations describes the constructor translation. The transformation step declares the abstract sort by the implementation sort and changes the constructor affiliation of the old constructors becoming operations. The equations of the constructor translation are parsed, type checked and inserted as axioms into the active specification. Moreover, all occurrences of constructors on the left-hand sides of constructive equations are exchanged by their implementation.

If the implementation of the old constructors are non-constructor terms, the data structure refinement may change semantic properties of the transformed equations. Additional transformations are required to achieve again constructive equations.

Refining constructor systems   The data structure refinements for introducing of a constructor system (see Subsection 8.4.2), enriching and reducing a constructor system (see Subsection 8.4.3 and 8.4.4) can also be performed by simple commands. The application conditions are checked automatically by the analysis algorithms. If these algorithms fail to prove the required syntactic criteria, LTS refuses the refinement and stops with a warning.

11.3.4   Refining the development graph

As specifications can be enriched by sorts, function symbols, and axioms, the import can be enriched by a new specification expression. This extends the development graph and forms an enrichment of the corresponding named specification. Similarly, a specification expression can be reduced by dropping parts of the import expression. Again this affects the development graph. Since the interface of the actual specification is reduced by this command, it must be assured that no specification of the development graph uses this import.

In order to use refinements that are performed along with a renaming of the specification, we can exchange an imported specification by a refinement of the development graph. This step may change relevant semantic properties. Hence additional transformations may be required by manual treatment.

11.4   Transformation strategies

The single-step commands can be combined into complex strategies using a fixed collection of strategy constructors. This idea was originally proposed in the LCF system [71]. LTS provides various pre-defined strategies that can be used in different situations. In the following we will describe the pre-defined strategies. For building user-defined strategies see Appendix C.4.5.

11.4.1   Fold/unfold strategy

As an example for a predefined strategy we implement the fold/unfold paradigm. The strategy aims at eliminating an operation from the right-hand side of an equation.

The strategy is presented in Fig. 11.1 in a syntactically sugared form. The strategy first invokes a case analysis based on the definition of the function. Each resulting transformation node is treated by repeatedly trying to apply the induction hypothesis and applying one rewrite step until there is no further possibility for rewriting. In the status field of the transformation nodes we record whether the node has already been treated and whether the transformation node succeeded.

```
step(inductf fname lpo)
whileLoop (isStatus "active")
      repeat
          ifSuc (step(applhyprl 1))
              skip
          else
              ifSuc (step(onerew))
                  skip
              else step(onerewall)
      ifCond (existsInRhs fname)
          setStatus ("fail")
          else setStatus("ready")
      postpone
endwhile
```

Figure 11.1: Fold/unfold strategy (in sugared syntax)

11.4.2 Fusion strategy

The fusion transformation consists of the fusion step which generates the new axiomatization, the derivation of an algorithmic axiomatization of the combine operations, and a simplification of the improved axiomatization. LTS provides a strategy that combines these sub tasks to a single strategy. The strategy consists of several specification transformations and fine tuning strategies. As argument the strategies expect a single axiom name or a list of the axiom names comprising the relevant function compositions.

After the fusion step a fine tuning strategy is executed that aims at deriving algorithmic combine operations.

Automatic derivation of the combine operations   In most cases the derivation of the combine operation is easy and can be achieved by several rewrite and generalization steps. In order to relieve the user of such work, LTS provides a strategy which tries to derive the combine operations automatically.

The strategy applies alternately a rewrite step and a sensible generalization step. If none of them is applicable anymore or if the derivation is finished, the strategy stops and either allows the user to finish the derivation manually or closes the derivation in case of success. A generalization step is sensible, if it eliminates a variable completely in an equation. The search for sensible generalizations is similar to the unbetasteps of [19]. Here the combine operation is derived by higher-order unification modulo one, so called, unbetastep.

Simplification   Finally, the algorithmic description can be used to simplify the new axiomatization of the synthesized functions. If the combine operations do not occur anymore in these axioms, the function symbols of the combine operation can be dropped.

11.4.3   Completion of data structure refinements

Data structures refined by algebraic implementations often lead to non-algorithmic specifications which require completing refinement steps. The generated equations are of the
form

$$abstr \circ f = f_{old} \circ abstr$$

The strategy for completing the data structure refinement tries to generate a constructive
equation for the new function symbol f. If the abstraction function symbol *abstr* is
specified completely, a case analysis is generated followed by simplification steps that
unfold the function symbol *abstr* and possibly some further simplification steps. The
strategy aims at achieving an equation of the form

$$abstr(f(t_{c,i})) = abstr(r_i)$$

where $t_{c,i}$ is the constructor term of the case analysis and r_i an arbitrary term. A decomposition step then yields the constructive equation $f(t_{c,i}) = r_i$. If the strategy fails, it
stops at that point and the user can finish the transformation manually.

11.5   Code generation

If a specification is detected to be algorithmic, it can be compiled into Standard ML code.
For each involved named specification LTS creates a file with an SML structure. For a
structured specification of the form **spec** $name[SP] = SE$; (Σ, E) the system generates an
SML structure with name *name* importing the structures that emerge from the compilation
of the imported specifications in SE. The body of the structure *name* contains a data
type for each constructor sort of Σ and a pattern defined function for each operation in Σ
based on the equations of E. According to Def. 5.1.8 each operation of Σ has constructive
equations in E contributing to a function declaration. The data structure constraints are
omitted which requires the proof that the generated implementation is behaviourally
equivalent to a model of the specification *name*. This means that generated functions
must be compatible with the data structure constraints.

The generation of the imported structures requires a recursive application of the code
generation to specifications occurring in SE. Signature morphisms are first applied to
the respective specification before code generation. Parameter specifications are handled
by vertical composition since the parameterization concept of structures in SML only
supports signatures as parameter. Parameter instantiation is resolved by union. Since
the module concept of SML does not provide horizontal composition with overlapping,
union compositions in the import are merged to one structure.

Chapter 12

Conclusion

In this chapter we review and discuss the results obtained in this thesis. In addition we outline future research in the area of mechanizing transformational programming.

12.1 Summary

This work was driven by the idea of providing a sound algebraic framework for mechanizing the transformation of specifications during the development of software systems.

As a first step towards this goal we decided to use equational algebraic specifications extended by higher-order concepts as specification language. The clear separation of syntax and semantics of algebraic specifications suits well for a mechanical treatment; the loose semantics chosen gives freedom in developing an implementation. Powerful structuring concepts make compositional specification and development techniques possible. The integration of higher-order concepts increases the expressibility of the specification language incorporating concepts of advanced functional programming. Yet, the specification language allowing arbitrary equations is more expressive than pure functional programs. The chosen compromise between algebraic specifications and functional programming concepts offers a coherent framework for both property oriented specifications and high-level algorithms.

The next step concentrated on providing a sound framework for the stepwise refinement of software systems starting with a requirements specification. The refinement of specifications is separated into two layers, viz. refining basic and structured specifications. As refinement relation we consider a generalization of the model inclusion relation which allows data structure embeddings and congruences. The proposed refinement relation preserves the behaviour of the specified function symbols and allows a stepwise refinement.

Refinement steps can be grouped into syntactic replacements achieving an equivalently axiomatized specification, restriction of possible implementations by design decisions, enrichments, and embeddings. Syntactic replacement steps and enrichments are used to prepare genuine design decisions; embeddings realize data structure refinements. The refinement of structured specifications is described using development graphs which comprise the import and parameter relations as well as the refinement relations between sub specifications. The refinement relation on structured specifications is compatible with the specification combinators of the specification language. The compositional development of software systems starts with a structured specification proceeded by a stepwise development of its components following correctness preserving refinement steps. The procedure of a compositional development can be summarized by first specifying the system in top-down strategy and then deriving an implementation in a bottom-up way.

Aiming at mechanizable transformations we introduced various syntactic manipulations realizing refinement steps on basic specifications. The basic transformation rules comprise specification enrichments and various logic and algebraic rules for the manipulation of single axioms. Although these elementary steps can be combined into more powerful steps, further wide-spanning transformations are desirable.

An important contribution of this thesis consists in the definition of wide-spanning mechanizable transformations for entire specifications, which affect several axioms and operations in one go. Two kinds of wide-spanning transformation steps are considered. The fusion transformation simplifies function compositions, where the innermost function symbol forms a catamorphism. The theory is based on algebra homomorphisms, which can be constructed by axioms showing a certain shape. The mechanization of the fusion theorem consists of two parts. First catamorphisms have to be detected by a syntactically sufficient criterion checking the shape of the involved axioms. As a second task the syntactic manipulation of a specification is defined constructing a new catamorphism by new axioms. The major benefit of the fusion transformation compared to the traditional fold/unfold procedure lies in the guidance for achieving a catamorphism as result. The fusion step can be performed in one large transformation instead of a series of small transformation steps requiring more user interaction.

The second wide-spanning transformation step concerns the refinement of data structures. Here a general theoretic framework is introduced, which also deals with higher-order sorts and function symbols. Based on this general framework we suggest several data structure refinements, viz. constructor introduction and enrichment as well as reduction of constructors, and constructor implementation. A general method of data structure refinement is given by algebraic implementations. Here, the representation and abstraction functions are inserted as function symbols into the specification and axiomatized. For all data structure refinements a syntactic manipulation rule is given and its correctness wrt. the general theoretical framework is proven. The data structure refinements constitute wide-spanning transformation steps towards an implementation by standard data structures. The abstract and comprehensible specification of abstract data types in the beginning of a development can be implemented in a stepwise way by ready-made standard data structures.

The suitability of the proposed approach and adequacy of the collection of introduced transformation steps are demonstrated by a case study. The mixture of small and wide-spanning transformations and the division of the overall development into sub developments concerning sub specifications suits well for a compact development process.

The feasibility wrt. the mechanization of the approach for developing software systems is validated by the Lübeck Transformation System. The complete collection of refinement transformations introduced in this thesis can be performed by LTS. Moreover, the system combines the transformation engine with the semantic analysis of higher-order theories in order to assist the user with his design decisions, to prove application conditions for refinements steps automatically, and to find out critical semantic properties. This combination leads to a better integration of computer-inferred information and user guidance. The transformation engine of LTS distinguishes two transformation modes: The specification mode provides refinements for entire specifications and development graphs and the fine-tuning mode focuses on single axioms for term and equation manipulations. The distinction between specification and fine tuning steps separates the concerns in a hierarchical way. A strategy language enables the formulation of user defined strategies combining several fine-tuning transformations to more powerful transformations.

A major contribution of this thesis consists of the presentation of mechanizable wide-spanning refinement steps and their implementation in a transformation system providing user-guidance and -assistance by analysis algorithms. For the fusion of function compositions a semantic foundation is laid on the basis of algebra homomorphisms. The mechanization of the detection of catamorphisms as well as the specification manipulations are introduced. The approach generalizes the fusion technique for functional programs to non-free data types and allows for specifying catamorphisms by a set of mutually recursive functions. Another class of wide-spanning transformation steps are the data structure refinements. Here, the thesis contributes to a general framework of data structure refinements comprising the extension of the theory to higher-order concepts. The suggested data structure refinements are incorporated into this framework and the syntactic manipulation schemes of such refinement steps are described. The mechanization of the proposed refinement steps is validated by LTS.

Further contributions contain the choice of the framework and the implementation of the approach by the Lübeck Transformation System. The framework forms a good compromise between expressibility of the specification language and mechanizability of the transformations steps. We provide a specification language that renders a property oriented specification of software systems possible and also allows for a high degree of tool assistance. The development process is structured in a compositional way by using a development graph. By implementing development graphs LTS supports the compositional derivation of software systems. The modular implementation of LTS can easily be extended by new transformation rules. Hence, the system provides a flexible platform for studying new transformation steps.

12.2 Experiences with the approach

Since 1998 the approach was successively elaborated and validated. Various case studies contributed to a sophisticated framework for transformational programming. So far we have carried out several case studies for derivations of higher-order functional programs, data structure refinements and stream processing functions [29] with the described approach. Most of the derivations have been performed or at least replayed with the Lübeck Transformation System.

The development of the booking optimizer described in Chapter 9 proves the feasibility of a compositional development technique as well as the usefulness of the introduced refinement steps. Modularized specification and development are essential in coping with larger specifications.

Another case study was the transformational derivation of a byte code verifier for expressions with dyadic operators compiled to a reverse polnish notation [25]. Here it becomes evident that the granularity of the refinement steps must be on the one hand fine enough to render sophisticated design decisions possible, and on the other hand coarse enough to handle sequences of fine-tuning steps to standard transformations in order to obtain an easy to survey overall development. Wide-spanning refinement steps support a better understanding of the essential design decisions.

The mechanization of the development appears to be feasible and the analysis algorithms assist the process well. The refinement of data structures allows the implementation of abstractly defined sorts by efficient standard data structures. Clearly, the degree of automatization increases if the specification shows an algorithmic shape.

A drawback of the presented approach is that the set of transformation rules is sometimes not flexible enough. Often the application of wide-spanning transformation steps requires a certain shape of a specification. In order to achieve this shape several preparatory transformation steps may be necessary. Sometimes the results of the wide-spanning transformation steps require a subsequent treatment. These preparation and completion steps complicate the overall derivation. Many preparation and completion treatments can be mechanized by LTS .

The rudimentary user interface invoking SML functions on the top level environment of Moscow ML must be improved in order to provide a system beyond the prototype status. First prototypes of graphical user interfaces show promising improvements towards the acceptance of this approach.

12.3   Future work

The approach of this thesis can be extended in several ways. For applying the approach to real world developments the specification language has to be enriched by syntactic sugar allowing infix notation and abbreviating notations. Moreover, further advanced concepts are desirable. As an example, subtyping of sorts forms an essential concept for specifying efficient data structures like, for example, search trees. In long term the specification language should evolve towards the common algebraic specification language CASL in order to be compatible with other tools. Furthermore, the integration of abstract errors [40] or partial functions is desirable when aiming at putting the approach into practice.

Extending the expressibility of the specification language requires of course additional transformation rules.

With regard to the transformation process we strive for widely applicable transformations that could replace part of the ad-hoc programming practiced nowadays by a more systematic and safer generation of an implementation. Therefore, future work in this field should provide wide-spanning transformation steps that embody the essential design decisions and abstract from preparation and completion steps. The development should comprise only few large transformation steps achieving an easy to survey overall derivation.

Concerning the transformation system LTS, future work will not only improve the prototype implementation. Rather we also continually head for improving the system environment, the user interaction, the rule basis, and the transformation engine. For a better acceptance of the system, the degree of mechanization must be increased making derivations that comprise the essential design decisions only possible. For the user interaction we experiment with different manipulation models, for example direct manipulations vs. meta programming. Moreover, a proof engine for the emerging proof obligations has to be provided by LTS. This can either be obtained by implementing the proof engine as a new module of LTS or by an interface to an existing proof system like PVS [66] or Isabelle [72]. Finally, we extend the standard prelude by ready-made specifications and possible implementations by theories for specific application areas, for example stream processing functions for distributed systems [81].

Bibliography

[1] S. Autexier, D. Hutter, H. Mantel, and A. Schairer. System description: Inka 5.0 - a logical voyager. In H. Ganzinger, editor, *Proceedings 16th International Conference on Automated Deduction, CADE-16, Trento, Italy*, volume 1632 of *LNAI*, pages 135–153. Springer, 1999.

[2] S. Autexier, D. Hutter, H. Mantel, and A. Schairer. Towards an evolutionary formal software-development using CASL. In C. Choppy, D. Bert, and P. Mosses, editors, *Recent Trends in Algebraic Development Techniques, 14th International Workshop, WADT'99, Bonas, France*, volume 1827 of *LNCS*, pages 73–78. Springer, 2000.

[3] J. Avenhaus. *Reduktionssysteme: Rechnen und Schließen in gleichungsdefinierten Strukturen*. Springer, 1995.

[4] F. Baader and T. Nipkow. *Term Rewriting and All That*. Cambridge Press, 1998.

[5] R.-J. Back and J. von Wright. *Refinement Calculus, A Systematic Introduction*. Graduate Texts in Computer Science. Springer, 1998.

[6] F.L. Bauer, R. Berghammer, M. Broy, W. Dosch, F. Geiselbrechtinger, W. Hesse, R. Gnatz, B. Krieg-Brückner, A. Laut, T. Matzner, B. Möller, F. Nickl, H. Partsch, P. Pepper, K. Samelson, M. Wirsing, and H. Wössner. *The Munich Project CIP: The Wide Spectrum Language CIP-L*, volume 183 of *LNCS*. Springer, 1985.

[7] F.L. Bauer, H. Ehler, A. Horsch, B. Möller, H. Partsch, O. Paukner, and P. Pepper. *The Munich Project CIP: The Program Transformation System CIP-S*, volume 292 of *LNCS*. Springer, 1987.

[8] F.L. Bauer, B. Möller, H. Partsch, and P. Pepper. Formal program construction by transformation – computer-aided, intuition-guided programming. *IEEE Transactions on Software Engineering*, 15:165–180, 1989.

[9] R. Behnke, R. Berghammer, and S. Magnussen. Supporting algebraic program derivation by PVS. In R. Berghammer, B. Buth, and R. Peleska, editors, *Workshop on Tools for System Development and Verification, Bremen, Juni 1996*, BISS Monographs, pages 22–40. Shaker Verlag, 1998.

[10] R. Berghammer. On the use of composition in transformational programming. In L.G.L.T. Meertens, editor, *Proceedings TC2 Working Conference on Program Specification and Transformation, April 14-17, 1986 Bad Tölz*, pages 221–242. North-Holland, 1987.

[11] M. Bidoit, R. Hennicker, and M. Wirsing. Behavioural and abstractor specifications. *Science of Computer Programming*, 25(2-3):149–186, 1995.

[12] M. Bidoit, D. Sannella, and A. Tarlecki. Toward component-oriented formal software development: an algebraic approach. In *Proc. Monterey Workshop 2002, Radical Innovations of Software and Systems Engineering in the Future*, 2002. To appear.

[13] D. Box. *Essential COM*. Addison-Wesley, 1998.

[14] M. Broy. Deductive program development: Evaluation in reverse polnish notation. In M. Broy and M. Wirsing, editors, *Methods of Programming*, volume 544 of *LNCS*, pages 79–99. Springer, 1991.

[15] M. Broy. (Inter-)action refinement: The easy way. In Manfred Broy, editor, *Program Design Calculi*, volume 118 of *NATO ASI Series F*, pages 121–158. Springer, 1993.

[16] M. Broy, B. Möller, and M. Wirsing. Algebraic implementations preserve program correctness. *Science of Computer Programming*, 7:35–53, 1986.

[17] M. Burstall and J. Darlington. A transformation system for developing recursive programs. *Journal of the ACM*, 1(24):44–67, 1977.

[18] F. Buschmann, R. Meunier, H. Rohnert, P. Sommerlad, and M. Stal. *A System of Patterns, Pattern-oriented Software Architecture*. Wiley & Sons, 1996.

[19] O. de Moor and G. Sittampalam. Generic program transformation. In S.D. Swierstra, P.R. Henriques, and J.N. Oliveira, editors, *Advanced Functional Programming '98*, volume 1608 of *LNCS*, pages 116–149. Springer, 1999.

[20] W.-P. de Roever and K. Engelhardt. *Data Refinement: Model-Oriented Proof Methods and their Comparison*. Number 47 in Cambridge Tracts in Theoretical Computer Science. Cambridge University Press, 1998.

[21] N. Derschowitz. Termination of rewriting. *Journal of Symbolic Computation*, 3:69–116, 1987.

[22] N. Derschowitz and J.-P. Jouannaud. Rewriting systems. In J. van Leeuwen, editor, *Handbook of Theoretical Computer Science*, volume B, pages 243–320. Elsevier Science Publishers, 1990.

[23] E.W. Dijkstra. Notes on structured programming. In O. Dahl, E.W. Dijkstra, and C.A.R. Hoare, editors, *Structured Programming*. Academic Press, 1971.

[24] A. Dold. Representing, verifying and applying software development steps using the PVS system. In V.S. Alagar and M. Nivat, editors, *Proceedings of the Fourth International Conference on Algebraic Methodology and Software Technology, AMAST'95, Montreal, 1995*, volume 936 of *LNCS*, pages 431–435. Springer, 1995.

[25] W. Dosch and S. Magnussen. Transformational derivation of a byte code verifier. In S.Y. Shin, editor, *Proceedings of the 15th International Conference on Computers and Their Applications (CATA '00). New Orleans, Louisiana, March 29-31, 2000*, pages 443–448. International Society For Computers and Their Applications, 2000.

[26] W. Dosch and S. Magnussen. Algebraic data structure refinement with the Lübeck Transformation System. In K. Indermark and T. Noll, editors, *Kolloquium Programmiersprachen und Grundlagen der Programmierung, Rurberg, Oktober 2001*, number AIB2001-11 in Aachener Informatik Berichte, pages 7–12. RWTH Aachen, 2001.

[27] W. Dosch and S. Magnussen. Computer aided fusion for algebraic program derivation. *Nordic Journal of Computing*, 8(3):279–297, 2001.

[28] W. Dosch and S. Magnussen. Lübeck Transformation System: A transformation system for equational higher-order algebraic specifications. In M. Cerioli and G. Reggio, editors, *Recent Trends in Algebraic Development Techniques: 15th International Workshop, WADT 2001, Joint with the CoFI WG Meeting, Genova, Italy, April 1-3, 2001. Selected Papers*, volume 2267 of *LNCS*, pages 85–108. Springer, 2002.

[29] W. Dosch and A. Stümpel. Views of a memory cell. In V.V. Kluev, C.E. D'Attellis, and N.E. Mastorakis, editors, *Advances in Automation, Multimedia and Videosystems, and Modern Computer Science*, pages 47–55. WSES Press, 2001.

[30] W. Dosch and B. Wiedemann. List homomorphisms with accumulation and indexing. In G. Michaelson, Ph. Trinder, and H.-W. Loidl, editors, *Trends in Functional Programming*, pages 134–142. Intellect, 2000.

[31] H.-D. Ebbinghaus, J. Flum, and W. Thomas. *Einführung in die mathematische Logik*. Spektrum Verlag, 1996.

[32] H. Ehrig and B. Mahr. *Fundamentals of Algebraic Specifications 1, Equations and Initial Semantics*, volume 6 of *EATCS Monographs on Theoretical Computer Science*. Springer, 1985.

[33] M. Feather. A survey and classification of some program transformation approaches and techniques. In L.G.L.T. Meertens, editor, *Proceedings TC2 Working Conference on Program Specification and Transformation*, pages 165–195. North Holland, 1987.

[34] U. Fraus. *Mechanizing Inductive Theorem Proving in Conditional Theories*. Number 334 in Informatik/Kommunikationstechnik. VDI-Verlag, 1995.

[35] U. Fraus and H. Hussmann. Term induction proofs by a generalisation of narrowing. In C. Rattray and R.G. Clark, editors, *The Unified Computation Laboratory*, pages 43–55. Clarendon Press, 1992.

[36] Z. Fülöp and H. Vogler. *Syntax-Directed Semantics, Formal Models Based on Tree Transducers*. EATCS. Springer, 1998.

[37] E. Gamma, R. Helm, R. Johnson, and J. Vlissides. *Design Patterns: Elements of Reusable Object-Oriented Software*. Addison-Wesley, 1994.

[38] G. Gentzen. Untersuchungen über das logische Schliessen. *Mathematische Zeitschrift*, 39:176–210, 405–431, 1934.

[39] A. Gill, J. Launchbury, and S.L.P. Jones. A short cut to deforestation. In *FPCA '93, Conference on Functional Programming Languages and Computer Architecture*, pages 223–232. ACM Press, 1993.

[40] J.A. Goguen. Abstract errors for abstract datatypes. In E. Neuhold, editor, *Formal Description of Programming Concepts*, pages 491–525. North-Holland, 1977.

[41] J.A. Goguen, J.W. Thatcher, E.G. Wagner, and J.B. Wright. Initial algebra semantics and continuous algebras. *Journal of the ACM*, 24(1):68–95, 1977.

[42] J.A. Goguen and W. Tracz. An implementation-oriented semantics for module composition. In G.T. Leavens and M. Sitaraman, editors, *Foundations of Component-Based Systems*, chapter 11, pages 231–263. Cambridge University Press, New York, NY, 2000.

[43] W. Guttmann, H. Partsch, W.Schulte, and T. Vullinghs. Tool support for the interactive derivation of formally correct functional programs. *Journal of Universal Computer Science*, 9(2):172–188, 2003.

[44] H. Herold. *Lex und Yacc: Lexikalische und syntaktische Analyse*. UNIX und seine Werkzeuge. Addison-Wesley, 1995.

[45] C.A.R. Hoare. An axiomatic basis for computer programming. *Communications of the ACM*, 12:576–580, 1969.

[46] C.A.R. Hoare. Proof of correctness of data representations. *Acta Informatica*, 1:271 – 281, 1972.

[47] M. Hofmann and D. Sannella. On behavioural abstraction and behavioural satisfaction in higher-order logic. *Theoretical Computer Science*, 167:3–45, 1996.

[48] G. Huet. Confluent reductions: Abstract properties and applications to term rewriting systems. *Journal of the ACM*, 4(27):797–821, 1980.

[49] G. Huet and B. Lang. Proving and applying program transformations expressed with second-order patterns. *Acta Informatica*, 11:31–55, 1978.

[50] D. Hutter. Management of change in verification systems. In *Proceedings 15th IEEE International Conference on Automated Software Engineering, ASE-2000*, pages 23–34. IEEE Computer Society, 2000.

[51] R. Juellig, Y. Srinivas, and J. Liu. SPECWARE: An advanced environment for the formal development of complex software systems. In M. Wirsing and M. Nivat, editors, *Algebraic Methodology and Software Technology*, volume 1101 of *LNCS*, pages 551–555. Springer, 1996.

[52] S. Kahrs, D. Sannella, and A. Tarlecki. The definition of Extended ML: a gentle introduction. *Theoretical Computer Science*, 173:445–484, 1997.

[53] J.W. Klop. Term rewriting systems. In T.S.E. Maibaum S. Abramsky, D.M. Gabbay, editor, *Handbook of Logics in Computer Science*, volume 2, pages 2–116. Oxford Science Publications, 1992.

[54] M. Lifantsev and L. Bachmair. An LPO-based termination ordering for higher-order terms without λ-abstraction. In J. Grundy and M. Newey, editors, *11th International Conference, TPHOLs'98, Canberra, Australia, 1998*, volume 1479 of *LNCS*, pages 277–293. Springer, 1998.

[55] J. Loeckx, H.-D. Ehrich, and M. Wolf. Algebraic specification of abstract data types. In S. Abramsky, D.M. Gabbay, and T.S.E. Maibaum, editors, *Handbook of Logic in Computer Science*, volume 5, pages 217–316. Oxford Science Publications, 2000.

[56] C. Lüth, H. Tej, Kolyang, and B. Krieg-Brückner. TAS and IsaWin: Tools for transformational program development and theorem proving. In J.-P. Finance, editor, *Fundamental Approaches to Software Engineering FASE'99. Joint European Conferences on Theory and Practice of Software ETAPS'99*, volume 1577 of *LNCS*, pages 239– 243. Springer, 1999.

[57] C. Lüth and B. Wolff. TAS — a generic window inference system. In J. Harrison and M. Aagaard, editors, *Theorem Proving in Higher Order Logics: 13th International Conference, TPHOLs 2000*, number 1869 in LNCS, pages 405–422. Springer Verlag, 2000.

[58] S. Magnussen. Programmentwicklung im Rahmen algebraischer Spezifikationen: Grundlagen, Fallstudien und Rechnerunterstützung. Master's thesis, Christian-Albrechts-Universität Kiel, 1996.

[59] Z. Manna and R. Waldinger. A deductive approach to program synthesis. *ACM TOPLAS*, 2(1):90–121, 1980.

[60] E. Meijer, M. Fokkinga, and R. Paterson. Functional programming with bananas, lenses, envelopes and barbed wire. In J. Hughes, editor, *Functional Programming Languages and Computer Architecture (FPCA'91)*, volume 523 of *LNCS*. Springer, 1991.

[61] K. Meinke. Universal algebra in higher types. *Theoretical Computer Science*, 100:385–417, 1992.

[62] K. Meinke and J.V. Tucker. Universal algebra. In S. Abramsky, D.M. Gabbay, and T.S.E. Maibaum, editors, *Handbook of Logic in Computer Science*, volume 1, pages 189–411. Oxford Science Publications, 1992.

[63] R. Milner, M. Tofte, R. Harper, and D. MacQueen. *The Definition of Standard ML (Revised)*. MIT Press, 1997.

[64] P.D. Mosses. CASL: a guided tour of its design. In J.L. Fiadeiro, editor, *Recent Trends in Algebraic Development Techniques. 13th International Workshop, WADT'98 Lisbon, Portugal, 1998*, volume 1589 of *LNCS*, pages 216–240. Springer, 1999.

[65] Y. Onoue, Z. Hu, H. Iwasaki, and M. Takeichi. A calculational fusion system HYLO. In R.S. Bird and L. Meertens, editors, *IFIP TC2 Working Conference on Algorithmic Languages and Calculi*, pages 76–106. Chapman and Hall, 1997.

[66] S. Owre, N. Shankar, and J.M. Rushby. User guide for the PVS specification and verification system. Technical report, Computer Science Laboratory, SRI International, Menlo Park, CA, 1993.

[67] S. Owre, N. Shankar, J.M. Rushby, and D.W.J. Stringer-Calvert. PVS system guide. Technical report, Computer Science Laboratory, SRI International, Menlo Park, CA, 1999.

[68] R. Paige. Transformational programming – applications to algorithms and systems. In *Proceedings of the 10th ACM POPL Symposium, Austin, Texas*, pages 73–87, 1983.

[69] H. Partsch. *Specification and Transformation of Programs – A Formal Approach to Software Development*. Springer, 1990.

[70] H. Partsch, W. Schulte, and T. Vullinghs. System support for the interactive transformation of functional programs. In *Proceedings of the International Workshop on Software Transformation Systems at ICSE*, pages 1–7. STS'99 Organizing Committee, 1999.

[71] L.C. Paulson. *Logic and Computation: Interactive Proof with Cambridge LCF*. Cambridge University Press, 1990.

[72] L.C. Paulson. *Isabelle: A Generic Theorem Prover*, volume 828 of *LNCS*. Springer, 1994.

[73] L.C. Paulson. *ML for the Working Programmer*. Cambridge University Press, 1996.

[74] A. Pettorossi and M. Proietti. Rules and strategies for transforming functional and logic programs. *ACM Computing Surveys*, 28(2):360–414, 1996.

[75] E.T. Ray. *Learning XML*. O'Reilly, 2001.

[76] W. Reif, G. Schellhorn, and K. Stenzel. Interactive correctness proofs for software modules using KIV. In *COMPASS'95 – Tenth Annual Conference on Computer Assurance*. IEEE press, 1995.

[77] D. Sannella and A. Tarlecki. Towards formal development of programs from algebraic specifications: Implementations revisited. *Acta Informatica*, 25:233–281, 1988.

[78] D.R. Smith. KIDS – a semi-automatic program development system. *IEEE Transactions on Software Engineering Special Issue on Formal Methods in Software Engineering*, 16(9):279–308, september 1990.

[79] D.R. Smith. Automating the design of algorithms. In B. Möller, editor, *Formal Program Development (IFIP TC2/WG 2.1)*, volume 755 of *LNCS*, pages 324–354. Springer, 1993.

[80] I. Sommerville. *Software Engineering*. Addison-Wesley, 6th edition, 2001.

[81] A. Stümpel. *Stream Based Design of Distributed Systems through Refinement*. PhD thesis, Faculty of Technology and Sciences, University of Lübeck, 2003. to appear.

[82] C. Szyperski. *Component Software – Beyond Object-Oriented Programming*. Addison-Wesley, 1999.

[83] D. van Dalen. *Logic and Structure*. Springer, 1997.

[84] P. Wadler. Deforestation: Transforming programs to eliminate trees. *Theoretical Computer Science*, 73(2):231–248, 1990.

[85] M. Wirsing. Algebraic specification. In J. van Leeuwen, editor, *Handbook of Theoretical Computer Science*, volume B, pages 675–788. Elsevier Science Publishers, 1990.

[86] M. Wirsing, H. Partsch, P. Pepper, W. Dosch, and M. Broy. On hierarchies of abstract data types. *Acta Informatica*, 20:1–33, 1983.

Appendix A

Operations and Notations for Indexed Families

In order to simplify the way how to deal with indexed families, we introduce operations and notations on families.

Let I, J be non-empty disjoint index sets and let G, H be I-indexed families of sets and D a J-indexed family of sets. Then let for all $i \in I$ and $k \in I \cup J$:

- $(G \times H)_i = G_i \times H_i$ (tuple family)

- $(G \cup H)_i = G_i \cup H_i$ (family union)

- $(G \cap H)_i = G_i \cap H_i$ (family intersection)

- $(G \setminus H)_i = G_i \setminus H_i$ (family difference)

- $(\emptyset)_i = \emptyset$ (empty family)

- $(\mathcal{P}(G))_i = \mathcal{P}(G_i)$ (power family)

- $G = H \Leftrightarrow G_i = H_i$ for all $i \in I$ (equality of families)

- $G \subseteq H \Leftrightarrow G_i \subseteq H_i$ for all $i \in I$ (subfamily)

- $G \supseteq H \Leftrightarrow G_i \supseteq H_i$ for all $i \in I$ (superfamily)

- $u \in G \Leftrightarrow$ there is $i \in I$ such that $u \in G_i$ (family membership)

- $(G \overset{+}{\cup} D)_k = \begin{cases} G_k & \text{if } k \in I \\ D_k & \text{if } k \in J \end{cases}$ (family extension)

Moreover, we denote functions on families as follows:

- $f : G \to P$ for a set P denotes an I-indexed family of functions f_i with $f_i : G_i \to P$.

- $f : P \to G$ for a set P denotes an I-indexed family of functions f_i with $f_i : P \to G_i$.

- $f : G \to H$ denotes an I-indexed family of functions f_i with $f_i : G_i \to H_i$.

- $f : G \to (H_i)_{i \in I}$ denotes an I-indexed family of functions f_i with $f_j : G_j \to (H_i)_{i \in I}$ mapping elements of $u \in G_j$ to families G.

Finally, we denote an I-indexed family of homogeneous relations $R_i \subseteq G_i \times G_i$ on an I indexed family G by $R \subseteq G \times G$.

Appendix B

Basic Refinement Calculus

We summarize the basic rules of the refinement calculus given in Chapter 6.

Specification enrichments and reductions

Signature enrichment

Let (Σ_1, E) be an algebraic specifications and the signature $\Sigma_1 = (S_1, F_1, C_1)$ be a sub-signature of $\Sigma_2 = (S_2, F_2, C_2)$ such that $C_{1,sc} = C_{2,sc}$ and $C_{1,(s \to sc)} = C_{2,(s \to sc)}$ for all $sc \in S_1$. Then

$$(\Sigma_1, E) \twoheadrightarrow (\Sigma_2, E).$$

Dropping hidden operations

Let $P = (\Sigma, E, \Sigma_v)$ be an algebraic specification with hiding and $f \in F \backslash F_v$ an algorithmic and terminating operation in P. If f does not occur in any equation $e \in E \backslash E_f$, then

$$(\Sigma, E, \Sigma_v) \twoheadrightarrow (\Sigma \backslash \{f\}, E \backslash E_f, \Sigma_v)$$

Enrichment of axioms

Let (Σ, E) be an algebraic specification and E_{new} a set of closed (Σ, X)-formulae. Then

$$(\Sigma, E) \twoheadrightarrow (\Sigma, E \cup E_{new}).$$

173

Reduction of axioms

Let (Σ, E) be an algebraic specification. Assume that $\vdash$ is a correct deduction calculus for proving formulae in $CGEN(\Sigma, E)$ and let E_{th} be a set of closed (Σ, X)-formulae such that $E \vdash \varphi$ for all $\varphi \in E_{th}$. Then

$$(\Sigma, E \cup E_{th}) \twoheadrightarrow (\Sigma, E).$$

Manipulation of terms and equations

Simplification

$$\frac{(\Gamma \; t_l = t_g(t_f(t)))}{(\Gamma \; t_l = (t_g \circ t_f)(t))} \qquad \frac{(\Gamma \; t_l = @ft_1 \ldots t_n)}{(\Gamma \; t_l = f(t_1, \ldots, t_n))} \qquad \frac{(\Gamma \; t_l = t_i)}{(\Gamma \; t_l = \#i(t_1, \ldots, t_n))}$$

$$\frac{(\Gamma \; t_l = t_t)}{(\Gamma \; t_l = \text{if } true \text{ then } t_t \text{ else } t_e)} \qquad \frac{(\Gamma \; t_l = t_e)}{(\Gamma \; t_l = \text{if } false \text{ then } t_t \text{ else } t_e)}$$

Iflifting

$$\frac{(\Gamma \; t_l = \text{if } t_b \text{ then } t_f(t_t) \text{ else } t_f(t_e))}{(\Gamma \; t_l = t_f(\text{if } t_b \text{ then } t_t \text{ else } t_e))}$$

$$\frac{(\Gamma \; t_l = \text{if } t_b \text{ then } (t_1, \ldots, t_t, \ldots, t_n) \text{ else } (t_1, \ldots, t_e, \ldots, t_n))}{(\Gamma \; t_l = (t_1, \ldots, \text{if } t_b \text{ then } t_t \text{ else } t_e, \ldots, t_n))}$$

Rewriting

$$\frac{(\Gamma \; t_1 = t_2[r\sigma]_p)}{(\Gamma \; t_1 = t_2)} \quad l = r \in E, \; t_2|_p \,\hat{=}\, l\sigma$$

Application of induction hypothesis

$$\frac{(\Gamma, (l = r, \tau, \prec) \; t_1 = t_2[r\sigma]_p)}{(\Gamma, (l = r, \tau, \prec) \; t_1 = t_2)} \quad t_2|_p \,\hat{=}\, l\sigma, \; l\sigma \prec l\tau$$

$$\frac{(\Gamma, (l = r, \tau, m) \; t_1 = t_2[r\sigma]_p)}{(\Gamma, (l = r, \tau, m) \; t_1 = t_2)} \quad t_2|_p = l\sigma, \; lt(m(l\sigma), m(l\tau)) = true$$

Induction

Let (Σ, X) be an algebraic specification. Assume that $sc \in SC$ is a constructor sort and $x \in Var_{sc}(t_1)$ a constructor variable occurring in the term t_1. Let $\{t_{c,1}, \ldots, t_{c,n}\} \subseteq T_{sc}^{Cons}(\Sigma, X')$ be a complete case analysis on the constructor sort sc, where X' is a family of fresh variables.

term induction:

$$\frac{\begin{array}{c}(\Gamma\tau_1, (t_1 = t_2, \tau_1, \prec) \ \ (t_1\tau_1 = t_2\tau_1)) \\ \vdots \\ (\Gamma\tau_n, (t_1 = t_2, \tau_n, \prec) \ \ (t_1\tau_n = t_2\tau_n))\end{array}}{(\Gamma \ \ t_1 = t_2)} \quad x \in Var_{sc}, \ \tau_i = \{x \mapsto t_{c,i}\} \ \ (1 \leq i \leq n)$$

measure induction:

$$\frac{\begin{array}{c}(\Gamma\tau_1, (t_1 = t_2; \tau_1, m) \ \ (t_1\tau_1 = t_2\tau_1)) \\ \vdots \\ (\Gamma\tau_n, (t_1 = t_2; \tau_n, m) \ \ (t_1\tau_n = t_2\tau_n))\end{array}}{(\Gamma \ \ t_1 = t_2)} \quad x \in Var_{sc}, \ \tau_i = \{x \mapsto t_{c,i}\} \ \ (1 \leq i \leq n)$$

Tuple unfold

$$\frac{(\Gamma\tau \ \ t_1\tau = t_2\tau)}{(\Gamma \ \ t_1 = t_2)} \quad \tau = \{x \mapsto (x_1, \ldots, x_n)\}$$

Decomposition

$$\frac{(\Gamma \ \ t_1 = t_2)}{(\Gamma \ \ f(t_1) = f(t_2))}$$

$$\frac{(\Gamma \ \ t_1 = t_1'), \ldots, (\Gamma \ \ t_n = t_n')}{(\Gamma \ \ (t_1, \ldots, t_n) = (t_1', \ldots, t_n'))}$$

Extensionality

$$\frac{(\Gamma \ \ t_f(x) = t_g(x))}{(\Gamma \ \ t_f = t_g)}$$

Generalization

Let $t_1, t_2, t_z \in T(\Sigma, X)$, $P_1 = \{p_{11}, \ldots, p_{1m}\} \subseteq Pos(t_1)$ the set of positions p of t_1 such that $t_1|_p \cong t_z$ and $P_2 = \{p_{21}, \ldots, p_{2n}\} \subseteq Pos(t_2)$ the set of positions p of t_2 such that $t_2|_p \cong t_z$. Clearly, the different occurrences of the term t_z do not overlap in the terms t_1 and t_2. Then for a fresh variable $x \in X_s$ we have:

$$\frac{(\Gamma \vdash t_1[x]_{p_{11}} \ldots [x]_{p_{1m}} = t_2[x]_{p_{21}} \ldots [x]_{p_{2n}})}{(\Gamma \vdash t_1 = t_2)}$$

Appendix C

LTS User Manual

This manual will refer to specifications and notions of the thesis, in order to show how system development can be supported by LTS. We will not go into the installation of the system but show how the system can be applied to the described case study of chapter 9. The manual describes the LTS version 1.0.

The Lübeck Transformation System (LTS) is a tool for the interactive development of software systems. Algebraic specifications extended by higher-order concepts can be loaded and transformed by various transformation commands. The system analyses each specification after loading and transforming in order to provide critical or desirable semantic properties.

C.1   Specification language

We illustrate the specification language of LTS by revisiting the case study presented in Chapter 9. The specification language is based on named specifications as introduced in Section 3.2. The notation is similar to the syntax used in Chapter 4. A grammar is presented in Appendix C.5. In the following we will explicate loading and displaying of specifications with LTS.

The specifications *Collection* and *MapColl* are loaded by invoking the function `loadspec`.

```
- loadspec("Collection.lts");
> val it = () : unit
- loadspec("MapColl.lts");
> val it = () : unit
```

With the command `specOutput` the loaded specification can be displayed on the screen. A specification can be written back to a file using the command `specOutputToFile`. This allows to save the state of the development and to proceed with it in a later session.

```
- specOutput("Collection");
```

```
spec Collection[Elem] = Nat ;
sorts
    coll = clear | newColl(elem) | addAll(coll,coll)
ops
    contains : (elem,coll)bool,
    addElem : (elem,coll)coll
vars x,y : elem,s,p,q : coll
axioms
    ass:  addAll(addAll(s,p),q) = addAll(s,addAll(p,q)),
    neutr1:  addAll(clear,p) = p,
    neutr2:  addAll(p,clear) = p,
    contains1:  contains(x,clear) = false,
    contains2:  contains(x,newColl y) = eqEl(x,y),
    contains3:  contains(x,addAll(s,p)) = or(contains(x,s),contains(x,p)),
    addElem1:  addElem(x,s) = addAll(newColl x,s)
end
```

The parameter specification `Elem` and the predefined specification `Nat` form the import part of the specification `Collection`. The remaining new part of the specification extends the import by further specification constituents. The variables used in the axioms must be declared explicitly in the `vars` section.

The specifications named in the import part must be loaded first. Hence, the order of loading specifications is crucial to guarantee a cycle-free import graph.

The specification `ProductEval` (see Subsection 9.1.2) imports the specification `MapColl` (see Subsection 4.2.3) and two renamed instantiations of the specification `Collection`.

```
- loadspec("ProductEval.lts");
> val it = () : unit
- specOutput("ProductEval");

spec ProductEval = Nat +
MPN as MapColl[Product fit elem/product,eqEl/eqProd,
               Nat fit elem2/nat,eqEl2/eqNat]
      [S1.*/SP.*,S2.*/SN.*] ;
ops
    getValOfColl : (SP.coll)nat,
    sum : (SN.coll)nat
vars s:SP.coll,t:SN.coll,u:SN.coll,n:nat,p:product
axioms
    getValOfColl1:  getValOfColl s = (sum o (@map getVal)) (s),
    sum1:  sum SN.clear = zero,
    sum2:  sum (SN.newColl(n)) = n,
    sum3:  sum (SN.addAll(t,u)) = add(sum t,sum u)
end
```

For the imported specification `MapColl` an alias is provided renaming all constituents of the signature by prefixing them with `MPN`. Moreover, the aliases `S1` and `S2` declared in the specification `MapColl` distinguishing the two different instantiations of `Collection` are renamed by `SP` and `SN` respectively. The alias `MPN` for the specification `MapColl` is not necessary. An alias can generally be omitted if the respective constituents of the new signature part are unique in the context of the specification. The function symbol `map`, for example, does only exist in the imported specification `MapColl` and is therefore unique in `ProductEval`. However, the symbol `coll` is imported via `MapColl` twice, once for collections of products and another time for collections of natural numbers. Therefore `coll` is not unique; it has to be qualified either by `SP` or by `SN`. Furthermore, the following syntactic conventions are used:

- Hiding is not allowed in the import expression of a specification, but signature elements of the new signature part can be hidden.

- The operators union + and extension ; associate to the left and ; has a higher precedence than +.

- The symbol o is reserved for function composition and cannot be used as sort symbol, function symbol or variable.

- For derived sorts an abbreviation can be defined in the sorts section.

- Declarations of function symbols are restricted to the form $f : (s_1, \ldots, s_n)s$, with $n \geq 1$ or $f : s$. The used sorts may also contain abbreviations for derived sorts. This syntax agrees with the syntax of the specification language CASL [64].

- In the input files comments begin with /* and end with */.

A loaded specification follows the life cycle of a specification described in Section 10.2.

C.2 How to navigate through system states

A sequence of refinement steps on a named specification of the development graph is initiated by the command `start_refinement(na)` where `na` is the name of the specification. The user of LTS refines a specification by invoking commands that manipulate the specification in an interactive way. Only the new part of the specification can be refined; imported specifications remain untouched. After a sequence of refinement steps the development graph can be updated replacing the original specification by the refined specification. Alternatively, the original specification resides in the development graph, and the refined specification is added along with an enrichment of the refinement graph (see Def. 5.3.10).

After starting a refinement with the command `start_refinement`, the system enters the specification mode. The fine tuning process on an axiom with name `ax` of the active specification can be initiated by the command `start_task(ax)`.

A	=	algorithmic		OLF	=	non-overlapping
C	=	constructive		CMPL	=	complete
L	=	left-linear		CATA	=	catamorphism
T	=	terminating		CNSTR	=	data type constraint

Figure C.1: Properties analysed by LTS

In the beginning of the fine tuning process, a transformation node is generated containing the selected equation. The new transformation node is pushed onto the top of the initially empty stack of transformation nodes. The transformation node on top of the stack can now be refined by invoking particular commands. Each command replaces the transformation node on top of the stack by a list of new transformation nodes. Alternatively, the transformation node on top of the stack can be postponed. Then it is moved to the bottom of the stack, and the next transformation node, if existing, becomes active.

After several refinement steps, the user can replace the start equation by the derived equations residing on the transformation stack. Checking in the derived equations into the active specification concludes the fine tuning process of the start equation.

LTS provides an undo command undo_ref() canceling the last transformation step. Any equation manipulations and specification transformations invoked for manipulating the active specification can be annulled by this function.

C.3 Analysing specifications

LTS checks various properties of a specification. The results are relevant for further development steps or code generation. Fig. C.1 lists the properties to be analysed along with their abbreviations. In the sequel, we shortly introduce the relevant notions.

For an equation we analyse whether its structure meets the patterns used in SML function definitions. The properties of a function symbol are derived from the properties of all contributing axioms of this function symbol. Finally, the properties of a specification are synthesized from the properties of the equations and the function symbols. The result of the analysis can be displayed using the command print_spec.

Properties of single equations

LTS checks every single equation whether it is constructive (see Def. 5.1.2). In this case, the equation contributes to the definition of the outermost operation on the left-hand side. The equation is then directed and associated with the definition of that function symbol.

If an equation proves to be constructive, LTS additionally checks whether the equation is left-linear (see Def. 5.1.4). Next, the system examines the terms on the left-hand and the right-hand sides whether they are both constructor terms of a constructor sort. If this applies, the equation is marked to constrain the constructor sort. Such equations are called data type constraints (see Def. 5.3.6). Finally, LTS tests whether the equation is terminating according to Def. 5.3.5. As reduction order LTS uses the lexicographic path order extended to higher-order terms without λ-abstraction [54].

Revisiting the specification ProductEval (see Section C.1), we identify the constructor sort coll constrained by the associativity of concatenation:

```
ass:  addAll(s,addAll(p,q)) = addAll(addAll(s,p),q)
<C L T CNSTR>
```

LTS also detects the termination of this equation. The equation

```
sum3:  sum(SN.addAll(t,u)) = add(sum t,sum u)
<C L T RF(sum)>
```

of specification ProductEval is constructive, left-linear and terminating. The equation contributes to the definition of sum indicated by the cross reference RF.

In fine tuning mode the user is endowed with additional checks, see Subsection 11.2.4, which can be invoked manually. For example, terms and equations can be tested whether they are in normal form or algorithmic. These properties guide the selection of further refinement steps.

Properties of function symbols

The properties of a function symbol are partly synthesized from the properties of the equations describing the operation. An operation is specified algorithmically if all contributing equations are left-linear and the set of all these equations is non-overlapping. Then this set of equations can be compiled into a function declaration in SML .

After testing whether a function symbol is specified completely (see Subsection 5.3.2), LTS checks the catamorphism property using the criterion of Def. 7.3.5.

Again we illustrate the analysis using the specification ProductEval from Section C.1. The three constructive equations

```
sum1:  sum (SN.clear)      = zero,
sum2:  sum (SN.newColl(n)) = n,
sum3:  sum (SN.addAll(t,u)) = add(sum t,sum u)
```

contribute to the definition of the operation sum. This function symbol is algorithmic, since the equations are left-linear and non-overlapping. The set {sum1,sum2,sum3} of equations covers all constructor patterns, therefore the operation sum is specified completely. The definition of the operation sum follows the inductive structure of the data type coll and forms a catamorphism.

```
sum : (coll)nat > PROP: A OLF C CATA CMPL
```

The catamorphism property is a prerequisite for the fusion step, compare Subsection 7.3.7.

Properties of specifications

The analysis of an entire specification is based on the properties of its function symbols and equations.

If all equations are terminating, the specification is terminating as well. The non-constraint equations are then checked whether they are constructive and non-overlapping. If this is the case and all function symbols are algorithmic, the specification is algorithmic as well. If the specification is terminating, LTS additionally tests whether the set of directed equations forms a confluent rewrite system. For this purpose LTS generates the set of critical pairs of terms and tries to join them by the rewrite system given by the axioms of the specification. If all critical pairs are joinable, the rewrite system is confluent [4].

The accompanying specification ProductEval is algorithmic, since all equations are constructive and non-overlapping, and all operations are algorithmic. LTS does not detect any critical pair, all equations are terminating – henceforth the associated rewrite system of the specification ProductEval is confluent. After loading the specification ProductEval, the properties analysed by LTS are shown by displaying the specification with the command print_spec:

```
spec ProductEval = Nat +
    ...
end
PROPERTIES:
      ALGORITHMIC
      CONFLUENT
      NONOVERLAPPING
      CONSTRUCTIVE
      TERMINATING
```

The specification ProductEval is algorithmic and can be translated into STANDARD ML using the command genCode.

C.4 Refining specifications with LTS

The transformation of a specification effects a refinement of its behavioural semantics. In this section, we survey the transformation commands and strategies offered by the Lübeck Transformation System. Each transformation command ensures a sound refinement step for the entire specification. We distinguish between the transformation of specifications and the manipulation of single equations.

`onerew`	Apply one rewrite step with all terminating equations.
`onerewall`	Apply one rewrite step with all equations.
`rew(rl)`	Apply one left-to-right rewrite step with equations `rl`.
`rewrl(rl)`	Apply one right-to-left-rewrite step with equations `rl`.
`unfold(f)`	Unfold the constructive function symbol `f`.
`fold(f)`	Fold the constructive function symbol `f`.
`nfl(rl)`	Compute normal form with equations `rl`.
`nf`	Compute normal form with all terminating equations.

Figure C.2: Fine tuning commands for rewriting

C.4.1   Fine tuning steps

In this subsection the commands for fine tuning transformations are summarized and the handling of the induction principle is described.

A sequence of fine tuning transformations is started by the command `start_task` supplying the name of an axiom of the active specification as parameter. During fine tuning several transformation nodes may emerge residing on the transformation stack. To proceed with the next node the command `dopostpone` moves the transformation node on top of the transformation stack to the bottom. After performing several fine tuning steps the resulting equations can be written back by the command `checkin_task` replacing the original axiom.

In the following we focus on the different commands for fine tuning steps. An overview of the commands is given in Fig. C.2, C.3 and C.4. The illustrated functions manipulate transformation nodes and return lists of transformation nodes. The functions are used as atoms for the construction of strategies, see Subsection C.4.5. There are standard strategies executing one command which can be invoked by prefixing the function names by `do`. Except for induction orders all arguments of the functions are of type string or list of strings.

An example session containing the usage of several fine tuning steps is traced in Appendix D.2.

Rewriting   The equations of a specification form a term rewriting system [21, 53] if directed from left to right. Several term manipulations can be done using the term rewriting system associated with a specification. The standard fine tuning steps for rewriting are summarized in Fig. C.2. Variants provide a location-oriented search of applicable redexes in the equation. As a result of the analysis process, axioms can be grouped contributing to the same function symbol. Thus, for constructive function symbols fold and unfold steps are provided applying rewrite steps with the concerning axioms.

Induction principle   The induction principle in LTS is based on *term induction* [35] as described in Subsection 6.2.1. We illustrate the corresponding refinement functions in Fig. C.3.

An induction consists of a case analysis and the generation of an induction hypothesis. Each induction requires a syntactic order or a measure function for measure induction. As syntactic orders LTS provides the lexicographic path order `lpo`, the reverse lexicographic path order `lpor` and the multiset-order `multset`. The induction process can be started with three commands. The command `induct` generates the case analysis based on the construction principle of the sort of the supplied variable; for each constructor one case is generated. The command `inductf` introduces a structural induction by a case analysis on the argument of the supplied function symbol — provided that this operation is specified completely. Both commands must be supplied with a syntactic induction order. The third command `minduct` resembles the command `induct`, but introduces a measure function symbol as a string which is parsed and type checked.

Inductions in LTS are complete case analyses which also cause the generation of induction hypotheses and the specialization of the substitutions for the resulting transformation nodes.

The commands `applhyp` resp. `applhyprl` apply the induction hypothesis in left-to-right resp. right-to-left direction. Variants provide a location-oriented search of applicable redexes in the equation. Assume the induction hypothesis matches a subterm. In case of a syntactic order, the system automatically compares the two terms. In case of a semantical order, the system applies the induction hypothesis in any case, but generates a proof obligation.

Miscellaneous steps   Miscellaneous fine tuning commands are illustrated in Fig. C.4. Further rewrite steps comprise, among others, the simplification of terms, the treatment of higher-order terms, the manipulation of conditions and of conditional terms. Further manipulations of equations are decomposition and generalization steps.

C.4.2   Specification enrichments and reductions

A specification can be enriched by adding new function symbols, sorts, and equations. The transformation commands `add_function`, `add_sort`, and `add_axiom` expect a string as argument which is parsed into the declaration of a function symbol, a sort or an axiom,

`induct(va,or)`	Introduce case analysis on constructor variable `va` with induction order `or`.
`inductf(f,or)`	Introduce case analysis based on the completely defined operation `f` with induction order `or`.
`minduct(va,mes)`	Introduce case analysis on constructor variable `va` with measure function `mes`.
`applhyp(i)`	Apply hypothesis number `i` in left-to-right direction.
`applhyprl(i)`	Apply hypothesis number `i` in right-to-left direction.

Figure C.3: Fine tuning commands for induction

`decomp`	Apply a congruence step.
	Assumption: Outermost function symbols are equal.
`caseb(b)`	Introduce a conditional term with condition `b`.
`iflift`	Lift conditional into an application.
`ifsimp`	Simplify term by several simplification patterns.
`gener(t)`	Generalize term `t` by a fresh variable.
`gener_heur`	Find a generalizable term and generalize it.
`catafusion`	Apply the fusion theorem for catamorphisms.
`swap`	Swap the two sides of an equation.
`applext`	Apply the extensionality rule to higher-order equation.
`comp2appl`	Transform a function composition into an application.

Figure C.4: Miscellaneous fine tuning commands

respectively. The required syntax follows the syntax of the specification language. The parsed argument is context checked and then inserted into the specification.

Axioms can also be deleted using the command `drop_axiom` which causes a proof obligation for the deleted axiom. Moreover, hidden algorithmic function symbols that are not used in other axioms than the contributing axioms can be dropped by the command `drop_function` which also deletes the contributing axioms.

The commands for specification enrichments and reductions are summarized in Fig. C.5.

As specifications can be enriched by sorts, function symbols, and axioms, the import can be enriched by a new specification expression. In LTS this can be done by the command `add_import`. The actual importing expression is combined by union with the added import. Similarly, a part of the import expression can be dropped using the command `drop_import`. However, since the interface of the actual specification is reduced by this command, it must be assured that no specification of the development graph uses this import.

In order to use refinements that are performed along with a renaming of the specification,

`add_function(fd)`	Enrich spec. with function declaration `fd`.
`add_constructor(cd)`	Enrich spec. with constructor decl. `cd`.
`add_sort(sd)`	Enrich spec. with sort declaration `sd`.
`add_variable(vd)`	Enrich spec. with variable declaration `vd`.
`add_axiom(ad)`	Enrich spec. with axiom declaration `ad`.
`drop_variable(x)`	Drop variable `x` from spec.
`drop_function(f)`	Drop function symbol `f` from spec.
`drop_axiom(ax)`	Drop axiom with name `ax`,
	generate proof obligation.

Figure C.5: Commands for specification enrichments and reductions

we can exchange an imported specification by a refinement of the development graph. This can be done with LTS by the command `exchange_import`. This step may change relevant semantic properties. Hence additional transformations may be required by manual treatment.

C.4.3   Fusion steps

The fusion step from Prop. 7.3.7 can be applied to an axiom of the active specification by first starting a fine tuning process with the corresponding axiom and invoking the command `catafusion`. The system checks first whether the axiom is of the form $h = (g \circ f)$. If the function f has been detected to be a catamorphism, the active specification is enriched according to Prop. 7.3.7. The original axiom is removed since the generated equations for the synthesized function symbol h replace it. The new equations emerged from the fusion step reside in tasks. In most cases they will be transformed after a fusion step in order to derive algorithmic combine operations. The new combine operations can be transformed into an algorithmic version and the occurrences of the combine operations in the new axiomatization of h can be unfolded. As a result the definition of the new catamorphism is independent of the new combine operations.

The fusion step can either be invoked in fine tuning mode by the command `catafusion` or by the fusion strategies presented later.

In order to cope with chains of function compositions like

$$h \;=\; f_1 \circ f_2 \circ \cdots \circ f_n \,,$$

LTS provides transformation steps to partition the composition into two composition chains by the command `dojoincomp(i,j,g)`. This introduces a new function symbol g and two equations

$$
\begin{aligned}
g &= f_i \circ \cdots \circ f_j \\
h &= f_1 \circ \cdots \circ f_{i-1} \circ g \circ f_{j+1} \circ \cdots \circ f_n
\end{aligned}
\qquad 1 \le i \le j \le n
$$

replacing the original axiom. Multiple partitions produce a set of $(n-1)$ equations each of which comprises only one function composition. Such axioms can then be handled by the fusion step.

The fusion strategy consists of several specification transformations and fine tuning strategies. The strategy can be invoked either by the command `catafuse` if a single function symbol forms a catamorphism or `homfuse` for a catamorphism with several function symbols. As argument the commands expect a single axiom name or a list of the axiom names comprising the relevant function compositions.

An example session with LTS demonstrating the fusion transformation is illustrated in Appendix D.1.

`refine_DS_L(ipl,sn)`	Refine data structure by L simulation according to `ipl`.
`refine_DS_Lm1(ipl,sn)`	Refine data structure by L^{-1} simulation according to `ipl`.
`refine_DS_Um1(ipl,sn)`	Refine data structure by U^{-1} simulation according to `ipl`.

Figure C.6: Commands for algebraic implementations

C.4.4 Data structure refinements

LTS provides functions for the data structure transformations described in Sections 8.3 and 8.4. The application conditions are either inserted as axioms into the specifications or — when using implicit data structure representations — evaluated by the analysis algorithms of LTS using sufficient syntactical criteria. User interaction then completes the refinement by inserting concrete axiomatizations of representation and abstraction functions (in case of an algebraic implementation) and deriving algorithmic axiomatizations of the involved function symbols. Here LTS provides strategies for automatically deriving algorithmic definitions. If a strategy fails, the user can manually complete the derivation introducing additional design decisions or proving suitable propositions.

Algebraic implementations LTS provides three different commands for algebraic implementations representing L, L^{-1} and U^{-1} simulations (see Fig. C.6).

The commands expect as parameters the abstract sort along with the implementation sort and a new name for the generated specification. After invoking the command LTS copies and renames the actual specification, transforms the signature and inserts new axioms for application conditions and new operations according to the manipulation schemes given in Subsection 8.3.1. Only the representation function symbols and the abstraction function symbols are inserted in the signature; there are no axioms defining algorithmically the behaviour which gives a maximum of freedom for the embedding. Finally, LTS inserts an edge into the development graph to record the refinement relation between the old an the new specification. This information can be used to exchange the old specification imported in another specification by a refined specification.

Revisiting the example refining stacks from Subsection 8.5.2 the command

```
refine_DS_Lm1("stack = (nat,array)","StackByArray");
```

generates the new specification.

Data structures refined by algebraic implementations often lead to non-algorithmic specifications which require completing refinement steps. This completion can be mechanized by the strategy `DSfoldunfold` providing an axiom name as argument.

Constructor implementation The command `implement_cons` realizes the principle of an constructor implementation from Subsection 8.4.1. The command requires three arguments, viz. the abstract sort, the implementation sort and a list of equations. The list of equations describes the constructor translation. The transformation step declares the abstract sort by the implementation sort and changes the constructor affiliation of the old constructors; they become operations. The equations of the constructor translation are parsed, type checked and inserted as axioms into the active specification. Moreover, all occurrences of constructors on the left-hand sides of constructive equations are exchanged by their implementation.

If the implementation of the old constructors are non-constructor terms, the data structure refinement may change semantic properties of the transformed equations. Additional transformations are required to achieve again constructive equations.

An example session for a data structure refinement using a constructor implementation is presented in Appendix D.2 .

Introduction of generation constraint   The command `intro_genConstraint` introduces a generation constraint for a loose sort, see Subsection 8.4.2. The command expects a loose sort as argument and inserts a generation constraint into the active specification using all function symbols which have the loose sort as result sort.

Enrichment of the constructor system   The command `add_constructor` allows the insertion of a new constructor. The application conditions from Prop. 8.4.8 are checked automatically by the analysis algorithms. If these algorithms fail to prove the required syntactic criteria, LTS refuses the enrichment and stops with a warning.

Reduction of the constructor system   Similarly, a constructor can be dropped from the active specification by the command `drop_constructor` . The necessary application conditions are checked by the analysis algorithms of the system. If the application conditions cannot be approved by the analysis algorithms, LTS refuses the reduction of the constructor system and stops with a warning.

C.4.5   Building and executing transformation strategies

The single-step commands can be combined into complex strategies using a fixed collection of strategy constructors. Internally, a single-step command maps a transformation node into a list of transformation nodes. The application of a strategy transforms a stack of transformation nodes into a new stack of transformation nodes. The transformation system also provides various predicates for formulating conditions in user-defined strategies. Pre-defined and user-defined strategies can be executed by the command `try` .

User defined strategies   The constructors for building strategies are summarized in Fig. C.7 .

The empty strategy `skip` has no effect. The strategy `postpone` moves the top of the transformation stack to the bottom. As a result the second transformation node, if existing, gets the focus of the next step. The strategy `step(f)` attempts to apply the command `f` to the top of the transformation stack. The constructor `scomp([s1...,sn])` combines a list of strategies `si` expressing the sequential execution of the associated refinement steps. The strategy `repeat(s)` repeatedly applies the strategy `s` until its application has no further effect on the transformation stack. The command `ifSuc(c,s,t)` denotes a conditional

```
skip
postpone
setStatus of string
step of (transfnode -> transfnode list)
scomp of strategy list
repeat of strategy
ifSuc of strategy*strategy*strategy
ifCond of (transfnode list -> bool) * strategy * strategy
whileLoop of (transfnode list -> bool) * strategy
```

Figure C.7: Constructors for transformation strategies

strategy. If the first strategy c succeeds, i.e. it changes the top transformation node, then the system proceeds with the second strategy s, otherwise with the third strategy t. The conditional strategy ifCond(cond,s,t) and the while strategy whileLoop(cond,s) both require a function cond mapping a transformation stack to a Boolean value. The conditional strategy executes s, if the condition cond evaluates to true and t otherwise. The while strategy repeats the strategy s as long as the condition cond holds. Note that the repeat and the while strategies may cause nontermination.

Predicates on the transformation stack For expressing conditions in formulating transformation strategies, LTS provides a collection of useful predicates for referencing the transformation stack, compare Fig. C.8.

isStatus(st)	Is the status of the actual tranformation node st?
isGeneralisable	Is the actual transformation node generalizable?
isSpecialisable	Can the actual transformation node be specialized?
isNormalform	Is the actual transformation node in normal form?
NormalformAll	Are all transformation nodes in normal form?
existsInRhs(f)	Does the function symbol f occur on the right-hand side?
isConstr	Is the actual transformation node constructive?

Figure C.8: Predicates on the transformation stack

C.4.6 Generating code

For code generation the function genCode(spec) can be invoked. For each involved sub-specification of the specification spec the command creates a file with an SML structure. Additionally, an SML structure for the specification spec is generated importing the structures of the involved sub-specifications. When generating SML code of a specification the constructors lead to data type definitions, whereas the operations yield function definitions. These declarations are inserted into the corresponding SML structures.

C.5 Syntax of LTS Specifications

specification	::=	"**spec**" *id paramspec* "=" [*impspec* ";"]
		[*sortdecls*] [*functdecls*] [*vardecls*] [*axiomdecls*]
		"**end**"
paramspec	::=	"[" *specparam* "]" [*paramspec*]
specparam	::=	*id*
	|	"**{**" [*sortdecls*] [*functdecls*] [*vardecls*] [*axiomdecls*] "**}**"
impspec	::=	*impspec* "**+**" *impspec*
	|	*impspec* "**;**" *impspec*
	|	"(" *impspec* ")"
	|	*id* "**as**" *impspec*
	|	*impspec* "[" *maplist* "]"
	|	*id aktparamlist*
	|	"**{**" [*sortdecls*] [*functdecls*] [*vardecls*] [*axiomdecls*] "**}**"
aktparamlist	::=	{ "[" *aktparam* "]" }*
aktparam	::=	*impspec* ["**fit**" *maplist*]
maplist	::=	*compid* "/" *compid* { "," *compid* "/" *compid* }*
sortdecls	::=	"**sorts**" [*sortdecl* { "," *sortdecl*}*]
functdecls	::=	"**ops**" [*functdecl* { "," *functdecl*}*]
vardecls	::=	"**vars**" [*vardecl* { "," *vardecl*}*]
axiomdecls	::=	"**axioms**" [*axiomdecl* { "," *axiomdecl*}*]
sortdecl	::=	*id* "=" "(" *compidlist* ")" *compid*
	|	*id* "=" "(" *compidlist* ")"
	|	*id* "=" *consdecl* { "|" *consdecl*}*
	|	*id*
compidlist	::=	*compid* { "," *compid*}*
consdecl	::=	*id* ["(" *compidlist* ")"]
functdecl	::=	*id* ":" "(" *compidlist* ")" *compid*
	|	*id* ":" *compid*
vardecl	::=	*id* { "," *id*}* ":" *compid*
axiomdecl	::=	*id* ":" *Paterm* "=" *Paterm*
Paterm	::=	*Pterm* {*Pterm*}+ "**o**" *Paterm*
	|	*Pterm* {*Pterm*}+
	|	*Pterm* "**o**" *Paterm*
	|	*Pterm*
Pterm	::=	*compid*
	|	"**@**" *compid*
	|	"(" *Paterm* { "," *Paterm*}* ")"
	|	"**if**" *Paterm* "**then**" *Paterm* "**else**" *Paterm*
	|	"**#**" *int Paterm*
compid	::=	*id* "." *id* | *id*

Appendix D

Sample Sessions with LTS

D.1 A fusion transformation

(magnusse@pcclt03): ltsw

```
Moscow ML version 2.00 (June 2000)
Enter 'quit();' to quit.
Loading prelude...
done.
> val it = () : unit
-----------------------------------------------------------------------
------Luebeck Transformation System------Version 1.0-----------------
-----------------------------------------------------------------------
------Institute of Software Technology and Programming Languages------
------University of Luebeck-------------------------------------------
-----------------------------------------------------------------------
------Soenke Magnussen---------April 2002----------------------------
-----------------------------------------------------------------------
> val it = () : unit
Loading user settings...
> val it = () : unit
[opening file "/home/magnusse/wiss/LTS/LTSdev/autostart.sml"]
Standard autostart Datei
> val it = () : unit
[closing file "/home/magnusse/wiss/LTS/LTSdev/autostart.sml"]
> val it = () : unit
done.
> val it = () : unit
[closing file "/home/magnusse/wiss/LTS/LTSdev/LTS.sml"]
```

- loadspec("Collection.lts");

```
> val it = () : unit
```

- *loadspec("MapColl.lts");*

```
> val it = () : unit
```

- *loadspec("Product.lts");*

```
> val it = () : unit
```

- *loadspec("ProductEval.lts");*

```
> val it = () : unit
```

- *start_refinement("ProductEval");*

```
spec ProductEval
sorts
ops
    getValOfColl : (SP.coll)nat < A OLF C CMPL  >
  H sum         : (SN.coll)nat < A OLF C ra(0) CATA CMPL >
axioms
    getValOfColl1: getValOfColl s = (sum o @map getVal) s
    < C L T >
    sum1          : sum SN.clear = zero
    < C L T >
    sum2          : sum (SN.newColl n) = n
    < C L T >
    sum3          : sum (SN.addAll(t,u)) = add(sum t,sum u)
    < C L T >
end
PROPERTIES:
      ALGORITHMIC
      CONFLUENT
      NONOVERLAPPING
      CONSTRUCTIVE
      TERMINATING
> val it = () : unit
```

- *catafuse("getValOfColl1");*

```
Trying to apply fusion theorem ... ok
Trying to derive compb.-op getValOfColl1-cop1_addAll... ok
Simplifying new axioms... ok
closing fusion strategy

spec ProductEval
sorts
```

```
ops
    getValOfColl : (SP.coll)nat < A OLF C ra(0) CATA CMPL  >
  H sum            : (SN.coll)nat  < A OLF C ra(0) CATA CMPL >
axioms
    getValOfColl1-clear  : getValOfColl SP.clear = zero
    < C L T >
    getValOfColl1-newColl: getValOfColl (SP.newColl p_9) = getVal p_9
    < C L T >
    getValOfColl1-addAll : getValOfColl (SP.addAll(s_10,s_11)) =
                                    add(getValOfColl s_10,getValOfColl s_11)
    < C L T >
    sum1                 : sum SN.clear = zero
    < C L T >
    sum2                 : sum (SN.newColl n) = n
    < C L T >
    sum3                 : sum (SN.addAll(t,u)) = add(sum t,sum u)
    < C L T >
    getValOfColl1-_ass   : add(add(n_1,n_2),n_3) = add(n_1,add(n_2,n_3))
    < L >
    getValOfColl1-_neutr1: n_4 = n_4
    < C L >
    getValOfColl1-_neutr2: add(n_5,zero) = n_5
    < C L T >
end
PROPERTIES:
> val it = () : unit

- drop_function("sum");

spec ProductEval
sorts
ops
    getValOfColl : (SP.coll)nat < A OLF C ra(0) CATA CMPL  >
axioms
    getValOfColl1-clear  : getValOfColl SP.clear = zero
    < C L T >
    getValOfColl1-newColl: getValOfColl (SP.newColl p_9) = getVal p_9
    < C L T >
    getValOfColl1-addAll : getValOfColl (SP.addAll(s_10,s_11)) =
                                    add(getValOfColl s_10,getValOfColl s_11)
    < C L T >
    getValOfColl1-_ass   : add(add(n_1,n_2),n_3) = add(n_1,add(n_2,n_3))
    < L >
    getValOfColl1-_neutr1: n_4 = n_4
    < C L >
    getValOfColl1-_neutr2: add(n_5,zero) = n_5
    < C L T >
```

```
end
PROPERTIES:
> val it = () : unit
```

- *drop_axiom("getValOfColl1-_ass");*

```
PROOF OBLIGATION:
caused by dropping Axiom: getValOfColl1-_ass

   add(add(n_1,n_2),n_3) = add(n_1,add(n_2,n_3))
END

spec ProductEval
sorts
ops
    getValOfColl : (SP.coll)nat < A OLF C ra(0) CATA CMPL  >
axioms
    getValOfColl1-clear  : getValOfColl SP.clear = zero
    < C L T >
    getValOfColl1-newColl: getValOfColl (SP.newColl p_9) = getVal p_9
    < C L T >
    getValOfColl1-addAll : getValOfColl (SP.addAll(s_10,s_11)) =
                                    add(getValOfColl s_10,getValOfColl s_11)
    < C L T >
    getValOfColl1-_neutr1: n_4 = n_4
    < C L >
    getValOfColl1-_neutr2: add(n_5,zero) = n_5
    < C L T >
end
PROPERTIES:
      CONFLUENT
      CONSTRUCTIVE
> val it = () : unit
```

- *drop_axiom("getValOfColl1-_neutr1");*

```
PROOF OBLIGATION:
caused by dropping Axiom: getValOfColl1-_neutr1

   n_4 = n_4
END

spec ProductEval
sorts
ops
    getValOfColl : (SP.coll)nat < A OLF C ra(0) CATA CMPL  >
axioms
```

```
    getValOfColl1-clear   : getValOfColl SP.clear = zero
    < C L T >
    getValOfColl1-newColl: getValOfColl (SP.newColl p_9) = getVal p_9
    < C L T >
    getValOfColl1-addAll  : getValOfColl (SP.addAll(s_10,s_11)) =
                                      add(getValOfColl s_10,getValOfColl s_11)
    < C L T >
    getValOfColl1-_neutr2: add(n_5,zero) = n_5
    < C L T >
end
PROPERTIES:
      ALGORITHMIC
      CONFLUENT
      NONOVERLAPPING
      CONSTRUCTIVE
      TERMINATING
> val it = () : unit
```

- drop_axiom("getValOfColl1-_neutr2");

```
PROOF OBLIGATION:
caused by dropping Axiom: getValOfColl1-_neutr2

   add(n_5,zero) = n_5
END

spec ProductEval
sorts
ops
    getValOfColl : (SP.coll)nat < A OLF C ra(0) CATA CMPL  >
axioms
    getValOfColl1-clear   : getValOfColl SP.clear = zero
    < C L T >
    getValOfColl1-newColl: getValOfColl (SP.newColl p_9) = getVal p_9
    < C L T >
    getValOfColl1-addAll  : getValOfColl (SP.addAll(s_10,s_11)) =
                                      add(getValOfColl s_10,getValOfColl s_11)
    < C L T >
end
PROPERTIES:
      ALGORITHMIC
      CONFLUENT
      NONOVERLAPPING
      CONSTRUCTIVE
      TERMINATING
> val it = () : unit
```

- checkin_spec();

```
Checking in

spec ProductEval
sorts
ops
    getValOfColl : (SP.coll)nat < A OLF C ra(0) CATA CMPL  >
axioms
    getValOfColl1-clear  : getValOfColl SP.clear = zero
    < C L T >
    getValOfColl1-newColl: getValOfColl (SP.newColl p_9) = getVal p_9
    < C L T >
    getValOfColl1-addAll : getValOfColl (SP.addAll(s_10,s_11)) =
                                      add(getValOfColl s_10,getValOfColl s_11)
    < C L T >
end
PROPERTIES:
     ALGORITHMIC
     CONFLUENT
     NONOVERLAPPING
     CONSTRUCTIVE
     TERMINATING
ok
> val it = () : unit
```

D.2   A data structure refinement

```
(magnusse@pcclt03:) ltsw
Moscow ML version 2.00 (June 2000)
Enter 'quit();' to quit.
Loading prelude...
done.
> val it = () : unit
-----------------------------------------------------------------------
------Luebeck Transformation System------Version 1.0------------------
-----------------------------------------------------------------------
------Institute of Software Technology and Programming Languages------
------University of Luebeck-------------------------------------------
-----------------------------------------------------------------------
------Soenke Magnussen---------April 2002-----------------------------
-----------------------------------------------------------------------
> val it = () : unit
Loading user settings...
> val it = () : unit
[opening file "/home/magnusse/wiss/LTS/LTSdev/autostart.sml"]
Standard autostart Datei
> val it = () : unit
```

```
[closing file "/home/magnusse/wiss/LTS/LTSdev/autostart.sml"]
> val it = () : unit
done.
> val it = () : unit
[closing file "/home/magnusse/wiss/LTS/LTSdev/LTS.sml"]
```

- loadspec("Collection.lts");

```
> val it = () : unit
```

- start_refinement("Collection");

```
spec Collection
sorts
     coll = clear | newColl(elem) | addAll(coll,coll)
ops
    contains : (elem,coll)bool < A OLF C ra(1) CATA CMPL  >
    addElem  : (elem,coll)coll < A OLF C CMPL  >
axioms
    ass      : addAll(addAll(s,p),q) = addAll(s,addAll(p,q))
    < C L T CNSTR >
    neutr1   : addAll(clear,p) = p
    < C L T CNSTR >
    neutr2   : addAll(p,clear) = p
    < C L T CNSTR >
    contains1: contains(x,clear) = false
    < C L T >
    contains2: contains(x,newColl y) = eqEl(x,y)
    < C L T >
    contains3: contains(x,addAll(s,p)) = or(contains(x,s),contains(x,p))
    < C L T >
    addElem1 : addElem(x,s) = addAll(newColl x,s)
    < C L T >
end
PROPERTIES:
      ALGORITHMIC
      CONFLUENT
      NONOVERLAPPING
      CONSTRUCTIVE
      TERMINATING
> val it = () : unit
```

- add_import("List[sorts elem fit T/elem]");

```
enriching importing to:
```

```
     Nat + List[{sorts elem} fit T/elem]

spec Collection
sorts
     coll = clear | newColl(elem) | addAll(coll,coll)
ops
     contains : (elem,coll)bool < A OLF C ra(1) CATA CMPL  >
     addElem  : (elem,coll)coll < A OLF C CMPL  >
axioms
     ass      : addAll(addAll(s,p),q) = addAll(s,addAll(p,q))
     < C L CNSTR >
     neutr1   : addAll(clear,p) = p
     < C L T CNSTR >
     neutr2   : addAll(p,clear) = p
     < C L T CNSTR >
     contains1: contains(x,clear) = false
     < C L T >
     contains2: contains(x,newColl y) = eqEl(x,y)
     < C L T >
     contains3: contains(x,addAll(s,p)) = or(contains(x,s),contains(x,p))
     < C L T >
     addElem1 : addElem(x,s) = addAll(newColl x,s)
     < C L T >
end
PROPERTIES:
      ALGORITHMIC
      CONFLUENT
      NONOVERLAPPING
      CONSTRUCTIVE
      TERMINATING
> val it = () : unit
```

- *implement_cons("coll", "list",*
["cl1: clear = nil",
"nC1: newColl(x) = cons(x,nil)",
"addA1:addAll(s,p) = conc(s,p)"]);

```
Applying Strat to: ass
Applying Strat to: neutr1
Applying Strat to: neutr2
Applying Strat to: contains1
Applying Strat to: contains2
Applying Strat to: contains3
Applying Strat to: addElem1


spec Collection
```

```
sorts
    coll = (list)
ops
    contains : (elem,coll)bool < OLF ra(1)  >
    addElem  : (elem,coll)coll < A OLF C CMPL  >
    clear    : coll           < A OLF C CMPL  >
    newColl  : (elem)coll      < A OLF C CMPL  >
    addAll   : (coll,coll)coll < A OLF C CMPL  >
axioms
    ass      : conc(conc(s,p),q) = conc(s,conc(p,q))
    < L >
    neutr1   : conc(nil,p) = p
    < C L T >
    neutr2   : conc(p,nil) = p
    < C L T >
    contains1: contains(x,nil) = false
    < C L T >
    contains2: contains(x,cons(y,nil)) = eqEl(x,y)
    < C L T >
    contains3: contains(x,conc(s,p)) = or(contains(x,s),contains(x,p))
    < L T >
    addElem1 : addElem(x,s) = conc(cons(x,nil),s)
    < C L T >
    cl1      : clear = nil
    < C L T >
    nC1      : newColl x = cons(x,nil)
    < C L T >
    addA1    : addAll(s,p) = conc(s,p)
    < C L T >
end
PROPERTIES:
> val it = () : unit

- rename_spec("CollByList");


spec CollByList
sorts
    coll = (list)
ops
    contains : (elem,coll)bool < OLF ra(1)  >
    addElem  : (elem,coll)coll < A OLF C CMPL  >
    clear    : coll           < A OLF C CMPL  >
    newColl  : (elem)coll      < A OLF C CMPL  >
    addAll   : (coll,coll)coll < A OLF C CMPL  >
axioms
    ass      : conc(conc(s,p),q) = conc(s,conc(p,q))
```

```
    < L >
    neutr1    : conc(nil,p) = p
    < C L T >
    neutr2    : conc(p,nil) = p
    < C L T >
    contains1: contains(x,nil) = false
    < C L T >
    contains2: contains(x,cons(y,nil)) = eqEl(x,y)
    < C L T >
    contains3: contains(x,conc(s,p)) = or(contains(x,s),contains(x,p))
    < L T >
    addElem1 : addElem(x,s) = conc(cons(x,nil),s)
    < C L T >
    cl1       : clear = nil
    < C L T >
    nC1       : newColl x = cons(x,nil)
    < C L T >
    addA1     : addAll(s,p) = conc(s,p)
    < C L T >
end
PROPERTIES:
> val it = () : unit

- drop_axiom("ass");


PROOF OBLIGATION:
caused by dropping Axiom: ass

    conc(conc(s,p),q) = conc(s,conc(p,q))
END

spec CollByList
sorts
    coll = (list)
ops
    contains : (elem,coll)bool < OLF ra(1)  >
    addElem  : (elem,coll)coll < A OLF C CMPL  >
    clear    : coll            < A OLF C CMPL  >
    newColl  : (elem)coll      < A OLF C CMPL  >
    addAll   : (coll,coll)coll < A OLF C CMPL  >
axioms
    neutr1    : conc(nil,p) = p
    < C L T >
    neutr2    : conc(p,nil) = p
    < C L T >
    contains1: contains(x,nil) = false
```

```
    < C L T >
    contains2: contains(x,cons(y,nil)) = eqEl(x,y)
    < C L T >
    contains3: contains(x,conc(s,p)) = or(contains(x,s),contains(x,p))
    < L T >
    addElem1 : addElem(x,s) = conc(cons(x,nil),s)
    < C L T >
    cl1       : clear = nil
    < C L T >
    nC1       : newColl x = cons(x,nil)
    < C L T >
    addA1     : addAll(s,p) = conc(s,p)
    < C L T >
end
PROPERTIES:
      TERMINATING
> val it = () : unit

- drop_axiom("neutr1");


PROOF OBLIGATION:
caused by dropping Axiom: neutr1

   conc(nil,p) = p
END

spec CollByList
sorts
     coll = (list)
ops
    contains : (elem,coll)bool < OLF ra(1)  >
    addElem  : (elem,coll)coll < A OLF C CMPL  >
    clear    : coll            < A OLF C CMPL  >
    newColl  : (elem)coll      < A OLF C CMPL  >
    addAll   : (coll,coll)coll < A OLF C CMPL  >
axioms
    neutr2   : conc(p,nil) = p
    < C L T >
    contains1: contains(x,nil) = false
    < C L T >
    contains2: contains(x,cons(y,nil)) = eqEl(x,y)
    < C L T >
    contains3: contains(x,conc(s,p)) = or(contains(x,s),contains(x,p))
    < L T >
    addElem1 : addElem(x,s) = conc(cons(x,nil),s)
    < C L T >
```

```
    cl1        : clear = nil
    < C L T >
    nC1        : newColl x = cons(x,nil)
    < C L T >
    addA1      : addAll(s,p) = conc(s,p)
    < C L T >
end
PROPERTIES:
      TERMINATING
> val it = () : unit

- drop_axiom("neutr2");


PROOF OBLIGATION:
caused by dropping Axiom: neutr2

   conc(p,nil) = p
END

spec CollByList
sorts
     coll = (list)
ops
    contains : (elem,coll)bool < OLF ra(1)  >
    addElem  : (elem,coll)coll < A OLF C CMPL >
    clear    : coll            < A OLF C CMPL >
    newColl  : (elem)coll      < A OLF C CMPL >
    addAll   : (coll,coll)coll < A OLF C CMPL >
axioms
    contains1: contains(x,nil) = false
    < C L T >
    contains2: contains(x,cons(y,nil)) = eqEl(x,y)
    < C L T >
    contains3: contains(x,conc(s,p)) = or(contains(x,s),contains(x,p))
    < L T >
    addElem1 : addElem(x,s) = conc(cons(x,nil),s)
    < C L T >
    cl1      : clear = nil
    < C L T >
    nC1      : newColl x = cons(x,nil)
    < C L T >
    addA1    : addAll(s,p) = conc(s,p)
    < C L T >
end
PROPERTIES:
      CONFLUENT
```

```
      TERMINATING
> val it = () : unit
```

- start_task("contains2");

```
TASK contains2
   contains(x,cons(y,nil)) := eqEl(x,y)

> val it = () : unit
```

- dorewoccrl(["or1"],nil);

```
TASK contains2
   contains(x,cons(y,nil)) := or(false,eqEl(x,y))

> val it = () : unit
```

- dorewrl(["contains1"]);

```
TASK contains2
   contains(x,cons(y,nil)) := or(contains(x,nil),eqEl(x,y))

> val it = () : unit
```

- dogener("nil");

```
TASK contains2
   contains(x,cons(y,X_1)) := or(contains(x,X_1),eqEl(x,y))

> val it = () : unit
```

- checkin_task();

```
spec CollByList
sorts
    coll = (list)
ops
    contains : (elem,coll)bool < OLF ra(1) CATA CMPL  >
    addElem  : (elem,coll)coll < A OLF C CMPL  >
    clear    : coll            < A OLF C CMPL  >
    newColl  : (elem)coll      < A OLF C CMPL  >
```

```
    addAll   : (coll,coll)coll < A OLF C CMPL  >
axioms
    contains1: contains(x,nil) = false
    < C L T >
    contains2: contains(x,cons(y,X_1)) = or(contains(x,X_1),eqEl(x,y))
    < C L T >
    contains3: contains(x,conc(s,p)) = or(contains(x,s),contains(x,p))
    < L T >
    addElem1 : addElem(x,s) = conc(cons(x,nil),s)
    < C L T >
    cl1      : clear = nil
    < C L T >
    nC1      : newColl x = cons(x,nil)
    < C L T >
    addA1    : addAll(s,p) = conc(s,p)
    < C L T >
end
PROPERTIES:
      CONFLUENT
      TERMINATING
> val it = () : unit

- map_strat_all(step(nf));

Applying Strat to: contains1
Applying Strat to: contains2
Applying Strat to: contains3
Applying Strat to: addElem1
Applying Strat to: cl1
Applying Strat to: nC1
Applying Strat to: addA1

spec CollByList
sorts
     coll = (list)
ops
    contains : (elem,coll)bool < OLF ra(1) CATA CMPL  >
    addElem  : (elem,coll)coll < A OLF C CMPL  >
    clear    : coll            < A OLF C CMPL  >
    newColl  : (elem)coll      < A OLF C CMPL  >
    addAll   : (coll,coll)coll < A OLF C CMPL  >
axioms
    contains1: contains(x,nil) = false
    < C L T >
    contains2: contains(x,cons(y,X_1)) = or(contains(x,X_1),eqEl(x,y))
    < C L T >
    contains3: contains(x,conc(s,p)) = or(contains(x,s),contains(x,p))
```

```
    < L T >
    addElem1 : addElem(x,s) = cons(x,s)
    < C L T >
    cl1      : clear = nil
    < C L T >
    nC1      : newColl x = cons(x,nil)
    < C L T >
    addA1    : addAll(s,p) = conc(s,p)
    < C L T >
end
PROPERTIES:
     CONFLUENT
     TERMINATING
> val it = () : unit

- drop_axiom("contains3");


PROOF OBLIGATION:
caused by dropping Axiom: contains3

   contains(x,conc(s,p)) = or(contains(x,s),contains(x,p))
END

spec CollByList
sorts
     coll = (list)
ops
    contains : (elem,coll)bool < A OLF C ra(1) CATA CMPL  >
    addElem  : (elem,coll)coll < A OLF C CMPL  >
    clear    : coll            < A OLF C CMPL  >
    newColl  : (elem)coll      < A OLF C CMPL  >
    addAll   : (coll,coll)coll < A OLF C CMPL  >
axioms
    contains1: contains(x,nil) = false
    < C L T >
    contains2: contains(x,cons(y,X_1)) = or(contains(x,X_1),eqEl(x,y))
    < C L T >
    addElem1 : addElem(x,s) = cons(x,s)
    < C L T >
    cl1      : clear = nil
    < C L T >
    nC1      : newColl x = cons(x,nil)
    < C L T >
    addA1    : addAll(s,p) = conc(s,p)
    < C L T >
end
```

```
PROPERTIES:
      ALGORITHMIC
      CONFLUENT
      NONOVERLAPPING
      CONSTRUCTIVE
      TERMINATING
> val it = () : unit
```

- checkin_spec();

```
Checking in

spec CollByList
sorts
     coll = (list)
ops
    contains : (elem,coll)bool < A OLF C ra(1) CATA CMPL  >
    addElem  : (elem,coll)coll < A OLF C CMPL  >
    clear    : coll            < A OLF C CMPL  >
    newColl  : (elem)coll      < A OLF C CMPL  >
    addAll   : (coll,coll)coll < A OLF C CMPL  >
axioms
    contains1: contains(x,nil) = false
    < C L T >
    contains2: contains(x,cons(y,X_1)) = or(contains(x,X_1),eqEl(x,y))
    < C L T >
    addElem1 : addElem(x,s) = cons(x,s)
    < C L T >
    cl1      : clear = nil
    < C L T >
    nC1      : newColl x = cons(x,nil)
    < C L T >
    addA1    : addAll(s,p) = conc(s,p)
    < C L T >
end
PROPERTIES:
      ALGORITHMIC
      CONFLUENT
      NONOVERLAPPING
      CONSTRUCTIVE
      TERMINATING
ok
> val it = () : unit
```